DANTE, ER

Dante, Eros,
& Kabbalah

Mark Jay Mirsky

SYRACUSE UNIVERSITY PRESS

Copyright © 2003 by Syracuse University Press
Syracuse, New York 13244–5160

All Rights Reserved

First Edition 2003

03 04 05 06 07 08   6 5 4 3 2 1

Excerpts from Renato Poggioli, "Paolo and Francesca," *PMLA* (1977) are reprinted by permission of The Modern Language Association. Copyright © 1977 The Modern Language Association.

Excerpts from Leonardo Olschki, *The Myth of Felt,* are reprinted by permission of the University of California Press. Copyright © 1949 Regents of the University of California, © renewed 1977 Leonardo Olschki.

Excerpts from Leo Strauss, *Persecution and the Art of Writing,* are reprinted by permission of University of Chicago Press, the present copyholder. Copyright © 1952 by The Free Press, a corporation.

Illustrations by Inger Johanne Grytting

The paper used in this publication meets the minimum requirements of American National Standard for Information Sciences—Permanence of Paper for Printed Library Materials, ANSI Z39.48–1984.∞™

Library of Congress Cataloging-in-Publication Data

Mirsky, Mark.
Dante, Eros, and Kabbalah / Mark Jay Mirsky.— 1st ed.
p. cm.
Includes bibliographical references and index.
ISBN 0–8156–3027–1 (pbk. : alk. paper)
1. Dante Alighieri, 1265–1321. Divina commedia. 2. Love in literature
3. Cabala in literature. I. Title.
PQ4432.L6M57 2003
851'.1—dc21
2003008004

Manufactured in the United States of America

To my great grandfather, Moses Mirsky,

remembered by his grandson, Wilfred, as a kabbalist,

and my children, Israel and Ruth,

to whom such knowledge might be precious.

Mark Jay Mirsky has received a National Endowment for the Humanities Senior Fellowship and an Editor's Award from the National Endowment for the Arts. He is the author of four published novels, *Thou Worm Jacob, Proceedings of the Rabble, Blue Hill Avenue,* and *The Red Adam;* a collection of novellas, *The Secret Table;* and several books of nonfiction, among them *My Search for the Messiah* and *The Absent Shakespeare,* the last nominated for a National Book Critics Circle Award. He is the editor of the English language edition of Robert Musil's *Diaries,* published by Basic Books and coeditor of the anthology *Rabbinic Fantasies* first issued by the Jewish Publication Society and reissued in the Yale Judaica Series. Mark Jay Mirsky's articles and fiction have appeared in the *New York Sunday Times Book Review,* the *Washington Post Book World, Partisan Review,* the *Progressive,* the *Boston Sunday Globe* and many other periodicals. He is the editor of the magazine *Fiction,* which he founded in 1972 with Donald Barthelme and Max and Marianne Frisch.

Contents

Acknowledgments

I INCURRED MANY DEBTS writing this book, a number confessed in its first chapter, which serves both as an introduction and a summary of the story that began this argosy, "Dante, Kaballah, and the New World," published in the *Denver Quarterly.* The citations through the text acknowledge how many times I consulted the translators of Dante and their notes. I could never have embarked on the enterprise without help from my colleague at The City College of New York, Frederick Goldin. He is not responsible for any of the mistakes I may have made, but his encouragement, correction of glaring errors, and advice gave me the confidence to explore at greater length the world of Dante's *Commedia.* Frederick Goldin invited me to sit in on his graduate class at the college on Provençal poetry and the Medieval romance. The notes I took had a long-lasting effect. His classroom again and again dissolved the boundaries of time, as the students sat in the presence of the courtiers and princes of Provence, the troubadours and trouveres. Professor Goldin translating anew from the texts in front of him evoked the laughter, verbal skill, and radical questions these poets dramatized for their audiences. To hear him recite was to receive a fresh impression of the courtly lyrics as they were sung before a blushing face.

Clara Claiborne Park went over an earlier version of this manuscript, making suggestions, commenting (some of her very apt observations I have preserved in my footnotes), and checking the accuracy of my quotation and translation. In the case of the latter I have tried to stay very close to the English cognates of the Italian, constantly referring the reader to the original.

I owe a debt to Max Frisch, whose novella, *William Tell,* which we published in the magazine *Fiction,* showed me the means of retelling myths of history and literature with skeptical relish. Was it in a restaurant by a lake in Zurich that I first sketched this portrait of Dante, watching Max's face for a sign of approval? This book has been many years in the making. Among its partisans was a good friend, now passed into the other world, Arthur Cohen. One poet I wished to show it to, Howard Nemerov, spoke so generously of my first novel that I was too embarrassed to send the manuscript on to him while he was alive, putting it off until I should have a more perfect argument. His remarks on Dante, however, gave me the heart early on to push forward.

I received golden words at the beginning of my career from the poet John Ciardi, whose translation of Dante was the first I was to read. In my long association at *Fiction* with Donald Barthelme, this great stylist was often my stern preceptor. My friendship with Edward Dahlberg was brief, for in the flesh he was hard to endure, but I often return to his essays on Melville, Thoreau, Whitman, memorizing lines. This book owes more to him than I can easily admit. Nor can I forget the poet and translator Anthony Kerrigan, in whose company I met Dahlberg. Tony was my elder brother through a span of many years, guiding my reading and commenting upon this manuscript in early drafts. I have to mention the help I received from Rabbi Ben-Zion Gold and Rabbi Meir Fund. They set me on the trail of a remark that I heard from Rabbi Joseph Soloveitchik, one that set my head spinning in circles I have noted in this manuscript.

Among other staunch friends of the book as it circulated in its earlier revisions were Russell Banks, Robert Creeley, Fanny Howe, Dorothea Straus, and Cynthia Ozick. Cynthia's kindness not just to me but to many writers struggling to be part of a conversation about literature has been an epic of generosity.

One obligation looms beyond all others among these acknowledgments. In November of the year 2000, my teacher, Albert Guerard Jr., passed away. He continued after my years at Harvard College and Stanford University to read my work with sharp, unstinting criticism. My debts to him cannot be found in particular footnotes but in the spirit of the whole. It was Albert who first taught me to look into a writer's stories and to decipher from the struggle of ideas, characters, unsolved questions, and metaphor a concealed outline that often lies behind a work of fiction—the writer's own portrait. And there is always another secret sharer in the work, to be discerned in those death masks set by writers like Howard Nemerov and Osip Mandelstam who, bending over the dead Father, take the mold off and scrutinize the impression. In my case Albert was the master who taught me the process.

Author's Note

I HAVE USED the obvious abbreviations for the three cantos of the *Commedia, Inf.* *(Inferno), Purg. (Purgatorio)* and *Par. (Paradiso).* For *La Vita Nuova*, it seemed easiest to use *Vita.* I have not cited lines of *La Vita Nuova* (several editions had different schemes of numbering them), but chapter headings on which all the editions I consulted agreed. The *Letters of Dante* are listed as *Epist.*, while the Grandgent edition of *La Divina Commedia* is referred to as *Commedia.* Several poems of Dante's are quoted from Fredi Chiappelli's edition of *Vita Nuova/Rime,* and I will refer to this as *Rime* rather than citing it under Dante's name and the edition's date. In referring to a note or to a translation from a specific edition of Dante's *Divine Comedy,* I have listed it under the author-date system, by its dates. When I refer, for instance, to a note from the Carlyle and Wicksteed edition of *The Divine Comedy* that was published by The Modern Library in 1932, I will cite the date to identify the particular edition (*Par.* 1932, 1:67–69). The line numbers are essentially the same in both the Sinclair and the Grandgent and Singleton editions of the three books of the *Divine Comedy,* but I have given precedence to the textual choices of the latter.

In citing one of the tractates of the Talmud, it is the Babylonian Talmud to which I refer, numbered in its editions according to the folio pages *a* and *b* of these divisions.

Commedia	*La Divina Commedia.* Edited and annotated by C. H. Grandgent, Revised by Charles S. Singleton. Cambridge, Mass.: Harvard Univ. Press. 1972.
Epist.	*Dantis Alagherii Epistolae: The Letters of Dante.* Translated by Paget Toynbee, 2nd ed. Oxford: Clarendon Press, 1966.
Inf.	Dante Alighieri. *The Inferno.*
Purg.	Dante Alighieri. *Purgatorio.*
Par.	Dante Alighieri. *Paradiso.*
Rime	*Vita Nuova/Rime.* Edited by Fredi Chiappelli. Milano: Mursia. 1973.
Vita	*La Vita Nuova.*

Dante, Eros, & Kabbalah

CHAPTER ONE

Dante in America

Exoteric literature presupposes that there are basic truths which would not be pronounced in public by any decent man, because they would do harm to many people, who, having been hurt, would naturally be inclined to hurt in turn him who pronounces the unpleasant truths. It presupposes, in other words, that freedom of inquiry and of publication of all results of inquiry, is not guaranteed as a basic right. This literature is then essentially related to a society which is not liberal. Thus, one may very well raise the question of what use it could be in a truly liberal society. The answer is simple. In Plato's *Banquet,* Alcibiades—that outspoken son of outspoken Athens—compares Socrates and his speeches to certain sculptures which are very ugly from the outside, but within have most beautiful images of things divine. The works of the great writers of the past are very beautiful even from without. And yet their visible beauty is sheer ugliness compared with the beauty of those hidden treasures which disclose themselves only after very long, never easy, but always pleasant work. This always difficult but always pleasant work is, I believe, what the philosophers had in mind when they recommended education. Education, they felt, is the only answer to the always pressing question, to the political question par excellence, of how to reconcile order which is not oppression with freedom which is not license.

—Leo Strauss, *Persecution and the Art of Writing*

> "O brothers," I said, "who through a hundred thousand
> perils have reached the west
> to this—such a little vigil
> of our senses that remains
> do not will to refuse the experience
> behind the sun, of a world without people.
> Consider the seed whence you spring.
> You were not made to live like brutes
> but to follow virtue and knowledge."
> My companions I made so eager
> with this little speech for the road
> that I could hardly have held them back
> and with our poop turned to the morning
> we made of the oars, wings for the mad flight.—*Inf.* 26:112–25

1

The subject of forbidden relations may not be expounded in the presence of
three, the work of creation in the presence of two, the chariot in the presence
of one, unless he is a sage and understands of his own knowledge. Whoso-
ever speculates upon four things, a pity for him! He is as though he had not
come into the world—what is above, beneath, before, and after.
                          —*Mishnah, Hagigah*, 11:1.

I WAS IN DANTE'S CITY, Florence, to steep in medieval humors, to read the
Commedia in the original, a notion husbanded through two earlier windings
through the *Divine Comedy* wholly in English. For several years in New York City,
during late breakfasts I had pinned myself to a table behind the steel facade of an
air conditioning unit in a Sixth Avenue greasy spoon where the syllables of Attica
chiseled the air. There I thumbed the pages of the *Inferno, Purgatorio, Paradiso*.
Politics, religion, romantic eroticism, Dante's obsessions were mine.

Now I wound up the twisting road past Settignano mornings, with a library
card admitting me to Bernard Berenson's villa, I Tatti. In the afternoons, the Italian of Dante facing John Sinclair's English translation in the Oxford paperback
edition echoed to its proper background, the noisy streets by the Ponte Santa
Trinità. Here, one could lord it over a whole table when the chairs outside were
dry, by the screams of scooters, hoot of auto horns, a cacophony muted in the
throat of the Arno rushing a few feet away. During the rain I bunched up with others in a corner of the friendly cafe, writing elbow to elbow.

Dante inhabited his city, but Dantiana was best enjoyed in exile above Florence in the library nooks where a shelf of books in English about Dante Alighieri
occupied about four square feet on Berenson's shelves. One morning in Florence
under a sky of lead plate reflecting a Puritan countryside that in suppression of its
colors glowed with blue, green, red specks through the gray earth, I took up the fat
volume *Dante Abroad* and heard its urbane author, Werner P. Friedrich, detail,
amused, the antique scholarship of two Englishmen of the Victorian schoolhouse,
E. H. Plumptre and W. E. Gladstone (the British Prime Minister):

Scholars are so generally agreed today that Dante did not ever go to Paris that the
assumption that he also studied at Oxford seems to be even more untenable and
hence is generally abandoned. Only Plumptre and Gladstone have ever really
championed that viewpoint and have tried to prove it through internal evidence
gleaned from the D.C.; Plumptre has even advanced a definite period, the two

years between Beatrice's marriage and the battle of Campaldino, during which Dante heartbroken roamed through France and crossed to England either by way of Flanders or by way of Cologne and the Lowlands—while Gladstone follows Boccaccio's biography of Dante in assuming that the poet visited France and England only later, during his bitter years of exile. (Friedrich 1950, 181)

Suckled on the fables of the Argentine exponent of *Ultraismo*, Jorge Luis Borges, for whom Kipling and other dusty busts of Victoria and Edward were heroes of man's existential predicament—I appreciated these antiquities not as knickknacks but as talismans. One might adventure in the tracks of Plumptre and Gladstone. In another volume, as a sarcastic aside, I found a suggestion. Angelina La Piana intoned, in superior tones, "Dante could not have known that following the direction he had chosen for their imaginary voyage, Ulysses and his companions would have landed somewhere on the coast of South America" (La Piana 1948, 1).

Dante *not* know. That statement was irreverent. No one who labors in the shadow of a work called the "Divine" ought to be quick to say that Dante, despite his archaic science, did not or "could not know" something so fundamental as his sailing directions. One ought to think out the implications of Ulysses and his bark heading toward Mexico.

And if Dante knew?

Perhaps Dante had gone! Why not send him, to America.

Dante, Dante in America.

A messenger of the god of Love, I sent him off, half divine, to meet in mid-Atlantic, the Mexican deity, Quetzalcoatl. The pumping hearts of men, torn out of their breasts, were offered to this American god. Dante would become his victim. The poet who returned to Italy would write and dream with an empty space in his chest and assume the guise of Quetzalcoatl, bird feathers. Boccaccio reports that Dante's mother had seen her son in a dream transformed from a man into a peacock (Boccacio 1904, 13). Dante as Quetzalcoatl, but feathered in the white down of the *Commedia*'s angels, a cannibal god of Love, eating his own and his beloved's heart? Does Dante not cry out in *The New Life* to Death to be his savior?

Into my fiction, stitched of Icelandic saga, anthropology, history, something bizarre, ominous, threaded. Dante must have thought about the space to which his townsman, Americus Vespucius, two centuries later, would give a name. Why send one's shadow, secret sharer, the hero Ulysses, out of the Mediterranean, contrary to the classical fable of the Ithacan's wanderings, push the mariner through the gates of Hercules into the uncharted Atlantic? Out here, Dante locates his island, *Purgatory,* the repository of his hopes, though he will reach it by a circuitous route, unknown to the Greek captains of antiquity.

(There was an America to which Dante went. We Americans still dream about it, subsumed under clichés like "The New Frontier" and "The New Society." We are ever coining names for this, the edge of Paradise that Columbus reported finding on his third voyage though no one believed him.)

I began to suspect that Dante was seeking the same land that the conquistadors, creaking in armor through the land of flowers, centuries later, sought in vain, the "true, the blushful" fountain of youth. The thirteenth- and fourteenth-century maps of surreal terrain had places more mysterious than the moon. I wondered about Dante and Kabbalah, the dream world of the thirteenth- and fourteenth-century Jews, and the cosmology of the *Zohar,* a text scholars believe to be antecedent by a generation to the *Commedia.* The inspiration for the *Zohar* supposedly came from Provence, the place where Dante derived his "sweet new style" to walk in the circles of Paradise. The dream geography of the Jewish mystics promised a flow of sexual bliss not only in maturity and old age but beyond.[1]

Maps of the world, half, three-quarters real, verifiable, spread out as well. Five months out from the European outer limit, Dante's Ulysses sees the island of Purgatory. From the familiar outline of the Bjarn islands off Greenland to the mysterious Marvel Strands of a new mainland, is only a six-day sail, according to *Erik's Saga.* Dante's Ulysses, however, grows old between Italy and the Strait of Gibraltar.

Dante Alighieri dreamed of that Atlantic voyage. He left a footnote, however, to an old brotherhood with the Vikings exclaiming in his letters, "Eia, facite, Scandinaviae soboles, ut cuius merito, trepidatis adventum, quod ex vobis est, praesentiam sitiatis," "Up then ye sons of Scandinavia and so far as ye may show yourself eager for the presence of him whose advent ye now justly await with dread" (*Epist.* 5:52, 60). He is calling on his fellow citizens of Florence, alluding to the tradition that they as Lombards are descended from Scandinavians. The late thirteenth century was alive with speculation about the world. Marco Polo had charted to the east. Dante, imagining an escape from this world, looked toward a geography beyond the Gates of Hercules, earthly and spiritual. The white falcons of Canada that were traded from its Arctic through Iceland to the kings of Europe cannot have come unaccompanied by tales of origin. Not only the real places explicit in the *Di-*

---

1. Harry A. Wolfson, professor of religious philosophy at Harvard University, remarked succinctly that Jewish cosmologies were "ethical" while Greek ethics tended to be "cosmological" (Wolfson 1977, 120). In the *Zohar* cosmology tends toward the sexual while trying to retain its ethical content. Martin Ritter, a scholar of Wolfson, maintains that Wolfson qualified several of his earlier generalizations as he matured, though this epigram seems astute.

vine Comedy, but the spiritual ones, began to come into focus: beyond the vague headlands of America, the Neoplatonic bulk of kabbalistic continents.

The language of metamorphosis points the way. In the poet Ovid, one finds the story of man become a finny god. The fisherman, Glaucus, tasted grass, which had revived a fish he caught, and became "the sea fellow of the other gods." The reference comes in the opening canto of *Paradiso*. Dante staring at Beatrice staring into the sun, a shimmering light runs through his body. He is transformed. "Gazing on her such I became within as was Glaucus tasting of the grass that made him the sea fellow of the other gods" (*Par.* 1932, 1:67–69). One notes several strands in Dante's exposition of the myth: metamorphosis into a divine being, luminescent flesh, a miraculous grass or reed, talisman of a rebirth, which effects both metamorphosis and resurrection (or reconstitution). Most striking perhaps is the poet's identity with a man turned into a god of the sea. This is what staring at Beatrice has done to him. Dante has "passed beyond humanity." He can not put the experience into words he claims, yet turns to a fable to describe the tale of transformation into divinity by a descent into the sea of Glaucus.

Dante's first motion on the true road in the *Commedia* is downward, through the depths of Hell, in the *Inferno*'s cantos. Summing up the myth of Glaucus, Dr. H. Oelsner and Phillip Wicksteed echo the eager thirst for metamorphosis that sounds in Ovid's account. The fisherman Glaucus, who tasted the grass, which "revivified" or resurrected his catch of fish, was "thereon . . . seized with yearning for the deep into which he plunged and became a sea god" (*Par.* 1932, 408). Dante's mind, always resonant to allusion, must have caught not only the religious image of the fish, but the lure of the sea's depths for Glaucus. Ovid's readers knew that the transformation of the fisherman involves the beautiful nymph Scylla in a disastrous metamorphosis and brings ruin to the crew of Ulysses. Furious about her change into a monster, Scylla eats the seafarers alive—not wholly lovely, this sea change. In the canto following the reference to Glaucus, Dante warns most of his readers to turn back from the wake of his bark into the "open sea," as Wicksteed translates it, or "deep," "*pelago.*" Only those rare souls who reach out for the "*pan de li angeli,*" "bread of the angels" (*Par.* 2:11) should set themselves in the furrows of his ship.

That bread is exactly what Glaucus has tasted, albeit in a pagan, magical context.

Why use the image of a ship? Dante goes by foot through Hell and Purgatory, as Osip Mandelstam points out both in rhythm and metaphor, except for a short ferry by boat and submarine (Mandelstam 1971, 68). In the Heavens Dante rises as if on wings. The Florentine poet wishes us to forget this at moments and confuse his journey with that of Ulysses who sails toward the Unknown. What about the deliberate confounding of river, sea, ocean and sky? A sense of cosmic waters is what Dante wants us to feel, and his deep, until we reach Purgatory, is specific. It is the Atlantic.

What was Dante's Atlantic?

It was the forbidden. The sea into which one dared not sail.

It was the river of death. And more.

It was the watery home of the isle of Purgatory.

Dante (above all a skillful commentator on information received: history, gossip, the religious myth of others, Ovid, Virgil, the Gospels, the lives of saints) rarely invents because his central invention, the journey toward Beatrice, will strain credulity. Dante makes an exception in the case of Ulysses. He invents a sailing toward the island of Purgatory out in the Atlantic. The commentators are at a loss to find any real precedents for it.[2]

Why? The critic John Freccero gives us an important part of the answer, commenting on the line from the second canto of the *Inferno*, "su la fiumana ove 'l mar non ha vanto," "Upon the stream where the sea cannot boast."[3] Virgil is describing to Dante the words uttered to him by Beatrice, who is quoting the charge by Lucy in Heaven to rescue Dante from the death that threatens him, "Upon the stream where the sea can not boast." John D. Sinclair translates *fiumana* as "flood" (*Inf.* 1972, 41). There is something of the primeval ocean in the image—Freccero demonstrates. It is "Oceanus, the father of all waters. . . . In the mythological cosmology of Homeric Greece, the river was thought to be the boundary of all reality. For this reason, the shield of Achilles had for its rim 'the mighty Stream of Oceanus'. . . . Beyond the boundary formed by the river lay the world of the dead, into which the river carried those who crossed it. Circe sends Odysseus to the 'deep flowing river of Oceanus and the boundaries of the world.'" (Freccero 1986, 60–61).

Again, "In the Book of Enoch, the prophet in his journey reaches the great river and the darkness of the west. . . . In the Gnosis, the Jordan was a cosmic river, the frontier between the world of the senses and the spiritual world" (61).

"In an exegetical tradition that extends from Philo Judaeus to Thomas

2. Dr. H. Oelsner, in his notes to the Modern Library edition (Carlyle and Wicksteed 1932, 142) states, "This account of Ulysses' voyage is entirely of Dante's invention."

3. In the sense of "honor," the word [I]vanto[I] has been used earlier in the same canto, line 25, which links Virgil's account of Aeneas as a traveler both to the underworld and to Italy, to Saint Peter's voyage to Rome. *"Per quest' andata onde li dai tu vanto,"* [through this voyage because of which you give him honor]. Dante thus suggests the parallels between the voyages of Aeneas, Saint Peter, and himself, journeys over real and spiritual waters. The notion of "honor" and "knightly combat, boast," clings to both uses of the word.

Aquinas, the etymology of the name 'Jordan' was said to be *katabasis autōn*, '*descensus eorum*,'" "' their descent' " (63).

In fact, the Hebrew root, YRD on which "Yaardan" or "Jordan" (the letter represented by *Y* used to be pronounced like English *J* in ancient Hebrew) is based, means exactly that, "to go down."

As John Freccero stresses, Dante is within an old tradition of religious adventure when he goes down into this spiritual deep. He is fighting death as Dante puts it, in waters "over which the sea can not boast." What Dante has done is to make these mysterious waters of resurrection flow through the ocean, the Atlantic.

Ulysses will skim the surface of the ocean and be swallowed up in its depths. Dante by contrast will willfully go down, change himself into a creature of the depths. At the beginning of *Paradiso* he refers back to Glaucus as an image of his metamorphosis. Dante, tasting the grass of the Resurrection thirsts for the deeps of the salt sea, its waters, the Atlantic. He cries triumphantly, in the last lines of *Purgatorio*, the canto before the mention of Glaucus: "I returned from the holiest waves / remade . . . to go up to the stars." The music of the Italian, with its sly spin through the *S*'s is worth speaking just to hear Dante spinning himself "higher." (Sinclair, to whose translation I am indebted, employs "ready" in place of the cognate "disposed" but I think the context calls for Dante's wink at his own rebaptism.)

> Io ritornai da la santissima onda
> rifatto sì come piante novelle
> rinovellate di novella fronda,
> puro e disposto a salire a le stelle.
>
> I returned from the holiest waves
> Remade—as new plants
> Renewed with new leaves,
> Pure and disposed to go up to the stars.
> (*Purg.* 33:142–45)

Dante is speaking of the sweet stream in the Garden of Paradise and aspiring to the empyrean above. Yet in the long perspective of the poem, the waters he bids his readers to return upon are the waves of the Atlantic, and the deep from which he has come up lies beyond the Gates of Hercules. The sense of his attraction for these real salt waters lingers through the whole of *Purgatorio* and *Paradiso*. For within them, I believe flashes a subterranean life, and it argues in Dante a radical notion of metamorphosis, of change, a desire to break away from conventional church cosmologies, to turn them upside down. To go down is also to turn revelation and salvation upside down. (In the Hebrew language the words for heaven and water flow through a common root, and the listener senses the mystery of creation in the syllables that speak of the waters above and below.) A stream of *gnosis* runs through Dante, wine dark and antinomian.

Did he have something to hide? Is there a secret *Commedia?*

In my first notes, I groped alone toward Dante's concealed "New Life." I need not have. Gershom Scholem,[4] the scholar of Jewish mysticism, told me in our first encounter during the 1970s to read Leo Strauss's *Persecution and the Art of Writing.* In a second meeting, two years later, I was scolded for not having taken the book up yet. It was an uncanny premonition by Scholem, to whom I had presented myself as a novelist, never mentioning my interest in Dante. It was not until this manuscript went into its second draft after Scholem's death, that I finally read the book he had recommended.

Strauss's thesis is that Maimonides, and philosophers in general before the seventeenth century, concealed from the vulgar, or a state bureaucracy of conventional authority, convictions that ran counter to popular prejudice or myth. Such concealment is the principle, I have come to believe, that the whole of *La Vita Nuova* and the *Commedia* (the later work taking its cue from the earlier), is organized upon.

> Persecution cannot prevent even public expression of the heterodox truth, for a man of independent thought can utter his views in public and remain unharmed, provided he moves with circumspection. . . .
>
> Almost the only preparatory work to guide the explorer in this field is buried in the writings of the rhetoricians of antiquity.
>
> Persecution, then, gives rise to a peculiar technique of writing, and therewith to a peculiar type of literature, in which the truth about all crucial things is presented exclusively between the lines. That literature is addressed not to all readers, but to trustworthy and intelligent readers only. It has all the advantages of private communications without having its greatest disadvantage—that it reaches only the writer's acquaintances. It has all the advantages of public communication, without having its greatest disadvantage—capital punishment for the author. . . .
>
> The fact which makes this literature possible can be expressed in the axiom

---

4. No one has yet written about the sexual root of Gershom Scholem's writing and its laughing defense of the anarchist in love and politics. I had confirmation of the former in several meetings, particularly our final one in his Jerusalem home.

that thoughtless men are careless readers, and only thoughtful men are careful readers. But it will be objected, there may be clever men, careful readers, who are not trustworthy and who after having found the author out, would denounce him to the authorities. As a matter of fact, this literature would be impossible if the Socratic dictum that virtue is knowledge and therefore that thoughtful men as such are trust-worthy and not cruel, were entirely wrong. (Strauss 1973, 24–25)

"Modern historical research, which emerged at a time when persecution was a matter of feeble recollection rather than of forceful experience, has counteracted or even destroyed an earlier tendency to read between the lines of the great writers or to attach more weight to their fundamental design that to those views which they repeated most often" (Strauss 1973, 31–32).

"Every decent modern reader is bound to be shocked by the mere suggestion that a great man might have deliberately deceived the large majority of his readers. And yet, as a liberal theologian once remarked, these imitators of the resourceful Odysseus were perhaps more sincere than we when they called 'lying nobly' what we would call 'considering one's social responsibilities' " (Strauss 1973, 35–36).

"Farabi ascribed to Plato the view that in the Greek city, the philosopher was in grave danger. In making this statement, he merely repeated what Plato had said. To a considerable extent, the danger was averted by the art of Plato" (Strauss 1973, 21).[5]

Alfred Ivry, in his work on Neoplatonic sources in Maimonides, speaks of the influence on the great Jewish philosopher of Shi'a Islam's doctrine of *taqiyya,* or deliberate deception. (In pages to follow, I will speak of the link between Maimonides and Dante.) There have been a number of books and articles on the pos-

---

5. In addition to Farabi, Strauss may have been indebted to a book by the eighteenth-century bishop of Gloucester—William Warburton's *The Divine Legation.* Maurice Pope, in *The Story of Decipherment,* remarks that Warburton writing about the antiquity of hieroglyphics theorized that the Egyptians had a "double doctrine." Pope elucidates, "What he [Warburton] means by it is that all ancient philosophers and philosophical sects that concerned themselves with morals, politics, legislation and such matters (therefore not the Ionians or the Epicurians) promulgated publicly the belief in future rewards and punishments since they thought that such a belief was politically useful or even necessary, but that they themselves rejected it as being untrue.

"To prove this strange proposition Warburton assembles a massive and impressive array of quotations, not only from what he calls the 'grand quaternion' of theistic philosophy—Pythagorean, Platonic, Peripatetic, Stoic—but also from individuals like Cicero whose letters and occasional remarks in speeches show that he personally thought of death as the end of feeling despite what he says in his public works devoted to the subject" (Pope 1999, 47).

sible link between the night journey of Muhammad and the poet's descent and ascent to "Other Worlds" in the *Commedia*. If the steps of Dante through Hell are, as the medievalist Frederick Goldin suspects, a confession of the poet's secret sins, Muhammad's position at the very nadir of that Inferno is certainly suggestive. I wonder, though, if Dante's deepest tie to Islam and Maimonides, by extension, does not lie in the artifice I find him practicing throughout the *Commedia*. This is the "artful dodge" that Strauss attributes to philosophers in general, and Ivry to the followers of the Shi'ite branch of Islam. "To assist the believer to accommodate himself to an imperfect and often hostile world, the Shi'a legitimized the practice of *taqiyya* paying lip service only to what they considered the exoteric dimensions of their faith. Consequently, Shi'a allegiance to the law and caliphate of Sunni Islam was always suspect" (Ivry 1995, 278).

Others have spoken of the content of Dante's philosophy.[6] It would be interesting to investigate what Strauss might call "the sociology" of Dante's philosophy, its relationship to the society in which Dante lived and his ability to express freely philosophic views. I want, however, to speak of the psychology of his expression, both as a poet and a philosopher. Philosophy is a way of imagining, of understanding, both the visible and invisible world. The whole *Commedia* alerts us that Dante's preoccupation with philosophy is to gain entrance into the other world, beyond, above. He dramatizes metaphysics. He is not content to personify wisdom or love in Virgil and Beatrice, but desires to measure, quantify, and describe the process by which the abstract becomes real. It is a possibility many writers toy with. In Dante it is not a conceit but part of the justification for attempting the work. Boccaccio describes Dante as a young man devoting himself with his whole body and process of thought, psychology, spirit, "soul," to philosophy's study, in order to lose or leave behind the distinction between body and soul.

> And enamored by the sweetness of knowing the truth of things locked up by heaven, and finding no other in this life more dear, wholly abandoning all other temporal anxiety, he gave himself up entirely to this alone, and in order that no part of philosophy should be left unscrutinized by him, he plunged with keen intellect into the profoundest depths of theology. Nor was the result remote from the intention: for thinking naught of heat and cold, of vigils or of fasts, nor any other bodily vexation, he reached by unbroken study to such a knowledge of the Divine Essence and the other Sequent Intelligence as may be compassed by

---

6. See, for instance, Etienne Gilson's *Dante the Philosopher* (1949) and Edmund G. Gardner's *Dante and the Mystics* (1968).

human intellect. And it was at diverse ages that he studied and learned the diverse sciences, so likewise it was diverse Places of Study that he mastered them under diverse teachers. (Boccaccio 1904, 7)

Michael Barbi, Dante's biographer, has footnoted the effects of abandonment. "According to Dante's own testimony, shortly after the year 1290 he applied his labors to philosophy with such zeal that 'in a short time, perhaps thirty months,' he began 'to be so keenly aware of her sweetness that the love of her drove away and destroyed every other thought.' Not more than two or three years had elapsed when 'having overtaxed his eyes with too much reading,' he felt his visual powers to be so weakened that 'the stars appeared to him to be shadowed by some white mist' " (Barbi 1966, 8).[7]

Again and again in the *Commedia* there is reference to an overdazzling light. The edge of the real is shadowed by the unreal. It does not stop at metaphor. Dante is searching for something real in the realm of philosophy and in his own fiction. He enters logic, perhaps ironic, in which he hopes to prove the reality of the unreal and to find the real flesh of the dead Beatrice.

He is the descendent of Orpheus, the ancestor of Don Quixote. He is pathetic and godlike. The encomium of the Spanish philosopher and novelist, Unamuno, on the poor knight of Castile, holds for the weeping cavalier of Tuscany. "The longing for immortality is rooted in the love of a woman, for it is there that the instinct for self-perpetuation triumphs over the instinct for mere self preservation; substance thus triumphing over appearance. The longing for immortality leads to the love of a woman, and thus it was that Don Quixote found both woman and Glory in Dulcinea: since he could not perpetuate himself in her by a child of the flesh, he sought to make himself eternal through her by spiritual deeds" (Unamuno 1976, 77). The voice of the Spaniard echoed in the conch of the triton, Edward Dahlberg, Saint Louis, Missouri: "What a woe was the uterus—a great sea trough through which four edenic rivers flow, one of milk, the second of honey, the third of balsam and the last of urine" (Dahlberg 1967a, 36).

Dante's philosophy, poetic theory, promises immortality, through the love of a woman.[8] Dante, Unamuno, Dahlberg, voyage down into the sea as uterus. For it is not so much over the waves that Dante journeyed but through them, down, in order to come up to the Heavens. This smacks of the *Zohar*, or Kabbalah—the text

---

7. The quotations are from the *Convivio*, II, xii, 7 and III, ix, 15.

8. This was a commonplace of Provençal poetry, the platonic ladder of ascension thought to have been borrowed from Moorish poetry as practiced in the Catalan regions bordering on Provence.

of thirteenth-century mysticism. In my combing of the Atlantic sea grasses I looked again at the fraternal embrace Dante gives the sea monster, Fraud. (The reader whose Italian does not flow easily, must pardon me for quoting the passage in full, but the secrets lie in the repetitions of the Italian. The English cognates will guide even the novitiate through the rapids. And words touched on in this crucial moment, like *"maravigliosa"*[9] heard from the lips of Dante's teacher just moments before, speak the riddles of the text.)

> Io avea una corda intorno cinta
> e con essa pensai alcuna volta
> prender la lonza a la pelle dipinta.
> Poscia ch'io l'ebbi tutta da me sciolta
> sì come 'l duca m'avea comandato,
> porsila a lui aggroppata e ravvolta.
> Ond' ei si volse inver' lo destro lato,
> e alquanto di lunge da la sponda
> la gittò giuso in quell' alto burrato
> "E' pur convien che novità risponda,"
> dicea fra me medesmo "al novo cenno
> che 'l maestro con l'occhio sì seconda."
> Ahi quanto cauti li uomini esser dienno
> presso a color che non veggion pur l'ovra,
> ma per entro i pensier miran col senno!
> El disse a me: "Tosto verrà di sovra
> ciò ch'io attendo e che il tuo pensier sogna;
> tosto convien ch'al tuo viso si scovra."
> Sempre a quel ver c'ha faccia di menzogna
> de' l'uom chiuder le labbra fin ch'el puote,
> però che sanza colpa fa vergogna;
> ma qui tacer nol posso; e per le note
> di questa comedìa, lettor, ti giuro
> s'elle non sien di lunga grazia vòte,
> ch'i' vidi per quell'aere grosso e scuro
> venir notando una figura in suso,
> maravigliosa ad ogni cor sicuro,

9. The word *maravigliosa* or "marvelous" will be spoken by Dante's master on earth, Bruno Latini, in the circle of the homosexuals, and it will be pronounced as a blessing on his student. Its appearance here in the description of the monster Fraud, is one of those conscious or unconscious weavings of the *Commedia* that give it such a "personal voice," to use the language of one of my teachers, Albert J. Guerard.

sì come torna colui che va giuso
talora e solver l'àncora ch'aggrappa
o scoglio o altro che nel mare è chiuso,
che 'n sù si stende, e da piè si rattrappa.

I had a cord cinched about me
and with this I thought one time
to take the leopard with the painted hide.
After I had quite untied it
Just as my leader had commanded
I gave it to him wound and coiled.
Then turning toward his right side,
and some distance from the edge,
he threw it down into that deep abyss.
"It has to be something novel that will answer,"
I said to myself, "to the novel signal
which my master so follows with his eye."
Ah how much caution men must take
next to those who look not only to the deed
but see into the thoughts with wisdom.
He said to me, "Soon comes up
what I await and what your thought dreams
soon will be discovered to your sight."
Always to that truth which has the face of a lie
a man ought to close his lips, to the limit he can
for without fault, it brings shame
but here I can not be quiet and by the notes
of this comedy, reader, I swear to thee
so they may not fail of long lasting favor
but that I saw though that gross and gloomy air
come swimming up, a figure
marvelous to any stout heart
like to the return of one who went down
awhile to loosen an anchor gripped on
a reef or something else which in the sea is shut
who stretching upward, draws in his feet.
(*Inf.* 16:106–36)

Now these lines echo of "something novel" indeed. Not having read Strauss, I only understood that Dante was hinting that "something new" (more than a mythological monster) was swimming up. But looking at *Persecution and the Art of Writing,* one might be reading a paraphrase, poet/philosopher in the place of "philosopher."[10] "For philosophic readers he [the philosopher] would do almost more than enough by drawing their attention to the fact that he did not object to telling lies which were noble or tales which were merely similar to truth" (Strauss 1973, 35). The expression "novel signal" tells us to read between the lines. "Always to that truth which has the face of a lie / a man ought to close his lips, to the limit he can / for without fault it brings shame / but here I can not be quiet, and by the notes / of this comedy, reader, I swear to thee, / so they may not fail of long lasting favor." Again Strauss sounds in my ears. "Reading between the lines is strictly prohibited in all cases where it would be less exact than not doing so. Only such reading between the lines as starts from an exact consideration of the explicit statements of the author is legitimate. The context in which a statement occurs, and the literary character of the whole work as well as its plan, must be perfectly understood before an interpretation of the statement can reasonably claim to be . . . correct" (Strauss 1973, 30).

The context, despite the coy disclaimers of scholars, their unwillingness to read Dante in a sexual context, is clear to me. Dante and Virgil, his master, understand each other so well in this regard that without words, but at a silent command, the follower unhitches the belt of chastity with which he thought to keep lust at bay, the leopard with the painted hide, and Virgil throws it to the monster Fraud, as the tastiest of baits. They are in the circle of the homosexuals. What this means Dante will hint at further on, but the direct linking of lust, the "notes of this comedy," and Fraud as a sea monster seems plain.

What is the *Commedia* but a giant fraud in which a truth will be buried? That line, "something shut within the sea," as the image of an anchor coming loose warns us: the drama of ending the sixteenth canto while we await the mystery figure swimming up: the ironic laughter of Virgil when he rhymes explosively, histrionically, almost like a circus master barking, "*aguzza,*" "sharp," with "*apuzza,*" "stink," to begin the seventeenth canto (*Inf.* 17:1–3) all trumpet—look between the lines!

The "embrace" of Fraud by Dante is stressed through the latter's very revulsion and fear. He is afraid to call out to Virgil to embrace him, but again, the latter anticipates and grasps him in his arms. A few lines before, the Mantuan instructs

---

10. In fact in the same paragraph Strauss himself draws the parallel. "From the point of view of the literary historian at least, there is no more noteworthy difference between the typical premodern philosopher (who is hard to distinguish from the premodern poet) and the typical modern philosopher than that of their attitudes toward 'noble (or just) lies,' 'pious frauds,' the 'ductus obliquus' or 'economy of the truth.' "

him to be "strong and ardent," to take his seat on the sullen Leviathan's back. It is "by such stairs" that they will "descend."

Leaving the circle of homosexuals in Hell, Dante plunges, on the back of Fraud, into the depths of the *Inferno,* Malebolge. It is from the circle of homosexuals, or to be more exact, hermaphrodites, *bisexuals,* that Dante will leave the scalding fires of Purgatory and enter into the Garden of Eden. At the moment he grasps the monster, Dante's direct admission of his secret or secrets, for which he resorts (with Virgil, or rather holding on to Virgil) to piggybacking on artistic Fraud, truth with the *face* of a lie (literal Fraud, by contrast, is described as the lie, or serpent with the *face* of truth, appearing as the just man) is still at least a book away. Dante's fellow poets, Cino da Pistoia and Bosone da Gubbio, whose testimony consigning Dante to his own Hell I will come to, give him a bench in the eighteenth canto, the canto after he alights from the back of Fraud. It is not hard to guess that fraud has most to do with Dante's sexual life.

In Hell, where he has many sins to front, contend with, his sin is not obvious. In Purgatory, however, a creature of the sea not unlike Fraud or Geryon appears. It comes in a unique form, a frightening nightmare, as if the literal voyage of the *Commedia* did not hold terrors enough to release it. In the dark before dawn, rising out of a night like a sea, in vapors of fog, the siren, the one who tempted Ulysses, takes shape before Dante.

> Ne l'ora che no può 'l calor dïurno
> intepidar più 'l freddo de la luna
> vinto da terra e talor da Saturno:
> —quando i geomanti lor Maggior Fortuna
> veggiono in orïente, innanzi a l'alba
> surger per via che poco le sta bruna—,
> mi venne in sogno una femmina balba
> ne li occhi guercia, e sovra i piè distorta,
> con le man monche, e di colore scialba.
> Io la mirava; e come 'l sol conforta
> le fredde membra che la notte aggrava
> così lo sguardo mio le facea scorta
> la lingua, e poscia tutta la drizzava
> in poco d'ora, e lo smarrito volto,
> com' amor vuol, così le colorava.
> Poi ch'ell' avea 'l parlar così disciolto,
> cominciava a cantar sì, che con pena
> da lei avrei mio intento rivolto.

"Io son," cantava, "io son dolce serena,
che ' marinari in mezzo mar dismago;
tanto son di piacere a sentir piena!
Io volsi Ulisse del suo cammin vago
al canto mio; e qual meco s'ausa
rado sen parte; sì tutto l'appago"

In the hour that the daily heat
can not overcome the cold of the moon
vanquished by the earth and sometimes by Saturn
when the geomancers their Fortune Major
see rise in the east before dawn
by a path that only a while stays dark
there came to me in a dream, a stammering woman
cross eyed, crooked on her feet
with maimed hands and of sallow hue.
I stared at her and as the sun revives
the cold limbs frozen by the night
so that look of mine quickened
her tongue, quite lifted her up
in a short time, and her numb face
as by the wish of love colored.
When she had her speech thus set free,
she began to sing so, that with pain
I would have had to turn my mind from her.
"I am" she sang, "I am the sweet siren
who beguiles the mariners in the midst of the sea,
so full of pleasure is it to hear me!
I turned Ulysses on his eager way
to my song, and he who is with me
rarely departs, so wholly I content him."
(*Purg.* 19:1–24)

Virgil has to call Dante three times to rouse him from this vision. In the nick of time, "a lady holy and alert," appears to chase the seductress off. Even Virgil is scolded in the dream for letting the creature approach Dante since the latter's attraction to such chimeras is plain. There is confession in the dream by the author— shame before his own experiences. When the lady "holy and alert" tears off the Siren's clothes, the stink from her "belly" awakes the poet. ("Belly" seems like a euphemism in this context—pointing to the vagina.) Language links Geryon, or Fraud, the Siren, Ulysses, and Dante. The "*puzzo*," "stink," of the Siren and the cry of

Virgil about Fraud, the monster who makes the whole world *"apuzza," "*to stink,*"* are in parallel. The call of Virgil to Dante, "Or sie forte e ardito," "now be strong and ardent," in mounting Fraud, is repeated later in the exclamation of Ulysses about his trip to the Unknown, "dentro a me l'ardore/ ch'i' ebbi a divenir del mondo esperto," "within me the ardor which I had to arrive at experience of the world." These repetitions *"ardore, ardito, puzzo, apuzza"* draw one into Dante's self-scrutiny.

There is a link between the Siren and Beatrice few have desired to pursue. To my ear, the final call of blandishment to Dante, "so wholly I content him" (with its implication that Ulysses *was* so contented), echoes the angry rebuke of Beatrice to the poet in the Garden of Eden. "My buried flesh should have moved you. / Never did nature or art present you / with a pleasure equal to the beautiful limbs in which I / was enclosed, and they are scattered in the earth." *"Carne sepolta," "*sepulchered flesh," will hypnotize Dante. The Siren's hideous body, unhappily, is a refraction of Beatrice's, if it be divested of its spiritual magic. The images of immersion in the waters of Paradise play on that metaphor of drowning to which the Siren summons the mariners. Scholars have imagined that Dante's citing of a liaison between Ulysses and the Siren is the result of the Tuscan's inability to read Homer either in the original or translation, his possible misunderstanding of the story.[11] But Dante invents a journey for Ulysses beyond the Gates of Hercules into the Atlantic, searching for unknown lands, knowledge, finding the mountain of Purgatory. Is it so improbable that Dante also deliberately sent Ulysses to a liaison with the Siren? If so, why?

The answer is exactly what I would reply to the question of why he had the Greek, Ulysses, discover Purgatory. Ulysses is the shadow self of Dante. If Dante's quest for knowledge and the flesh of Beatrice is not hallowed by the Holy One, he becomes evil and impious. And there is good reason for Dante to believe that his search is unhallowed.

Dante's attraction to the Siren in Purgatory riddles his ambivalence about his own search. It is through the embrace of Fraud and the abandoning of chastity that Dante hopes to come to Paradise. Yet it may be that it is not Beatrice but the Siren who is beckoning him. He must chance it. His grasp of words that touch and feel, his intuition as a poet grounded in the sensations of his flesh tells him that lust is the way. (This is the plain sense of the action when Virgil throws the Friar's cord around Dante's middle as both bait and fish line into the Inferno's abyss.) Hearing Dante's disgust at Geryon, one can easily lose sight of the fact that the Florentine must unloop the cord of religious discipline and lure the monster up be-

---

11. See the notes of C. H. Grandgent as revised by Charles S. Singleton, in *La Divina Commedia,* on pages 474–75.

fore he and Virgil can proceed. Fraud is not a sideshow freak in the *Inferno*. The creature is one of Dante's guides.

> To that truth which has the face of a lie
> a man ought to close his lips, to the limit he can
> for without fault, it brings shame
> but here I can not be quiet.

My speculations on Dante and the erotic vibrations of the *Commedia* recalled to me the reading I had done in the *Zohar,* where dreams speak of knowledge of God through a spiritualized sex. I began to wonder whether Hell, Paradise, and Heaven in Dante were constructed out of similar ideas.

Moses de Leon, the reputed author of the *Zohar,* was dependent on Maimonides. Dante's philosophical tutor, Thomas Aquinas, was a careful student of the twelfth-century Jewish philosopher. Shlomo Pines, in the introduction to his translation of Maimonides' *The Guide of the Perplexed,* speculates on the basis of a designation of the prophet Moses in the *Inferno,* that Dante had read Maimonides in Latin translation. The Neoplatonism of the thirteenth century underlay both the new mysticism of the Kabbalists and the dreams of the poets in Sicily and Bologna—texts that sought to draw together philosophic and erotic longing.[12]

12. For Maimonides' fascination with Neoplatonism, see Alfred Ivry's remarks in "Islamic and Greek Influence on Maimonides' Philosophy": "It is in Plotinus's writings, lastly, that Maimonides would also have found the concept of an act of knowing which is immediate and intuitive, a type of knowing which goes beyond that couched in rational propositional logic, a knowledge which reaches out in a-rational ways to comprehend the rationally incomprehensible. It is this kind of knowledge which Plotinus calls 'ignorance,' which is an ignorance, in the words of the *Theology of Aristotle,* 'more sublime than any cognition,' *dhalika jahl ashrafu min kulli ma'rifah.* In this 'ignorance' man realizes, for Plotinus, the ultimate unity of being with which his soul yearns to unite, a unity such as is known only to the Universal Intelligence, and beyond that, in an even more mysterious way, to the Pure One. This ultimate and primary state of unified being is depicted by Plotinus as a state of love, and it is as an act of love, of 'pure love,' that the intelligible world, the world of essential being, proceeds from the One. Man shares in this divine love, and is transformed by it. He becomes aware of it when he exceeds his rational limits and gives himself to that perception of a reality, which is not evident to our senses, or to our intellect.

"It is this non-empirical and radically idealistic direction of Neoplatonic thought, with its monistic inclinations, which Maimonides must have found hard to take. Yet the vision and the means of attaining it did appeal to him. In his introductory (7) and closing remarks in the *Guide* (637) we find him speaking, respectively, of moments of sudden lightning like flashes of inspiration and of acts of divine loving-kindness, *hesed:* experiences which are not meant to be synonymous with normative acts of intellection or with the process of emanation as normally understood. Elsewhere Maimonides speaks also of our ignorance of God's nature, an ignorance which is a form of knowledge (1:58, 137;

It was to Dante's advantage to know and absorb the lessons of the Kabbalah.

From below must come the impulse to move the power from above. . . . It is from below that the movement starts and thereafter is all perfect. . . . It is thus the yearning from below that brings about the completion from above.

So the verse "and Isaac brought her into his mother Sarah's tent" (Gen. 24:67) our masters have interpreted to mean that the Divine Presence came to Isaac's house along with Rebecca. According to secret doctrine, the supernal Mother is together with the male only when the house is in readiness and at that time the male and female are conjoined. At such time blessings are showered forth by the supernal Mother upon them. (*Zohar* 1978, 1:35a,50a)[13]

Perhaps Dante's descent through the sea on Fraud's back was literal and symbolic, sexual and . . .

Mystical?

Dante's descent recalled a passage of Gershom Scholem.

The visionary journey of the soul to heaven is always referred to as the "descent to the Merkabah." The paradoxical character of this term is all the more remarkable

---

59; 1390); leading ultimately to a 'worship' and 'love' that goes beyond our understanding of normative cognition (3:51, 620f). For Maimonides these phenomena exist, and they would have received a measure of philosophical legitimization for him best through Neoplatonic teachings. Moreover, those teachings offered him the formulations, which he found most compatible with traditional Jewish beliefs" (Ivry 1986, 150–51).

According to Ivry, Maimonides was not eager to have his debt to Neoplatonism known, as it brought into question his adherence to Aristotle.

"It is the Aristotelian corpus of commentaries, which he is prepared to recommend to Samuel ibn Tibbon. Alfarabi, Ibn Bajja and Avicenna are regarded highly for their Aristotelianism, though the admixture of Neoplatonic thought in that Arisotelianism would only have increased Maimonides' admiration. Neoplatonism straight, however, was too much for Maimonides to accept, its metaphysics considered bizarre and its logic probably regarded as arbitrary.

"Yet despite his own training and life-long convictions, Maimonides reveals in the *Guide* a marked susceptibility to Neoplatonic perspectives, themes and ideas. . . . Maimonides utilizes Neoplatonic sources to strengthen and patch over the weak spots in his Aristotelian edifice. . . . The *Guide* was written, then, I dare say, not only *for* the perplexed, but *by* the perplexed" (1986, 151).

13. Scholem cites these quotes in the *Zohar* as 1:34a (in the Soncino translation 1:35:a) and 1:49b (Soncino 50a), respectively.

because the detailed description of the mystical process nonetheless consistently employs the metaphor of ascent and not descent. The mystics of this group call themselves *Yorde Merkabah,* i.e., "descenders to the Merkabah [chariot]" . . . we only know of their existence in Babylonia, from where practically all mystical tracts of this particular variety made their way to Italy and Germany; it is these tracts that have come down to us in the form of manuscripts written in the late Middle Ages. (Scholem 1961, 47)

It is not hard to hear the echo, *Yorde,* Jordan (The Hebrew Y was once pronounced like a J), and to wonder. If Dante knew about the tradition of a descent into a river over which the sea cannot boast, might he also know something of Jewish mysticism? It is not necessary to think that he actually was an enthusiast for the *Zohar,* as was Pico da Mirandola, several hundred years later, in Florence. Ideas of the *Zohar:* of reaching the Unknown through sexual congress with a woman who embodies the Female Presence of the Holy One, Blessed be He: the yearning from below summoning the Presence from above: an imaginary universe built of Neoplatonic concrete, all have a close cousinship in the world of the *Commedia.* Dante feels that without Beatrice he is imperfect. According to the *Zohar,* man was created imperfect, even in the Garden of Eden. "Only when Eve was made perfect, was he made perfect too."

The perfection of a rabbinical scholar, or of a Florentine gentleman through a woman, her love, strikes up the music of Provence where the rules of courtly love in the West were first defined. Dante openly acknowledges his debt to Provence and gives its poetics and language the highest of compliments, writing several lines of the *Commedia* in Provençal. He carries on his "game" within its court rules. The love of a woman, according to the troubadours, had a spiritualizing effect and acted as a ladder on which the lover could ascend to Heaven. It was a form of education in Platonics in which woman reflected the light of a heavenly idea. The troubadours sang that the more difficult love was to attain, the farther off the beloved, the higher, more valuable that love. In Provençal poetry there is also an earthy, comic strain, the *leis de con,*[14] laws of the cunt, as William IX trilled, and Platonics crosses at times in these poets with amoral behavior. What is so far away and hard to "attain" as a bird in another man's cage? Realities of court life play the bass fiddle to the soprano notes of Platonics. Dante carries the irony implicit in

14. For a discussion of the *leis de con,* see Frederick Goldin's remarks (1973b, 5–19). Refer to note 29, chapter 9.

the rules into another realm. His adulterous liaison has as its worshiped object a lady already dead—a woman at a dread distance, on a far shore.

The conceit is touched with pathos, crossed with coarse obscenity. It has what one art critic speaking of the sculpture of Florence described as a "sinister purity" (Stokes 1968, 106).[15] It also mirrors one of the deepest riddles of man which the medieval church was obsessed with, the worship of a human body caught in death.

If Dante places his beloved beyond this world and its touch, its consummation, his problem becomes how to get to her. Ought he to call his mistress down and to what purpose? Should she be an intercessory saint? He could carry on a courtship again with her on this earth only within the bounds of propriety or else risk a lewdness that would dissipate the moral authority and probably the beauty of his lines. A saint only as a companion? Dante wanted to resume the courtship. This could only be done with impunity in the afterlife. But how would the rules of courtly love conform to the natural laws of Heaven?

The answers to Dante's dilemma lay in Neoplatonic philosophy, studied in Provence earlier in the century at the end of which he reached maturity. The Heaven of the *Zohar* and other Neoplatonic universes created by the Spanish Jewish mystics under the sway of Provence's mysticism and philosophy bears many points of reference to Dante's. These men were not just mystics. Their mysticism was a response to the threat of rational philosophy to the religious imagination. They belonged to the same circle as Dante, the avid readers of Greek and Arabic texts interpreted by the theologians and rabbis of the thirteenth century. Historians of philosophy have testified to the crossings between Jewish and Christian minds at this juncture in European thought. From Arabic to Hebrew to Latin was a route by which many texts became available. Did the new Kabbalah, dreaming, reach the ears of Christian readers of philosophy?

The emanation of matter from nothingness obsessed medieval philosophers and theologians trying to understand the act of creation. It was an essential question for a cosmological poet—Dante or Moses de Leon—whose characters passed from the earthly to the transcendent realm. They must naturally wonder at the physics of the divine and human transformation. For both, the theories of Plotinus and Neoplatonism are indispensable. Maimonides had spoken of the substance of the prophetic dreams, taking his photographs against the silver backing

---

15. "Florentine artists show us the antinomy of their heritage. The most emotional may also be the most reserved. Not however, when the emotions are principally of love. Thus the slightly sinister purity of Florentine tenderness" (Stokes 1968, 105).

of the Neoplatonic negative, that is—"the is that is not," the substance that is not substantial, dream substance.[16] The coarser questions of courtship are expressed in the *Commedia* through the physics of this material, which sparkles with the crystals of Creation. It is no wonder that the drama of light, the notion of a theater of light, which is dramatic in the *Zohar,* is also found in the *Commedia.*

16. This will become critical for Dante in Purgatory, where he has a long discussion on the subject of the substance of visions with the Latin poet, Statius. For Maimonides, too, the perplexing question of miraculous phenomenon and visions are solvable only through Neoplatonism. See Ivry's anatomization of the paradoxes into which Maimonides is drawn, trying to remain consistent in a discussion of the visions of Moses.

"Maimonides . . . declares in *Guide,* i. 46 that all prophetic visions of the Divine are really of forms created by God. The events described in prophecy thus have an objective correlate, though not the one first supposed. Accordingly, says Maimonides at *Guide* ii. 33, the voice of the Lord heard at Sinai was really a 'created voice,' with all the effects previously described. This interpretation would seem to save the 'objectivity' of the event itself, as well as of Maimonides' interpretation of it, but for his insistence that Moses' prophecy was from God himself, unmediated by any other form or substance. The created forms in which miracles appear, if taken literally, are just the sort of imaginative construct, however 'real,' which Moses, on Maimonides' own reading, did not require. Belief in a 'created voice' at Sinai, thus reduces Moses' prophecy to that of other prophets, his perceptions differing from theirs in degree but not in kind. . . .

"As in classical Neoplatonic thought, diverse phenomena give way to substances that are more comprehensive, though less understood and these in turn point to higher realities and to the One who is above all else and responsible for it. The literal as well as the interpretative symbols used are all of only partial efficacy, and we are left without any real understanding of how God communicated his will to man.

"The overriding purpose of these biblical representations, Maimonides says in i. 46, is to establish belief in God's essence, that of a living being who is both aware of itself and of others, and who is ultimately responsible for all others. This responsibility is seen as executed through the process of emanation, as we have said, and it is here too that the Neoplatonic element is dominant, albeit in principle more than in detail" (Ivry 1991, 137).

HEAVENLY INTERCOURSE

A VISITOR ARRIVED FROM JERUSALEM. The poet Michal Govrin, a student of Gershom Scholem, sat in my studio and we spoke of Moses de Leon, the *Zohar*, and Dante. I was intrigued by a talmudic tradition that holds that David, King of Israel, committed his sin of adultery as a form of worship. Had Dante heard of it? The doctrine of *shogeh bah tomid*, to be ravished, wandering, erring, in excess always, seeking love of God—love of Beatrice in the uppermost limits of Dante's Heaven was also love of God. Michal told me that there was a chapter of the *Zohar* missing in the Soncino Press's abridged English translation describing the sexual intercourse of the dead in Paradise. I begged the gift of translation. I had also mentioned the theme of divine rapture, *shogeh bah tomid*. From the Holy City some weeks later came the passage with this note.

Dear Mark,
So my intuition was even more striking as the passage from the Zohar starts with your "shogeh"! and goes into a detailed description of the heaven of virtuous women and their special sexual intercourse with the virtuous men in heaven—a summit of the body Jewish conception—Paradise as a tremendous love (physical love) palace.[1]

Both the *Zohar* and the *Commedia* are about man's desire to penetrate the secrets of the afterlife. Both draw on Neoplatonic philosophy to give body to their dreams of this space beyond the world. If Dante's poem is a lyric of adultery, Dante's fascination with David must be obvious. To find the *Zohar* using the language of the Talmud about David was a surprise to me. And it is used in just that passage which describes the copulation of the virtuous in the afterlife—a moment I believed of consuming interest to Dante.

The central searcher of the *Zohar*, the second-century sage Simeon ben Yohai,

---

1. Letter to Mark Jay Mirsky from Michal Govrin, Jerusalem, 1983.

is meeting with his honored guests from the world on high. The night darkens. The members of the Divine Academy cry out to the sage, "O holy pious one, Light of the world, take this tablet, this lamp, and write!" They begin to impart to him a secret of the world beyond. It is the time for the members of the Heavenly Yeshiva to visit their graves. For the Holy One, Himself, is about to enter His Garden and sport with the righteous. The word "sport" is fraught with connotations of the erotic. As the ghostly rabbis rise, flying off, they promise to return the next day, to reveal more mysteries. They have already secured permission.[2]

Rabbi Simeon ben Yohai bursts into tears, groans with joy as the sages whirl upward around him:

> "Let her be as the loving hind and pleasant roe. Let her breasts satisfy thee at all times. And be thou ravished always with her love" (Prov. 5:18). Torah, Torah, light of all the worlds. How many seas and rivers and sources and springs spread out from you on all sides? Everything from you! All upper and lower beings exist by your merit. Spiritual light radiates from you! Torah, Torah, what can I say to you? You are the loving hind and the pleasant roe. The above and the below are your lovers. Who merits to suckle properly from you? Torah, Torah, the sport of your Master! Who can reveal or tell your mysteries and hidden things?
>
> "He cried and put his head between his knees and kissed the dust."

The lines that Rabbi Simeon cries out above, "Let her be as the loving hind. . . . Let her breasts satisfy thee at all times. And be thou ravished always with her love," from Proverbs, which refer to "the wife of thy youth" were interpreted by the sages as a metaphor for the love between a scholar and the study of the Law, Torah. Why a hind or deer? The most radical construction was put on this metaphor by Samuel h. Nahmani, in *Talmud Bavli,* who read it as an animal fable. The study of Torah (and the excitement that a *new* understanding in the law brings) is as sensual and blissful an experience as sleeping with a virgin whose vagina is as tight as a hind's. Maimonides noticed this passage and alluded to it in trying to explain the passion of man for God. It seems certain that Moses de Leon in repeating it intended a commentary on Maimonides (perhaps ironic), for it is the cry that introduces the *Zohar*'s exposition of lovemaking of the dead in Paradise.

The members of the Heavenly Academy who have come to sit with Rabbi Simeon must fly away to "visit" their graves. The word for "visit" has the connotation in Hebrew of sexual intercourse. Linked to the Holy One's coming to "sport"

---

2. For a fuller text of this passage see *Zohar* 1985.

with them in their graves through the Garden of Eden, "visit" means, in the context of what is to come, to "couple" male and female.

Rabbi Simeon, left to contemplate, sees in the morning's first dim glow a sacred light, images of the Temple in Jerusalem that lights up the heavens in its glow. He rejoices, the light is hidden and messengers from Heaven come, bringing greetings from the head of the Heavenly Yeshiva. They inform Rabbi Simeon that above: "[M]any new 'old things' were innovated in Torah that night."

"Please," he begs, "Tell me one of them."

In a long, tortuous interpretation they begin to reveal mysteries of procreation. "A spirit that goes naked in that world without children—his wife is made a vessel to be built up by him. What is the reason? His wife is the lamp that is lit by him; the two of them constitute one lamp. One light proceeds from the other. If this one is put out, it is relit from his very own light [which is in his wife], because they were one light." The metaphor of light is introduced but it is shadowed by the idea of a mysterious, supernatural semen.

Rabbi Simeon makes an unusual and blunt request. What happens to women in the world above? "Are they worthy to rise above into that world? What is it like for them there?"

In a flutter of wings, one of the ghostly rabbis flies off to get permission to reveal these secrets. He returns crying:

> Rise, Rabbi, your portion is worthy—rise! Because of you we see and are worthy of several hidden upper things. How much joy seized us when they gave us permission to reveal to you all that you wish. The Head of the Heavenly Academy has gone out to us and said, "Greet the son of Bar Yochai Rabbi Simeon. The place of Bar Yochai—has it not been kept empty several days? No one will approach it. He is worthy."
>
> . . . all the members of the Yeshiva went out and I asked permission that the son of Yochai should ask this question. Because of this they showed me what I did not know before.
>
> O Rabbi! Six halls they showed me with so many different pleasant things. [It was] in the place where the veil is drawn in the Garden, for from that veil onward, men do not enter at all.

Four pious women, Bitya, the daughter of Pharaoh; Serach, the daughter of Asher; Jochabed, the mother of Moses; and Deborah, the prophetess, sit here with "tens of thousands and thousands" of women, all of whom have deserved wide places of light in Heaven. Toward the curtain behind which they lounge, come the images of appropriate great men. Moses. At set times Moses visits his foster mother, Pharaoh's daughter; Joseph approaches Serach. The women rise to greet them. Between the visits the women sit studying the Law, Torah, and singing and listening to the angels praise their names. And beyond these women are the halls of the matriarchs of the Jews, Sarah, Rebecca, Leah, Rachel, in even holier solitude.

"All day they are by themselves, as I told you, and the men as well." Suddenly in the middle of the night, the gardens of study, of psalmody, secrecy, begin to buzz with sexual life. "Every night all of them gather as one. For the hour of intercourse is in the middle of night. Both in this world and in that world. The intercourse of that world is the cleaving of soul with soul: light with light. The intercourse of this world is body with body." In this copulation of the heavenly all is seemly, there are no matches between men and animals, or mothers and sons.

> And all is proper, species after species, intercourse after intercourse, body after body, intercourse of that world is light after light. The halls of the four matriarchs are called the Halls of the Trusting Daughters and I was not worthy to see them. Their portion is worthy of the righteous. Men and women who take the straight road in this world deserve all the pleasures of that world.
>
> O Rabbi, Rabbi! If you were not the son of Yochai, it would not be permitted to be revealed. The intercourse of that world is more fruitful than the intercourse in this world. In their intercourse, the intercourse of that world, in their desire (to be) one, when their souls cleave one to the other, they produce fruits and light goes out from them. They become lamps. And these are the souls of the proselytes who convert. They all go into one hall.
>
> When the dead who are righteous couple in the Heavens, their union is not barren or fruitless. No, they give birth to the souls of those who will convert to Judaism.
>
> Hearing this, Rabbi Simeon bent over and kissed the dust. He said, "Word, Word. I sought you from the day of my birth and now a word has been made known to me from the root and source of all."

Is it important to Dante that there is sexual intercourse among the dead in Paradise?

Beatrice is dead.

Dante, however, still desires Beatrice. Does Beatrice desire him? She will tell him, "[H]ow in the opposite way my buried flesh should have moved you," in the Garden of Eden. "Never did nature or art present you with a pleasure equal to the beautiful limbs in which I was enclosed."

Does Dante desire before this rebuke a purely "spiritual" Beatrice?

Has he desired the Beatrice who walked on earth?

If Dante is seeking sexual intimacy with Beatrice in Heaven, "intercourse," he will have read with some trepidation the Gospel of Matthew. Jesus has ridiculed the notion of marriages in Heaven.

The same day came to him the Sadducees, which say that there is no resurrection, and asked him, Saying, Master, Moses said, If a man die, having no children, his brother shall marry his wife and raise up seed unto his brother.

Now there were with us seven brethren: and the first, when he had married a wife, deceased, and, having no issue, left his wife unto his brother: Likewise the second also, and third, unto the seventh. And last of all the woman died also. Therefore in the resurrection, whose wife shall she be of the seven? for they all had her.

Jesus answered, and said unto them, Ye do err, not knowing the scriptures, nor the power of God. For in the resurrection they neither marry, nor are given in marriage, but are as the angels of God in heaven.

Matthew 22:23–30 seems to put a stop to any hope of encountering Beatrice's flesh in Paradise.[3] Dante, however, is skilled in paradoxes. The prohibition against marriage in Heaven presents him with an opportunity. The statement of Jesus can be read as a tacit dissolution of the bonds of marriage in the realm where all, men and women, live as angels. Since there can be no marriage, there will be no question of adultery. What can Beatrice allow Dante in the highest circles of Divinity? This is the burning question of *Purgatorio* and *Paradiso*.

3. Dante, in setting out in a journey to find a woman in the other world, was flirting with heresy. Jesus, warning that there was no marriage in Heaven, presumably meant no sexual intercourse. Yet Jesus, in proffering his own body as a spiritual substitute, had offered an idealized idea of union, a substitute that suggests a reflection of Plato's ideas. See Harold Bloom's remark, "The historical difference between the Yahwist and Akiba *is* Plato, and this influx of Athens into Jerusalem saved Judaism" (Bloom 1987, 31). This observation about postbiblical Jerusalem, however pungent, is qualified by the early Christian embrace, the rabbinical refusal, of Platonic tendencies when it comes to sexual experience. Despite the *Zohar*'s reconstruction of midrash on the basis of Neoplatonic ideas, even this late Jewish midrash insists on sexual rather than purely intellectual experience in Heaven. Saint Bernard could show Dante his way by adoring the body of Jesus, and speaking of the divine kiss, but Dante substitutes a real woman, Beatrice. The Platonic notions of the Italian poets, like their Provençal predecessors, hoping to bring together the act of copulation and the spiritual ascent, reflect a romanticism to which rabbinic Judaism since the thirteenth century has often been sympathetic.

This raises another question. Did Dante, on the earth, have intercourse with the real Beatrice in the flesh?

One ought to look again at Dante's poetry before his descent into Hell, his ascent of the mountain of Purgatory. I will come to what Dante hopes for with Beatrice in Heaven. What about their love on earth?

CHAPTER THREE

SEDUCED BY BEATRICE?

And then so much of him passed into me, he
Disappeared—I know not how.

—*Vita 9*

AS I TOOK UP *La Vita Nuova,* Dante's early work, with suspicions of the poet's connection to Kabbalah, to the search for the Holy One between the thighs of a wife, mistress—a woman beloved beyond death—a story, previously hidden, seemed to reveal itself. As a lyrical manual of young love, the poem is often obscure as far as a lover's emotions are to be discerned. The narrative line yields to dry prosaism. In the collection of love songs with their prose explanations I began to suspect a method. Was a lover concealing confessions in the tedious?

To go to so much trouble over a girl, woman, with whom Dante had but a distant romantic affection, did not seem true to the direct temperament of the poet. Has Dante slept with Beatrice? If it is so, *La Vita Nuova,* a document close to the event, ought to reveal it.

The chastity of Beatrice Portinari and Dante is an important myth for scholars. But it is a hypothesis not an axiom. I hope to accumulate evidence to the contrary, not for the sake of biographical certainties but in order to read the poetry in a new way. The portrait of Dante sketched by Boccaccio adds some weight to my suspicions.

And assuredly, I blush to be forced to taint the fame of such a man with any defect: but the order of the things on which I have begun in some sort demands it: because that if I held my peace concerning those things in him which are less worthy of praise, I shall withdraw much faith from the praiseworthy things already recounted. So I do plead my excuse to him, himself, who perchance even as I write, looketh down with scornful eye from some lofty region of heaven. Amid all the virtue, amid all the knowledge, that hath been shewn above to have be-

29

longed to this wondrous poet, lechery found most ample place not only in the years of his youth but also of his maturity: the which vice, though it be natural, and common, and scarce to be avoided, yet in truth is so far from being commendable that it cannot even be suitably excused. But who among mortals shall be a righteous judge to condemn it? Not I. Oh the infirmity, oh the brutish appetite of men! What power cannot women exercise over us when they choose, seeing what great things they can do even when they choose not. Attractiveness and beauty and natural appetite and many other things are working for them without pause in the hearts of men. (Boccacio 1904, 55)

Boccaccio wrote these lines in his *Life of Dante,* composed in the generation after the poet's death. He knew men who had known Dante Alighieri personally. The chastity of Beatrice Portinari is questionable when an admirer with Dante's reputation writes of her with intimacy.

✦   ✦   ✦

ALL POETS have a pathological need to confess. *Life Studies* is not a new conception but an old collection. If Dante wanted to speak about seduction, adultery, he had to be artful, even deceitful. He had full need of an "exoteric" text in the manner of the Ismai'ili Neoplatonists.[1] The knives of Beatrice's kinsmen, her husband's, would be sharp to avenge any direct admission. He had to mask his unburdening from the crowd, "confuse the ignorant," and deflect the literal-minded. In the fourth of the forty-two chapters of *La Vita Nuova,* he tells us many of his friends, some with "malicious curiosity," were attempting to learn about him "that which above all I wished to keep secret." In the fifth chapter, that is, still at the very beginning of the work, when he is discussing his methods of procedure for the whole, he announces his intention of using "a screen for the truth." Dante is referring to pretending to be in love with one lady, in order to throw the scent off the trail of his affection for Beatrice, but it echoes strangely, this lover's stratagem, of Strauss's prescription for describing the secret intent of a work which is best concealed from the vulgar. If it is Dante's device in the first critical moment of his love when it attracts the world's attention, it is not hard to think that it might be a device he resorts to for what must be concealed at large in *La Vita Nuova,* and again in the *Commedia.* If the device is employed to shield his conventional attentions to

---

1. For the doctrine of deliberate deception or *taqiyya* as practiced by the Ismai'ili Muslim philosophers in particular, see both my quotations from Alfred Ivry's work in the introduction and notes in the next chapter, "Dante Bewildered."

Beatrice from the citizens' attention, it would certainly be appropriate to "screen" from the regard of readers too sober his confession about Beatrice's chastity.

Dante's seduction begins in *The New Life.* In that book's last lines Dante promises to join Beatrice. This conceit returns to the man lost in his middle age. It calls for a strange form of fraud or disguise as if to answer the White Angel who intones to him in *La Vita Nuova,* "Fili mi, tempus est ut pretermictantur simulcra nostra," "My son it is time to do away with our pretendings" (*Vita* 12). *Simulcra* has the connotations of "pretendings," "disguises," "similitudes."

Without the pretense, the fraud, the chaste disguise, there will be no comedy, and perhaps no new life. Why does Dante flee from the Old World to the New, the isle of Purgatory, in the *Commedia,* eating his heart over the absent love of adolescence?

Does Dante confess in *La Vita Nuova* to sleeping with his adolescent love? More shocking, while she lived, did he dream, even hope, for a dead Beatrice. Is she responsible for his seduction, he for her death?

◆ ◆ ◆

DANTE SEDUCED? Is that the secret of *La Vita Nuova?* Has a lover concealed evidence, yet made it beat through the poem with suppressed joy; hymning of his beloved a divine virgin in recompense for earthly adultery? "Ecco la fiera con la coda aguzza," "Behold the beast with the sharp tail" (*Inf.* 17:1). Behold the monster—Fraud.

Under the noses of generations of readers—so well has the author covered his act, who has come forward to assert it? Is the *Commedia* a comedy whose smile begins in *La Vita Nuova?*

Under the measured repetitions of *The New Life,* the summations, the tender professions of innocence and the showers of tears, deep in the rustling lines of the poetry lies the nude body of an adolescent girl. We will catch only a faint glimpse under the gauze of her scant cloth in the arms of Love. "Nude except for a scanty blood colored cloth" (*Vita* 3). Why has Dante shown us Beatrice almost unrobed? He wishes to show himself with her, naked.

It is the first secret of Dante—his mistress has enjoyed him—but only one who will lie with his poetry deserves to know.

I too did not understand until now this brother who extends the blessed bread not of a woman's body.

Dante has taken the Divine Presence in adultery, as David did. [2] The sin will

---

2. This infatuation of David's with God—*Shiggayon l'Dovid,* David's reeling, erring, outpouring, or ravishment—was responsible, according to rabbinic storytelling, for King David's sin with

drive him round in circles. Afterward, looking upon his beloved Beatrice, dead—guilt will stalk him until he has built the catafalque of the *Commedia*.

The whole is a vast funeral, a round pyramid or burial chamber, a ziggurat in reverse. The Etruscan is born again in the Florentine Renaissance, an architecture that bores down through the rocky catacombs of the Tuscan hills. To go up, one must go down, this is Dante's mature wisdom, the wisdom of Heraclitus, of the Hebrew mystics in the chariot literature of Babylon. In *Purgatorio,* Dante will bless the act he has confessed to in *The New Life.* A messenger's open wings are the gates to Paradise. Come, cries an angel, "Con l'ali aperte che parean di cigno," "With wide opened wings which seemed of swan" (*Purg.* 19:45–46). Dante enters into his own tomb to taste Beatrice's lips, bring himself against her breasts, within her thighs, "*l'ali aperte*" "wide opened wings."

Seek love within an ossuary? That is a greater adventure than to cross the Gates of Hercules and sail the unknown seas. Purgatory and Paradise as places lie always out of reach, but as ideas they are a breath away in death. "Venite." It is the invitation through the gates of Eden.[3]

> "Venite, qui si varca,"
> parlare in modo soave e benigno,
> qual no si sente in questa mortal marca.
> Con l'ali aperte, che parean di cigno,
>
> "Come, here is the passage,"
> spoken in manner so exquisite and benign
> as is not heard in these human bounds.
> With wide opened wings which seemed of swan.
> (*Purg.* 19: 43–46)

All through *La Vita Nuova*, Dante calls out weeping for death. His disclaimers of lust are gauze, however, for his appetite. Why is seduction in Dante linked to death and how are both part of Dante's search for God? As the poet comes near Beatrice in the fifteenth chapter of *La Vita Nuova,* Love warns him to flee, for the emotion is too much "for this world." The intoxication, inebriation of love turns the stones of the street into the portals of death's kingdom. They are gravestones.

Bathsheba. It seems to be related to Maimonides' concept of *shogeh bah tomid,* being wrapped up in God, which I alluded to in my second chapter. I will expand on the conception of holy sin and its possible influence on Dante in the chapter "Dante and King David."

3. Note that this invitation comes after the attempt by the siren to seduce Dante. The language has a muted eroticism, suggesting the downy rape of Leda by Zeus in the persona of a swan.

e per la ebrietà del gran tremore
le pietre par che gridin: "Moia, moia!"

and through the drunkenness of the great tremor
the stones seem to cry: "Die, die!"
(*Vita* 15)

Dante links dying to courtship? Is this just the language of extremes? Dante's gift is for the concrete. He speaks what he says, death is real. Love, seduction, has been real for him too.

What seduction?

In the first chapter of *La Vita Nuova*, a brief thirty-three words or so, Dante mentions in a rather dry, offhand way, several important things. In Latin the poet announces, "Here begins the new life." He remarks that he is copying this from "the book of my memory" and adds, "There is nothing really worthy reading before this chapter." This third comment, a footnote to the two before, cannot help but jolt the contemporary mind. For in chapter 2 of *La Vita Nuova* it becomes plain that Dante is talking about events that took place when he was nine years old.[4] Now with the exception of one pained, but nonspecific cry about "mommies" in the *Commedia*, references to an actual father and mother are nonexistent. The poet talks of distant ancestors with self-confessed pride and speaks not only of Beatrice, but of her father. Dante has discounted, however, those first years of life that psychiatry, that twentieth-century metaphysics, tells us looms so large in determining human behavior. If it *is* only the eighteenth- and nineteenth-century novelists like Fielding, Sterne, Austen, Dickens, the Brontes, Eliot, Dostoyevsky, and their successor, Freud, who taught us to consider childhood important—why does Dante even allude to his?[5] Dante wants us to know that an experience wiped childhood from his "book of memory" or reduced it to a cipher not worth mentioning.

4. Barbara Reynolds points out in the notes to her edition of *La Vita Nuova* that "Dante indicates that he was almost nine years old when he first saw Beatrice (traditionally in May, 1274)." And that "by saying that the heaven of the fixed stars had moved one twelfth of a degree to the east since the birth of Beatrice, Dante indicates that she was eight years and four months old" (*Vita* 1969, 104–5).

Dante speaks of his own age and Beatrice's, however, in terms of parallel nines, giving their movement toward each other in childhood and adolescence the gravity of religious myth. Not only does he not mention the figure eight, but even the disparity of almost a year is made to balance through the repetition of "near" and "ninth." "She appeared to me, near the beginning of her ninth year and I first saw her, near the end of my ninth" (*Vita,* 2).

5. The ancient epic seems to anticipate the importance of childhood—the Isaac and Joseph stories, the folklore surrounding the infancy of biblical heroes, Abraham, Moses, the Gilgamesh cycle.

A reader does not have to look far from the first chapter of *La Vita Nuova* for that event. Immediately in the second chapter of *La Vita Nuova,* Dante introduces Beatrice, to whom he attributes his real birth. And he speaks about her in terms that will awaken the suspicion of one who takes the notion of truth through indirection seriously. "And through her image which stayed continually with me, was the confidence of Love to be Lord over me, it was of such noble virtue that it never once suffered me to be ruled by love without the faithful counsel of reason (regarding those things wherein such counsel would be useful to hear). Since to dwell too long on the passions and actions of such early years may appear to speak of something fabulous, I shall leave them, and pass over many things which can be imagined from the example of these" (*Vita* 2). What things? What fabulous actions and passions?

And again, "I tell how I wish to speak of her in order not to be hindered by vileness." What "vileness"? "First I speak of the eyes which are the beginning of love. . . . And, that every vicious thought may be put aside, remember you who read what is written above—that the greeting of this lady, that which was the operation of her mouth, was the end of my desires while I could receive it" (*Vita* 19).

"The denial that there is anything wrong, when we know that it is impossible that there should be anything wrong, is itself wrong." This is the maxim of al-Junayd, quoted by the Muslim theologian, Ibn Khaldun.

The "vicious" or "perverse" thought once spoken of by Dante, can not be "put aside . . . discarded . . . extinguished." In a poem that follows, Dante will cry, then faint under the flickering shades of two adulterous lovers, Francesca and Paolo—hearing a tale that one can only conclude, echoes his own, the seduction of the beloved through a book, words, description of a smile, illicit romance.

In the second chapter of *La Vita Nuova,* Beatrice first appears to the reader, as she has to the boy Dante, "dressed in the most noble of colors, a modest and chaste blood red, bound round and adorned in a guise appropriate to a young girl's youth." Why should the poet remember so particularly the color, *"umile e onesto, sanguigno,"* "modest and chaste, blood red," and refer to it as *"nobilissimo,"* "most noble"? Why yoke a bloodstain together with chastity, modesty of hue—or using closer cognates, humility and honesty of hue? Why the emphasis on the fact that this blood-red cloth, chastely "bound her round and adorned her in a guise appropriate to her youth"?

The answers are to be found, again, close at hand. In the very next chapter of *La Vita Nuova* the opposite of the "modest and chaste" is presented. Mark Musa translates this last phrase as "subdued and decorous" (*Vita* 1965, 3). Nine years precisely to the day, after the last of their childhood meetings, Dante Alighieri sees Beatrice Portinari again and receives her greeting. He goes home, faint, having experienced "the very ends of bliss" or beatitude. Intoxicated, he lies on his bed to dream and has a vision. The "Lord" whom Dante anticipated in chapter 2 materializes and declares that he is the poet's master, saying many other things that Dante Alighieri does not understand. Who can concentrate on what Love, Dante's lord and master, is *saying?* What is Love *doing?*

A few hours ago, Dante saw Beatrice dressed in pure white between two ladies. Now in the lap of Love, a god whose aspect the poet describes as both "terrible and full of joy" Dante descries a person. "Ne le sue braccia mi parea vedere una persona dormire nuda, salvo che involta mi parea in uno drappo sanguigno leggeramente; la quale io riguardando molto intentivamente, conobbi ch'era la donna de la salute, la quale m'avea lo giorno dinanzi degnato di salutare," "In his arms I seemed to see a person sleeping nude, except that she appeared to be covered in a scanty blood-red cloth, upon whom looking intently I recognized as the lady of the salute who earlier that day had deigned to greet me." There are endless echoes between chapters 2 and 3 of *La Vita Nuova,* words deliberately repeated—but none is as striking to me as the *sanguigno,* blood red. An almost naked girl appears in the arms of Love before the sleeping, intoxicated Dante. The poet heightens the drama by descrying her first as a dim figure, "a person," until staring hard he recognized who is lying in this state—Beatrice. This is not the girl who has yet to attain the age of nine "bound round and adorned in a style suitable to her years." The color too has undergone a remarkable metamorphosis while remaining red. The texture and light of the red has changed. Beatrice is wrapped in something less than a filmy negligee. Yet the color, blood red, throws us back on the first red dress. (The word "suitable" or "appropriate" becomes almost ironic in the context of the eighteen-year-old woman and her flimsy apparel.)

In chapter 2, Beatrice and Dante, the girl approaching nine, the boy just past it, are still children with the freedom to run around corners, play hide-and-seek, find each other in closets. Has something happened in the back of a room, behind a stairway? When the gauze of red appears, which Rossetti translates as a "blood colored cloth," it recalls Beatrice's robes as a child. Why has Dante bound them so tightly to her in her ninth year? Is he hinting the very opposite, that they have put their arms around each other, unbound, revealed secrets of the first swellings of sex? Why has that child of nine, the girl, Beatrice, so touched the boy, Dante that he trembles and his "animal spirit" says, "Now your bliss has appeared"?

They hardly acknowledge in words what happened. It may all have been mute, the grave, eight-year-old girl not speaking to the boy—summoning him to an empty back room of the Portinari mansion out of sight of adults, in dumb show. Those first motions of a girl revealing nakedness to a boy some months older—no need of words. Words would betray the bliss.

Whatever happened at nine—nine years later, it bears fruit—here nine, the months of pregnancy, seem to Dante a magical number. Now Beatrice, seventeen years old, does address him. Dante is triumphant in his third canto. "The first time she had ever spoken to me." Barbara Reynolds glosses, "Dante must have heard her voice before, but it appears from this that she had not previously addressed him directly" (Reynolds 1969, 106).

The words, the gestures, the "sweet greeting" of the girl are swept up in a conflict between the erotic and the puritan, a drama whose actors are both lovers and figures in a Christian passion. Beatrice eats the heart of Dante. One cannot help recall the eating of the body of Jesus by the faithful. Is Dante the divinity or is the image meant to suggest that he has lost his heart to Beatrice? Beatrice has lain as if dead under the red veil. Adrian Stokes's phrase, "the slightly sinister purity of Florentine tenderness" (Stokes 1968, 106), echoes with Dante Alighieri's imagination of this young woman. Only the legendary Florentine "reserve" masks the action.

It is not only an erotic rite the two adolescents perform, but a religious one, as thirst for experience of God becomes part of the seduction. It is present, however, from the first meeting of the two. At nine, to the boy, Dante, Beatrice "did not appear as the daughter of a mortal man but of a god" (*Vita* 2). At the moment it is spoken, this seems only the language of poetic hyperbole. Dante quotes it from the *Odyssey* of Homer, the middle-aged man's appreciation of the young princess, Nausicaa, who looks boldly at the naked man coming out of the woods, hiding his private parts with a bush.[6] In chapter 3, the hyperbole of chapter 2 becomes real. The almost naked Beatrice timidly eats a heart. The act of eating makes man one with God in Christian tradition. The force of the beloved eating her lover's heart—that is comprehensible. They become one through a poetic cannibalism. That Beatrice and Dante become immortal through the eating of the heart—that religious act is not so readily admitted. If Beatrice is a goddess, Dante ought to have eaten her heart. This is the Christian offering. But it is Dante's heart in the manner of an Aztec sacrifice, cruel, mocking, which is consumed. The image remains a riddle. Dante is not beyond seeing himself as a surrogate for Messiah. In a ceremony both pagan and Christian, Beatrice, after eating Dante's heart, ascends

---

6. A number of critics believe that the quote comes from Aristotle's seventh book of *Ethics*. I discuss the controversy in footnote 2 of my final chapter, where the question of Dante's specific knowledge of Homer through Latin filters is taken up.

A reference to the warlike Achilles may be seen as appropriately ironic in the context of Beatrice's stroll through Florence at the age of eight, but an allusion to the princess Nausicaa, still a young girl in pigtails, radiant, unafraid in the presence of a stranger, seems more likely, given the context in which Dante is speaking.

with the God of Love. Boccaccio, who graphically describes the aura of eroticism that surrounded Dante's life, is also sensitive to the spiritual claims radiating from the poet. "Were it lawful so to say, I would declare that he had surely become a God upon the earth" (Boccaccio 1904, 144). This is the assertion of Boccaccio's biography.

Dante's solipsism has deep roots in his work. It is difficult to understand him without referring to his dreams of being the Messiah. In his letters the poet speaks in the voice of the Hebrew, Lord of Hosts, addressing himself to the Roman cardinals:

> Perchance in indignant rebuke you will ask: "And who is this man who, not fearing the sudden punishment of Uzzah, sets himself up to protect the Ark, tottering though it be? Verily I am one of the least of the sheep of the pasture of Jesus Christ: verily I abuse no pastoral authority, seeing that I possess no riches. By the grace therefore, not of riches, but of God, I am what I am." (*Epist.* 8: 144)

Dante knows his Bible and what "I am what I am" implies in the mouth of its speaker.

> And Moses said unto God, "Behold when I come unto the children of Israel, and shall say unto them, 'The God of your fathers hath sent me unto you,' and they shall say to me 'What is his name?' What shall I say unto them?"
>
> And God said unto Moses, "I am that I am": and He said, "Thus shalt thou say unto the children of Israel, 'I AM hath sent me unto you.'"[7]

It is the secret, forbidden, personal name that God announces to his prophet Moses from the burning bush. Dante declares, "I am a nobody, 'the least of the sheep,'" but a moment later the burning in his breast forces him to cry out, "'I am what I am.'"

Is this one of the secrets of *La Vita Nuova*? Beatrice is Jesus but to that goddess-messiah, is Dante lover, brother, father?

When Beatrice eats Dante's heart in the third chapter of *La Vita Nuova*, it is

---

7. *The Holy Scriptures according to the Masoretic text,* English version translated and revised by Alexander Harkavy, Exod. 3:13–14. Note the difference between Toynbee's "I am what I am" and Harkavy's "I am that I am." The exact meaning of the Hebrew is in dispute. Alternate translations include, "I will be what I will be," "I am He who Exists," "I am He who Endures." For Canaanite parallels, see Frank Moore Cross, *Canaanite Myth and Hebrew Epic,* 66–69. Also, "I am who I am," see Umberto Cassuto, *A Commentary on the Book of Exodus,* 36–40; and Moshe Greenberg, *Understanding Exodus,* 78–84.

the glowing organ of the living god. Modern readers will hear William Butler Yeats's lines, see in the winding cone of purgatory, his gyre:

> I saw a staring virgin stand
> Where holy Dionysus died,
> And tear the heart out of his side . . .

It is the rite of God's death. "Were it lawful so to say, I would declare that he had surely become a God upon the earth." Boccaccio has heard one of his master's hints and echoed it. Dante makes it clear in *La Vita Nuova* that he aspires to the form of the god of Love.

> Suddenly love became so great a part of me that as
> if transformed in aspect I rode on that day. . . .
> And then so much of him passed into me, he
> disappeared—I know not how. . . .
> (*Vita* 9)

> Whoever had wished to know love might have done
> so by looking into my trembling eyes.
> (*Vita* 11)

The death of Beatrice is part of a ritual of seduction. *La Vita Nuova* has not one, but three seductions. Something passes between Dante and Beatrice in their childhood when she is in her ninth year. She draws him back into the closets in a damp house and dazzles him with nakedness. Does the precocious girl initiate him into her mystery so that the first touch of a female body, Beatrice's, is a flame of the erotic that he can never forget? "Fabulous," he calls it, and it is—the first clumsy, holy touching in a forgotten room when the adults are absent. At eighteen, she appears again. Dante lifts the thin red veil from Beatrice's breasts. They begin a dance that will end in adultery, the poem's final seduction, which Dante feels as a religious passion. Adultery, warns the Talmud, remembering the sin of David and Bathsheba, leads to murder. Despite Dante's religious rhetoric, it is Beatrice who dies. But not before her invitation as a married woman to the poet.

Death, to which Dante looks forward, will be another consummation for him of this adultery, though the narrator of *La Vita Nuova* will not understand the drama at first. How can he? The purgation of the sin lies far ahead in unwritten cantos of the *Inferno* and *Purgatorio.* But that the seduction threatens death, he knows from the third chapter of *La Vita Nuova.*

Long before Beatrice's death, Dante is given a vision of her corpse. The veil, like the gauze that covered her young body at the very beginning of this early poem, is lifted. Dante stares upon her nude and feels her "peace." The way to the beloved's "true humility," that is—perfection of the erotic and spiritual life, lies in death. Beatrice is blissful and hauntingly beautiful as "the naked and the dead," that modern jingle.

> "Più nol ti celo:
> vieni a veder nostra donna che giace."
> Lo imaginar fallace
> mi condusse a veder madonna morta:
> e quand'io l'avea scorta,
> vedea che donne la covrian d'un velo;
> ed avea seco umilità verace,
> che parea che dicesse: "Io sono in pace."
>
> "I shall not hide anything from you:
> come now to see our lady lying."
> My false imagining
> led me to see my lady dead
> and as I looked at her
> I saw ladies covering her with a cloth;
> she had with her true humility,
> it was as if she said: "I am at peace."
> (*Vita* 23)

This is the twenty-third chapter, just before the crucial four chapters in which the deed of adulterous seduction is confessed. It seems almost as if Dante had willed the death of his beloved for the great sin they commit. This is the bass drum of psychology! As a mythologist, one might assume that the death of a human being destined to be a god, goddess, is the most rapturous form of love in which one could share. Death, a synonym among the Elizabethans for sexual bliss, is something Dante *desires!*

> Morte, assai dolce ti tegno
> tu dei omai esser cosa gentile,
> poi che tu se' ne la mia donna stata.

. . .

Death, I hold you very sweet
you must be henceforth a gracious thing
since you have been with my lady.

Death and love, Dante's mourning and his consummation, are devoutly mixed. He walks from her bier to her bed.

Then I parted, every dole consummated
And when I was alone
I said, staring toward the high realm
"Blessed, beautiful soul, he who sees you!"
You called to me, just then, by your kindness.
(*Vita* 23)[8]

At the moment of mourning, the voice of his beloved calls to him. He seeks her in death. He hears first her voice, and in a moment he will see her smile. Two chapters before, in 21, this smile appeared, a foreshadowing of bliss to come, as is the call here.

In the next four chapters, (ch. 24–27), Dante will receive the glance of Beatrice, her acquiescence, her body. His joy in consummation will be interrupted brutally by news of her death: *coitus interruptus.* Only for an instant will Dante enjoy Beatrice.

The seduction begins in chapter 2. The word that alerts is *sanguigno.* A "blood colored cloth" is the translation of D. G. Rossetti (*Vita* 1977, 550). The addition of cloth takes a certain liberty with the text, but has the nineteenth-century poet understood better than later translators Dante's metaphor? Why use a word, *sanguigno,* which has the connotation of bloodstained for the wrappings that drape the child? Why use it again in the next chapter—3, for the gauze that covers the girl of eighteen? Is it the blood of the maidenhead at eighteen, or the anticipation of puberty at nine?[9] Is Beatrice wrapped in a veil stained with the token of virginity?

8. Note the use of *consumato* with its sexual overtone.

"Poi mi partia, consumato ogne duolo: / e quand'io sera solo / dicea, guardando verso l'alto regno: / 'Beato, anima bella, chi te vede!' / Voi mi chiamaste allor, vostra merzede."

9. The question of the onset of menses in the Middle Ages is complex. It varied from northern Europe, where it was late, to southern Europe, where it came earlier. Diet and social class also played a role. Marriages at twelve, however, were not uncommon, as the reader of Boccaccio will quickly discover, and betrothals occurred much earlier. It is unmistakable that Beatrice is portrayed as being precociously mature at eight years old. She creates a stir in the streets more appropriate to a woman than to a child.

It is the blood of Jesus as Lamb, certainly, but it speaks of other things in the procession, under the veil.

Dante first invests this girl at the brink of nine with an awesome seriousness, adulthood. At seventeen, he strips this away, unveils her. Her glance sends him, eighteen years old, into delirium. Dante's ambiguous clue lies in the word *sanguigno*.

The delirium of the eighteen-year-old Dante introduces another word that will serve as a metaphor for spiritual and sexual experience, *dolcezza*.

> While passing down a street she turned her eyes to that part where I was most afraid and because of her inexpressible courtesy that today is rewarded in the eternal life, she greeted me so honestly that it appeared as if I saw then all the ends of bliss. . . . I was so overcome with sweetness [*dolcezza*] that I departed from everyone as if intoxicated.

Just what Dante means by "*dolcezza*" [sweetness] is obscure at the beginning of *La Vita Nuova*. But in this same chapter 3, he strips off the "pure white" vestments of the afternoon's meetings, when Beatrice was "between two ladies of high bearing, both older than herself," her chaperones. The white stripped away points to the gauze of red, their common meeting in the arms of Love. The unwrapped, enticing girl, holds the eighteen-year-old Dante's naked heart:

> Allegro me sembrava Amor tenendo
> meo core in mano, e ne le braccia avea
> madonna involta in un drappo dormendo.

> Joyous Love seemed to me holding
> my heart in hand, and in his arms he had
> my lady, wrapped in a cloth, sleeping.

For Love, when Beatrice awakes, feeds the young man's heart to her.

> Poi la svegliava, e d'esto core ardendo
> lei paventosa umilmente pascea.

> Then he awoke her and of that burning heart
> Humbly he fed the fearful lady.

Dante calls this act of eating—a mythical but also a sexual act, which calls for a sexual organ—the eating of his "heart." He will not be vulgar. The girl fills him with terror as well as humility as she does it. But he has just boasted that he has experienced "all the ends of bliss." And a friend assures Dante, who has babbled to him of it, "I think that you beheld all worth." For in spite of the veil Dante has thrown over the act, love is joyous and substantial.

Dante can remember the *hour* of Beatrice's invitation, her promise ("three o'clock in the afternoon"), the *hour* of their consummation ("the first of the last nine hours of the night"), that is, "the fourth hour of the night," the fourth (just as in the fourth stanza after the dream of her death he will describe another consummation) and her weeping departure—yet does not know whether "his happiness changed into the bitterest weeping and weeping," *whether it has happened or not!*

Not a pale courtly love but a burning terror struck one—joy of Beatrice, of her fiery womb, haunts Dante. Has it happened or not? He seeks her in the street. He hurries to the church. He stares and, desperate that he will reveal their secret, he is forced to the game of using another as a blind.

(Does Dante expect even the charitable to believe this explanation for his running this way and that among the girls of Florence? Beatrice has seen him. He strains at the same explanation for looking into other eyes in chapters 35, 36, 37, of *La Vita Nuova*. Obsessed with the eternal, Dante is candid about a limited attention span in the here and now. Beatrice's charity must forgive him.)

◆   ◆   ◆

NOW HE TRAVELS on "la via d'Amor."

> Or ho perduta tutta mia baldanza
> che si movea d'amoroso tesoro;
>
> Now all my boldness is lost
> that sprang from amorous treasury.
> (*Vita* 7)

The omens of death multiply. Dante cannot be reduced to an Italian cavalier, a knight of the broken heart. A spark of Isaiah lodges in him. On the way to forbidden love in the *Commedia,* he passes the circle of the damned, the penitent, the corrupt—and shakes with prophetic anger and humility. In the midst of courtship, he hears Death coming, coming to dismember his beloved. He has wept for other ladies too. A dead friend of Beatrice's receives the tribute of his verse.

Hear how Love gave her honor
For I saw him lament in his very form
Over her charming lifeless image.
(*Vita* 8)

Frozen ground and snow evoke his love. So in the sestina "To the Dim Light"
as translated by Rossetti.

Utterly frozen is this youthful lady
Even as the snow that lies within the shade:
For she is no more moved than is a stone
By the sweet season which makes warm the hills
And alters them afresh from white to green
Covering their sides again with flowers and grass.
When on her hair she sets a crown of grass
The thought has no more room for other lady:
Because she weaves the yellow with the green
So well that Love sits down there in the shade—
Love who has shut me in among low hills
Faster than between walls of granite stone. . . .
A while ago I saw her dress'd in green—
So fair, she might have waken'd in a stone
This love which I do feel even for her shade:
And therefore, as one woos a graceful lady,
I wooed her in a field that was all grass
Girdled about with very lofty hills.
Yet shall the streams turn back and climb the hills
Before Love's flame in this damp wood and green
Burn, as it burns within a youthful lady,
For my sake, who would sleep away in stone
My life, or feed like beasts upon the grass,
Only to see her garments cast a shade.
How dark so'er the hills throw out their shade
Under her summer green the beautiful lady
Covers it, like a stone cover'd in grass.[10]

10. *The Portable Dante,* 625–27. This is the translation of D. G. Rossetti. Two liberties with the
text must be noted. See the version by Foster and Boyde, *Dante's Lyric Poetry* pp. 163–165. They ren-
der lines 28 and 29, "Hence I have desired her in a fair *grass* field—as much in love as ever a *woman*

Is the lady alive or dead? Is she merely hard-hearted or beyond all feelings except pathos? Dante's language takes root in the hard stone. His lady covers it with her garments, and he woos her as a shade in the grass. "Shade" in Dante's Italian has the same double meaning as in contemporary English, denoting both shadow and ghost. The sestina probably dates from before the death of Beatrice and refers to another woman. It illustrates, however, Dante's funereal passion. Love is inseparable from pathos, tears; Beatrice alive, finds this an "annoyance" (*Vita* 12). Dante is always weeping; even in Eden on the summit of Purgatory, she has to scold him on that account.

Yet death deepens love: sorrow, as he sings, brings it to maturity, to the divine.

> "Spirto in cui pianger matura
> quel sanza 'l quale a Dio tornar non pòssi."

> "Spirit in whom weeping matures
> that without which one can not return to God."
> (*Purg.* 19:91–92)

Dante is not one to confine himself to weeping with shadows. He knows the delights of what can be touched, grasped. His letters detail one of these affairs of the heart,[11] his biographer, Boccaccio, alludes to many, and even in *La Vita Nuova,* he is constrained to admit that his behavior has become infamous in Florence. "For this reason, the multitude of voices that viciously defamed me . . . refused me that sweetest greeting of hers in which lay all my bliss" (*Vita* 10). "But Beat-

---

was": and the final three lines, "Whenever the *hills* cast darkest *shadow,* this young *woman* makes it disappear beneath a fair *green,* as one makes *stone* disappear under *grass.*"

11. *Epist.,* Epistola IV, 39. "It befell, then, that after my departure from the threshold of that court (which I since have so yearned for), wherein, as you often remarked with amaze, I was privileged to be enrolled in the service of liberty, no sooner had I set foot by the streams of Arno, in all security and heedlessness, than suddenly, woe is me! Like a flash of lightning from on high, a woman appeared, I know not how, in all respects answering to my inclinations both in character and appearance. Oh! how was I dumbfounded at the sight of her. But my stupefaction gave place before the terror of the thunder that followed. For just as in our everyday experience the thunderclap instantaneously follows the flash, so, at the sight of the blaze of this beauty, Love, terrible and imperious straightway laid hold on me. And he, raging like a despot expelled from his fatherland, who returns to his native soil after long exile, slew or expelled or fettered whatsoever within me was opposed to him. He slew then that praiseworthy resolve which held me aloof from women and from songs about women . . . he fettered my free will. . ."

rice," he cried from canzone to canzone, "it is you I am gazing at, you I am sleeping with, you I am embracing in all these others!"

Love answers: "My son, it is time to do away with our pretendings" (*Vita* 12).

Even as he drops the cover or excuse of using another to address Beatrice, *La Vita Nuova* initiates a secret action, which Dante Alighieri would want to obscure. For at this moment, Dante, under the direction of the White Angel, begins to prepare the drama of his third sharing of dream with Beatrice. What has happened before to him, at nine, or eighteen, may be real or fantasy. (Though the reader will note that in this twelfth chapter, in which Love tells him to forget about other women and to concentrate directly on wooing Beatrice, there are two references to Dante as a child. The poet goes to bed after Beatrice's rebuff, "like a little boy sobbing from a spanking." And Love orders him to write a poem in which the fact that Dante has belonged to Beatrice since childhood will be stated, declaring as well that Love will be a witness and testify to this.) Dante decides *this* is the moment of opportunity.

Beatrice has scorned him. She has rebuked him. The knowing glance that they shared in the street, that "excess of sweetness" which was his "intolerable bliss" which transformed his body until it "passed and surpassed his capacity" (*Vita* 12) is no more. He comes to a wedding. Her wedding? And she laughs at his tears. He weeps again. He cries.

> e quand'io vi son presso, i' sento Amore
> che dice: "Fuggi, se 'l perir t'è noia."
> Lo viso mostra lo color del core
> che, tramortendo, ovunque pò s'appoia;
> e per la ebrietà del gran tremore
> le pietre par che gridin: "Moia, moia."
> Peccato face chi allora mi vidi
> se l'alma sbigottita non conforta.
>
> When I am near you, I hear Love
> Who says, "Flee if to die is fearsome to you."
> My face shows the color of my heart
> Which fainting, leans wherever it can
> And through the drunkenness of the great trembling
> The stones seem to cry, "Die. Die."
> It is a sin to see me then
> And not comfort that bewildered soul.
> (*Vita* 15)

Silence.

Vegno a vedervi, credendo guerire:
e se io levo li occhi per guardare
nel cor mi si comincia uno tremoto.

I came to see you, hoping to be cured:
but if I raise my eyes to look
within my heart begins a quaking.
(*Vita* 16)

A rebuke comes from her friends.

One of them, turning her eyes toward me, called me by name, speaking these words. "To what end do you love this, your lady, since you are not able to endure her presence? Tell us, for certainly, one may agree that the end of such love must be bizarre." When she had spoken these words, not only she, but all that were with her, began to observe me, waiting for my reply.

Then I spoke these words to them. "Ladies, the end and aim of my love was but the greeting of that lady of whom I believe you are speaking: wherein alone I found that bliss which is the end of all my desires. And now that it has pleased her to deny me this, Love, my Master, of his great mercy has placed all my bliss there where it will not come to less."

Then those ladies began to talk among themselves: and as I have sometimes seen rain fall mixed with the beautiful snow, so I seemed to hear their words come out mixed with sighs. And when they had spoken among themselves awhile, again, she addressed to me, that lady who had first spoken to me, these words. "We pray you will tell us where this bliss abides?"

I answered her so, "In those words which praise my lady."

She rejoined, "If your speech is true, those words you wrote describing your condition would have been fashioned with another intent."

Then I, thinking of these words, parted from them deeply ashamed and as I walked, I said within myself, "Seeing that there is so much bliss in those words which praise my lady, why did I abide to speak otherwise?" (*Vita* 18)

Is the cue that the "ladies who have intelligence of love" give Dante *not* that he should content himself by writing poetry about Beatrice, but that he should stop whining, writing plangent verses, cold and rainy with sighs? Let her feel the pleasure and warm passion love inspires.

Now words begin to fill the air, silver snares through the streets of Florence. Stooping in their gowns, tripping after the bright flutter: the lines are caught by others, fondled:

> Escono spirti d'amore inflammati
> che feron li occhi a qual che allor la guati
> e passan sì che 'l cor ciascun retrova:

> Spirits of love go out flashing
> that pierce the eyes then of anyone who sees
> passing through so that each one finds the heart.
> (*Vita* 19)

Dante touches the sacred string. The virginal stars of Heaven are not exempt. Even the Holy One, Blessed be He, whom Dante envies for possession of Beatrice, bends with pleasure to the sound of the psalmist's love. Whatever is feminine in the Divine Presence must come to embrace the earnest song that now rises. Poetry—Beatrice, the poetry you willed is all about you. Dante's rhymes lift from the table and pass from lip to lip.

> Ballad, I wish you to find Love
> and with him go before my lady
> so that my excuse which you sing
> my lord can explain to her. . . .
> Remain with her
> explain about your servant what you wish
> and if she through your prayer pardon me
> let her announce in a beaming appearance, peace.
> (*Vita* 12)

In the street, the girls are singing under Beatrice's window.

> Help me to go about, for I am sent
> to her whose praises do adorn me.
> (*Vita* 12)[12]

Her husband, perhaps, in innocence, repeats a few words at the table.

12. While this is out of sequence in terms of composition in the developing drama, the lines date from the hour of the White Angel's instructions to Dante on the wooing of Beatrice. At the end of the stanzas in chapter 12, Dante tells his verse to go before Beatrice at the moment when they will be likely to win him honor. This moment does not come until now, in chapter 19.

And if you do not wish to go in vain,
stay not where vulgar ones may be:
contrive, if you can to be plain
only with women or men of courtesy.
(*Vita* 19)

If for a moment Beatrice turns away, hoping to escape Dante's love? The words are circulating among her friends, handmaidens, courteously entreating them on doorsteps, in hallways:

Ladies who understand of love,
with you I wish to speak about my lady,
not that I think to perfect her praise,
but to explain and ease my mind.
(*Vita* 19)

But Beatrice, her friends, know to whom they are written. Can she help it? "Love and the gracious heart are but one thing" (*Vita* 20), as the sage Guinizelli sings in his ditty.[13] Dante is praising her. Her friends, husband, brother, are singing her litany through Florence: the solitary city fills with psalms of Beatrice. Dante does not come before her but when Beatrice meets him, the alleys are ringing with the lines of one who made himself ridiculous on her account. The city in his voice peals her name:

Ov'ella passa, ogn'om ver lei si gira,
e cui saluta fa tremar lo core,
sì che, bassando il viso, tutto smore.

Where she passes, every man turns toward her,
and her hello makes the heart tremble,
so that it blanches, lowering its gaze.
(*Vita* 21)

Can Beatrice avoid her lover? His verses are being cried, when men spin round to stare. Dante is before her in the street. His eyes averted from her snub, rebuke. He stops, waits. . . .

---

13. Dante quotes this line at the beginning of chapter 20 of *La Vita Nuova*.

> Ogne dolcezza, ogne pensero umile
> nasce nel core a chi parlar la sente.

> Every sweetness, every humble thought
> is born in the heart of one who hears her speak.
> (*Vita* 21)

She has spoken to him! And looking up, Dante bursts into open song.

> Quel ch'ella par quando un poco sorride,
> non si pò dicer né tenere a mente,
> sì è novo miracolo e gentile.

> Her appearance as she smiles a bit
> one can not speak or hold it in the mind
> so new and gracious a miracle it is.
> (*Vita* 21)

Dante sings of miracles. He has *won* forgiveness. But he craves more. His lines of praise have won "two actions of her mouth . . . her sweet manner of speaking . . . her miraculous smile." But Dante desires "*ogne dolcezza,*" every sweetness. And only death can win that from his Beatrice, wed them in its tears. The White Angel in his sheet, his pure winding sheet, sits by the doors of Beatrice.

Her father dies.

Now she too must cry. Now she too must taste the bitterness of loss. She weeps.

> Vedestù pianger lei, che tu non pui
> punto celar la dolorosa mente?

> Did you see her weep, that you can not
> hide the depth of your sorrowful thought?
> (*Vita* 22)

Dante has looked, through the window, into the eyes of Beatrice and died with her.

> Ell'ha nel viso la pietà sì scorta,
> che qual l'avesse voluta mirar
> sarebbe innanzi lei piangendo morta.

. . .

> She had in her face pity so plain,
> that whoever had wished to stare
> within her presence would, weeping, take his death.
> (*Vita* 22)

Dante stares. The poet who will take his steps into Hell feels the embrace of Death here—at this very moment—(if not before, in his mother's death, but that is a matter for lost volumes of Dante's thoughts). Here and now he takes the hand of Beatrice—over her father's bier. Dante will walk after her father, for Beatrice. The poet goes home to his bed to die.

"Nine days," he lies in a "severe illness" suffering "intense pain" and in that daze, in "delirium," "convulsed," the mantle of prophecy falls upon him: he sees the bier of Beatrice. And he begs to accompany her:

> Morte, assai dolce ti tegno. . . .
> Vieni, chè 'l cor te chiede.
>
> Death, I hold you so sweet. . . .
> Come to me, my heart calls you
> (*Vita* 23)

Wandering between Heaven and earth, Dante discovers the gates he will promise at the end of *La Vita Nuova* to return to—gates to the land of death. "Certain faces of ladies with hair in disarray appeared to me and they were saying, 'You too will die.' And after these women, other terrible and frightening appearances cried to me, 'You are dead.'" The streets are filled with wild women. The stars are turning pale, weeping. Birds fall dead to the earth. Multitudes of angels rise—in front of them a pure white cloud.

> Levava li occhi miei bagnati in pianti,
> e vedea, che parean pioggia di manna.
>
> I raised my eyes bathed in tears
> and saw those that seemed a rain of manna.
> (*Vita* 23)

In the next chapters there will be lovemaking, erotic jubilation, but in this, the twenty-third, the writer pauses—the origin of spiritual and bodily love is death. It is from the heights of death that Beatrice calls to Dante, in the very last line of the chapter (*Vita* 23). Does the same warning that comes to Dante in this chapter, come to Beatrice? "You too will die."

Dante speaks for himself and for Beatrice. In the anguish of death over the body of her father, they have exchanged a vow of love. Dante has been privileged to see Beatrice's corpse in the twenty-third chapter and pledged his death, his love beyond death. He has promised her immortality, a love beyond death. He has begged for her blessing.

While weeping for her father, Beatrice has heard Dante's voice, the angels. "You too will die." She has heard, "You are dead." In these words she passes the boundary of human fear. How then can there be any hurt in Dante and his love? He will be her cavalier beyond the bier. She lies, as the poet has seen her, in the care of her ladies, the red cloth of woman's blood now pure white.

> Ed avea seco umiltà verace,
> che parea che dicesse: "Io sono in pace."
>
> She had with her true humility,
> it seemed she said: "I am at peace."
> (*Vita* 23)

Dante Alighieri and Beatrice Portinari understand each other at the end of this chapter (ch. 23) in a way that, despite many backslidings on the poet's part, will never be forgotten. Their love is not for life but death. She has entered that kingdom a few steps with her father. Since Dante has promised to follow her, she takes her lover's hand on earth.

Only a few moments are left. His vision is true. She sees it too. It is time for the consummation, not for the *"consumato ogne duolo"* (*Vita* 23) but for the brief consummation of life.

It lies before me so plain I look away in shame.

> After this vain dream, I happened one day to be sitting in certain place, thoughtful, when a tremor took hold of my heart as if I were in the presence of my lady. Then a vision of love came to me and he seemed to come from that place where my lady lived and he said not aloud but within my heart, 'Now bless the day I entered into you, for it is fitting that you do.' And with that my heart was so full of gladness that I could hardly believe it to be mine, and not another's heart. (*Vita* 24)

This is chapter 24. The clouds of sighs and death of the twenty-third have lifted, dispelled by the sound of Beatrice's call. Soon the woman he has transposed to the stars, Beatrice Portinari, *Bice,* that fierce child of his poem, lauded, glorified, adored, until I must jog my memory to remind myself she was married, *"Bice"* will appear, smiling, arm in arm with *"Primavera,"* "Spring." Who can that be? What company is Beatrice keeping in the streets of Florence?

> Shortly after these words which my heart spoke to me with Love's tongue, I saw coming toward me a certain lady who was very famous for her beauty, and of whom that friend I have already called the first among my friends had long been enamored. This lady's right name was Joan, but because of her loveliness or at least it was so imagined, she was called of many Primavera (Spring) and went by that name among them. Then I looked again, and saw behind her, following, the miraculous Beatrice. (*Vita* 24)

Joan? Joan is the paramour of Guido Cavalcanti. That bodes ill for sainthood. This ballad, pastoral of Guido's, is one of the lyrics Lady Joan has been listening to:

> In a wood I found a shepherdess
> more beautiful than any star it appeared to me.
> Blond hair she had in little curls
> eyes full of love, a rosy face:
> with her rod she pastured lambs
> and barefoot, bathed in dew
> she sang as if she was enamored
> adorned with everything to please.
> At once I saluted her with love
> inquired if she had company
> and sweetly she replied to me,
> alone, alone through the woods she went,
> said, "Know when the birds sing
> then desire—to have a lover is in my heart."
> When she told me of her condition
> and through the woods I heard the birds sing
> I thought to myself, now is the moment
> to take pleasure with this shepherdess.
> "Excuse me," I asked, "would she only allow me
> to kiss and embrace her?"
> My hand she pressed with amorous wish
> and said she had given me her heart

she led me under the fresh leaves
there where I saw flowers of every color
and I felt so much of joy and sweetness
the god of love—I appeared to see.[14]

The pastoral of Guido Cavalcanti holds an important clue to the moments of pastoral in *La Vita Nuova*. What shepherding is going on under the "fresh," "cool," or "new" leaves, *"freschetta foglia,"* the lovers are covered, their nakedness masked. Tumbling in beds of new flowers is a sly hint of maidenhair, and maidenhead, making love under the spring leaves. A concealed play on the nickname of his girl-friend Joan, *Primavera,* spring, by Guido, seems clear, for the shepherdess of the pastoral is otherwise a creature in an erotic fairy tale. Dante takes up the nickname of Joan, Primavera, in *La Vita Nuova*. He makes certain that the reader understands that this Primavera is the beloved of Guido Cavalcanti, "first among my friends." Why?

He signals to his auditors in Florence who "have intelligence of love," that he means to speak of Beatrice through Guido's words about Joan. Guido's indiscretion allows Dante to be discreet. Thus, Dante's lines in chapter 24:

> L'una appresso de l'altra maraviglia;
> e sì come la mente mi ridice,
> Amor mi disse: "Quell'è Primavera,
> e quell'ha nome Amor, sì mi somiglia."

> One marvel after another;
> And so as my memory recalls,
> Love said to me: "The first is Spring,
> The other has the name of Love, she so resembles me."

14. For this translation I am indebted to my colleague Frederick Goldin, whose version of it appears in his *German and Italian Lyrics of the Middle Ages* (Goldin 1973a, 332–33): In un boschetto trova' pasturella / più che la stella bella al mi'parere. / Cavelli avea biondetti e ricciutelli / e gli occhi pien d'amor, cera rosata: / con sua verghetta pasturav' agnelli, / discalza, di rugiada era bagnata: / cantava come fosse 'nnamorata: / er' adornata di tutto piacere. / D'amor la salutai mantenente / e domandai s'avesse compagnia, / ed ella mi rispuose dolcemente / che sola sola per lo bosco gïa, / e disse: "Sacci, quando l'augel pia / allor disia 'l me' cor drudo avere." / Po' che mi disse di sua condizione, / e per lo bosco augelli audio cantare / fra me stesso diss'i: "Or è stagione / di questa pasturella gio' pigliare." / Merzè le chiesi sol che di baciare / e d'abracciare se le fosse 'n volere. / Per man mi prese, d'amorosa voglia, / e disse che donato m'avea 'l core: / menommi sott'una freschetta foglia / là dov'i vidi fior d'ogni colore; / e tanto vi sentio gioia e dolzore / che'l dio d'amore mi parea vedere.

"Marvel" after "marvel"? One "marvel" follows another? What follows "spring"? "Summer!"

What is spring—the promise? What is summer—the fulfillment? Joan brings in Beatrice and we can imagine why Love sings, "Now bless the day I entered into you" (*Vita* 24). Indeed Love "remained awhile with me. I saw and heard certain things." Through such euphemisms the bald facts of the first assignation between Dante and Beatrice are given the spiritual colors of abstraction.

Now, in the twenty-fifth chapter comes a euphemism, a diversion, worthy of a master. Dante declares, are you "puzzled at my speaking of Love as if it were a thing in itself, as if it were not only a spiritual but a bodily substance?" Bravo—a philosophical disquisition on the substance of Love and the *"lingua di si,"* the use of bold, everyday speech, the vernacular, while the lovers, Dante and Beatrice, are under the "foliage" proving that love is "substantial" indeed. They are murmuring to one another and not in Church Latin or even the exalted stanzas of Virgil. Such "leaves" are not "fresh" but dry, a far denser "cover" for romance.

Above, perched over the tree trunks, Aeolus, god of wind, is blowing nonsense through the bushes, quoting the *Aeneid*, Lucan, Horace, and Ovid's *Book of the Remedy of Love*. "And in order that a gross person may not take liberty with what I have said, I add that neither did the poets who wrote thus, do so without reason, nor should they who rhyme today, have no reason in what they write, for great shame would come on one who rhyming under the dress of metaphor or rhetorical color, who when being questioned, could not denude those words of such dress in the guise of what he had truly intended." Puzzle at the "denuding."

"Great shame" or "embarrassment"? Dante does not fear it. There is not a line of poetry in chapter 25 of *La Vita Nuova*. It is about the language of yes, the tongue of yes. Who has need for "spiritual" or "intellectual substance" (translate it either way) when he knows that Love is "a body" (*Vita* 25).[15]

Dante's head is ringing. "This most tender lady of whom I spoke in what has gone before, came into such great favor among men, that when she came down the street, people ran to see her. This brought me marvelous happiness when she drew near anyone: such modesty was brought to his heart that he dared neither to lift his eyes or return her salutation, and to this, many who felt it, could bear witness to one who can't believe. She went along crowned and clothed in humility, showing not a bit of pride for all that she saw and heard: when she had gone by, many cried, 'This is no woman but one of the beautiful angels of the sky.'

---

15. Dante here addresses playfully the question of the substance or "body" of love. In the *Commedia*, as I hope to show, this topic will take on a much more critical importance, as Dante tries to understand the nature of the body and its capacity for experience, erotic and intellectual, in the afterlife.

Che dà per li occhi una dolcezza al core,
che 'ntender no la può chi no la prova:
E par che de la sua labbia si mova
un spirito soave pien d'amore,
che va dicendo a l'anima: "Sospira."

So that she gives through the eyes a sweetness to the heart,
he who has not felt it can not understand it:
And it seems that from her lips there moves
an exquisite spirit full of love
that goes speaking to the soul:"Sigh."
(*Vita* 26)

"*Dolcezza*," sweetness! This is the key, that sweetness, that singing of orgiastic delight. It runs through the desirous sigh of *Sospira* like sap and drips into the next sonnet. Her face, which no one can recall "che non sospiri in dolcezza d'amore," "who does not sigh in the sweetness of love." [16]

The final stanzas of this series of days that began nine cantos before, the sonnet in the twenty-seventh chapter of *La Vita Nuova* celebrates this unexpected ecstasy.

Sì lungiamente m'ha tenuto Amore
e costumato a la sua segnoria,
che sì com'elli m'era forte in pria,
così mi sta soave ora nel core.
Però quando mi tolle sì 'l valore,
che li spiriti par che fuggan via,
allor sente la frale anima mia
tanta dolcezza che 'l viso ne smore,
poi prende Amore in me tanta vertute,
che fa li miei spiriti gir parlando,
ed escon for chimando
la donna mia, per darmi più salute.
Questo m'avvene ovunque ella mi vede,
e sì è cosa umil, che nol si crede.

16. The reader is asked to play the kabbalist as Dante requests in chapters 28 and 19 of *La Vita Nuova*. "As the number nine has taken a place many times among the preceding words, wherefore its appearance can not be without reason . . ." (28). Note that by adding the 2 and the 7 of the amorous Arabic numeral 27, one comes to the ineffable 9, three times three, a fertilized, eroticized trinity. And it is in chapter 27 that the fireworks of love explode.

So long has Love held me
and bred me to his Lordship,
that he who first seemed harsh,
now is a delightful thing within my heart.
But when he robs me of my power,[17]
so that the spirits flee,
then my frail soul feels
so much sweetness, my face pales.
then Love puts such power in me,
that he makes my spirits go about speaking,
and rushing out calling
my lady, to give me some greeting.
This comes to me wherever she sees me [18]
and this thing is so humble, that it's not believed.

These are "the lineaments of Gratified Desire." Give me "power." I have "so much sweetness, my face pales." The lover who sighs, "Give me some greeting." And confesses, "This comes to me wherever she sees me. And this thing is so humble, humbling as it happens to me [Rossetti, on the edge of confessing his secret thought cannot help but shade his translation, the *"cosa umil,"* rendered not as "humble" but "sweet"], it is hard to believe." Love, *dolcezza*, is a *"cosa soave"* and a *"cosa umil,"* an exquisite, delightful, humbling, *"sospira"* between her thighs. Is it happening? It is hard to believe.

◆   ◆   ◆

17. "Power" here is translated for the word *"valore."* Further down I use it for *"vertute."* Both words carry the connotations of virtue, worth, and power. They are employed with these varying shades throughout the *Commedia* by Dante. At this point we are passing from the spiritual to the sexual "power." Dante is speaking of a sudden flush of renewed sexual passion.

18. Dante has previously told us in chapter 12, without equivocation, that in Beatrice's "greeting" lay his "bliss." One wonders if his euphemisms do not allude to an early failure to satisfy Beatrice's sexual appetite. He describes himself lying after "intolerable bliss": like a *"cosa grava inanimata,"* "a thing heavy and inanimate." Is this a postcoital melancholy? Why does he speak of Beatrice's greeting as a *"soverichio dolcezza,"* "excess of sweetness," which "many times passed and surpassed his capacity"? This is early on in chapter 11. By chapter 28, a more mature Dante can control himself and cry with enthusiasm that though he may faint away after the first rush, "Love puts such power in me," that he goes rushing out again. This is the boast of the bridegroom, rejoicing in his chamber. It has biblical sanction. As for Beatrice, she is ready wherever he is. "Whenever" or "wherever," translate as one will, Dante is "humble" before her, wonderstruck at her powers, which are "hard to believe."

"HOW ALONE THE CITY SITS that was full of people" (*Vita* 28).[19] Dante tolls the funeral bell on the edge of his bed, in lamentation, sodden with *dolcezza,* nectar. He cannot believe it. He begins to count like a Kabbalist, distracted, hoping to find her on his fingers. "The first hour of the ninth day of the month . . ." (*Vita* 29) and the "ninth month of the year . . ." and "in the year of our Lord in which the perfect number was nine times multiplied within that century." Holy Nine? Dante gives his obvious reasons, the root of the Trinity, but adds, "Perhaps a more subtle person would see in this yet a more subtle reason" (*Vita* 29). Nine is the number of the months of pregnancy. Nine months more and he might have fostered a child on his Beatrice. Nine more revolutions of the moon and their love would be more than a passing image. Who had deprived him of his prophecy, his beloved?

Who is worthy as a rival? It must be *"l'etterno sire,"* the Holy One, Blessed be He, who, "marveling" and "seized with sweet desire . . . bade her to Himself aspire" (*Vita* 31). Why?

Beatrice as a woman has been too much for Dante. "She has passed and surpassed his capacity." She has *"tanta vertute."* Dante is bested by Beatrice and The Holy One, *"l'etterno sire"* who "sees that this obnoxious life / is not worthy of such a lovely thing!" "vedea ch'esta vita noiosa / non era degna di sì gentil cosa!" (*Vita* 31).

"Vita noiosa," obnoxious life. Soon enough Dante is circling the city with his tears, advertising his grief, drawing sighs from windows and balconies. Soon he has lured the eyes of another to him and he does not scruple to lift his wet face:

> Quando guardaste li atti e la statura
> ch'io faccio per dolor molte fiate.
> Allor m'accorsi che voi pensavate
> la qualità de la mia vita oscura.

> When you beheld the appearances and the posture
> that I had through sadness many times.
> Then I realized that you were meditating upon
> the nature of my dark life.
> (*Vita* 35)

He sighs. "Indeed with that lady is that Love / he who makes me go thus weeping" (*Vita* 35). He sees there, "Color of love, appearance of pity / have never so

---

19. Dante is quoting Lam. 1:1.

miraculously touched face of a lady" (*Vita* 36). Beatrice fortunately has gone to the highest Heaven. There she hears Dante whispering to his new amour, "I strongly fear my heart will break, / I'm not able to keep my ruined eyes / from you, time after time, staring" (*Vita* 36).

Dante is slipping away. "This is a lady tender, beautiful, young and wise, and appearing perhaps through the wish of Love in order that my life be peaceful" (*Vita* 38).

Beatrice returns. She reigns in the kingdom to which Dante has brought her. He resumes the robes of childhood

> so that I seemed to see that glorious Beatrice with that blood red [*sanguigne*] clothing with which she first appeared to my eyes and she seemed young, the same age at which I first saw her. Then I began to think of her, going back methodically through the past, my heart beginning sadly to repent of the desire which so vilely it had allowed to master it for several days, despite the constancy of reason, and casting out this evil desire, all my thoughts turned back to their most tender Beatrice. And I can say that from then on with all my shameful heart I began to concentrate on her so, that now my sighs were many times apparent. (*Vita* 39)

Dante is dreaming, not of the Beatrice whom he has made love to in the bed of adultery, nor of the Beatrice he has seduced in adolescence, but of the girl almost nine years old, grave and innocent in her childhood gowns. Let them depart, hand in hand, down the dark alleys of Florence, under the shadows of the feudal towers. What they do with each other is a mystery, shameful or no.

Only who is the spirit dressed in white who strides after the children—a pagan god of Love? So Dante understood when he became one with it. Or is this a masquerade? Has the angel who came to instruct Dante how to woo and be wooed by Beatrice been Death? Has Dante taught Beatrice how to die and betrayed his love into pale hands? Or is it Beatrice who, anticipating death, has taken Dante's soul from among the living?

The poet cries in chapter 33: " 'Come to me,' I said with so much love, / I envy everyone who dies."

CHAPTER FOUR

BEWILDERED

OUTLINING A DRAMA in which Dante Alighieri is thinking about seduction beyond death, I see a door in the *Commedia* swing open. Does Eros play as large a part in Dante's world as in his biographer Boccaccio's, but a mystical Eros?

Dante's begins in bewilderment, sympathies he hardly dares to admit, willing to entertain heresies. Torn between desire for fame, lust for women, piety, humility, Dante spins. As he ages, the contradictions send him around faster and faster until he must go down in order to come up.

He is a man bewildered in a wood, bewildered in his life, bewildered in his body. "Smarrito." The journey to Heaven starts in Hell.

◆   ◆   ◆

SMARRITA, we begin with the poet and that word, "lost, bewildered, confused, wild."

> Nel mezzo del cammin di nostra vita
> mi ritrovai per una selva oscura
> che la diritta via era smarrita.
>
> In the middle of the road of our life
> I found myself in a dim wood
> Where the direct way was lost.
> (*Inf.* 1:1–3)

We hear it again and again. The road is confused, and his footsteps on it. He is bewildered, dashed up against the rocks, *smarrita,* gone astray, knocked out of his wits, off his course. But Dante means something more, and he does not reveal it until *Purgatorio,* when he gives the word another meaning. The Siren's face in the frigid cold of the morning is *smarrito* (*Purg.* 19:14) wan, bewildered—numb. Frigid. Dante is confused, drained, and numb in his member. Take the measure of his comedy.

Dante Alighieri, bewildered, made a religious epic out of adulterous love, his Beatrice married to another man. This Lancelot of Florence rides toward a dead married woman. Is it important—the biographical fact? The civic events of Florence give so much of the epic its power and the personal pathos of the poet's banishment. That the woman he idolizes, Beatrice, taken up into Heaven, was married to another is a stark fact of the poem.

To release Dante from the terror of his sin is the burden of the *Commedia,* a comedy not only of revenge upon political adversaries but of impossible, forbidden love. This pathos is absent in Dante's disciple, Geoffrey Chaucer. A sweetness of voice, gentle self-mockery, substitute. Dante never laughs at his rhyme the way Chaucer does, ribbing himself in *The Canterbury Tales* as a jangling poet, "nat worth a toord."[1] Dante's comedy, self-parody, has to do with his character, not rhyme.[2] His love is comic, ironic, the task of the poem to *sublimate* (falling into our own jangling), to make an act or dream of sin,[3] love's offering to God.

Did Milton's Lucifer dream so of his sin?

Milton had a sadder, more prosaic experience of women—lost his key to Paradise. He elevated a devil into a hero, guardian angel of his poem. Milton's own

---

1. It is rumored that Chaucer was the victim not the perpetuator of adultery. Chaucer parodies his voice in the character of the absurd Sir Thopas, who contributes to the *Canterbury Tales* a rhyme so bad that even the unlettered Bartender begs him to be done with it. ". . . 'By God,' quod he, 'for pleynly at a word / Thy drasty ryming is nat worth a toord! / Thou doost noght elles but despendest tyme. / Sire, at o word, thou shalt ne lenger ryme.'"

2. In the very midst of Paradise's circles Dante will scramble into the arms of Beatrice crying like a baby so that she has to soothe him with, "Thou art in Heaven . . . all is holy here" (*Par.* 22:7–8), he will make himself ludicrous, never his song.

3. Did Dante commit the sin of adultery only in his heart or did he sleep with Beatrice before or during her brief married life? Most scholars find the idea of an actual coitus reprehensible. Albert J. Guerard told me that a colleague of his, one of America's most distinguished Dante critics, responded to an early draft of this manuscript with the remark: "Mirsky is the Philip Roth of Dante scholarship." To one reading Dante's biographer, Boccaccio, it is manifest that the world of Florence offered a plethora of opportunities to imaginative lovers. Adultery is never justified in Dante as it is in *The Decameron*. Boccaccio's criticism of marriage as an institution, however, his attack on sexual hypocrisy, his defense of woman's right to freedom married or not, and his praise of discretion, make one think again about Boccaccio's attraction to Dante. In the Florence that Boccaccio has made so vivid, but a few years distant from Dante's, why should a liaison with Beatrice be unthinkable?

pathos, despite his blindness, was not sufficient. *Paradise Lost* is not a comedy [4] but an historical epic. Dante, a "modernist," wrote a sexual confession.

King David, poet, prophet, and adulterer, has blood on his hands. The Talmud tolls, "Adultery leads to murder." Dante would wonder about Beatrice in the other world. Could he freely enjoy her in Paradise? Has he wanted her dead? Can he meet her in the Neoplatonic visions of his head? Has he *imagined* what happened between them? A book, in which Dante would meet Beatrice for that "New Life" he boasted of, might save him from the confusion that threatens to overwhelm his will to go on.

Smarrita—the first terror of this confusion in the middle of his life, is literal. He is lost. To be lost is to be forgotten. This is the ground of his first steps in Hell. At the beginning of the *Commedia,* Dante starts with those who envy every other fate, "e la lor cieca vita e tanto bassa, / che 'nvidiosi son d'ogni altra sorte," "and their blind life is so low, / that they are envious of every other fate" (*Inf.* 3:46–47). This theme of those who are forgotten, who have lost their chance for fame, is curiously echoed by Chaucer in *The House of Fame.* With customary modesty, Geoffrey begs before the goddess of fame to be forgotten. His disciple's request would have horrified Dante.

> "Maestro, che è quel ch'i' odo?
> e che gent' è che par nel duol sì vinta?"
> Ed elli a me: "Questo misero modo
> tengon l'anime triste di coloro
> che visser sanza 'nfamia e sanza lodo."

> "Master what is it I hear?
> And what people are these so vanquished by pain?"
> And he to me: "This is the miserable way
> those sad souls keep who
> lived without infamy or praise."
> (*Inf.* 3:32–36)

> "Fama di loro il mondo esser non lassa;
> misericordia e giustizia li sdegna:
> non ragionaiam di lor, ma guarda e passa."
> · · ·

4. A friend annotates, "Not a comedy in the sense of a work grounded in an ironical relation of described events and their interior/ulterior meanings." Needless to say, Milton's epic is never funny.

> "Report of them the world does not allow;
> Pity and justice disdain them:
> Speak not of them, but stare and pass."
> (*Inf.* 3:49–51)

When the soaring eagle brings Chaucer to windy heights, asking,

> "Artow come hider to han fame?"
> "Nay for sothe, frend," quod y.
> "I came noght yder, graunt mercy,
> For no such cause, by my hed!
> Sufficeth me, as I were ded,
> That no wight have my name in honde.
> I wot myself best how y stonde."
> (Chaucer 1957a, 1872–78)

Such is the English poet's rejoinder to his own pretensions. In Hell his teacher, Dante Alighieri, speaks of fame as the one antidote against the Inferno's pain. The damned beg to be remembered as if it were a gift, a balm for eternity. The wayfarers in Purgatory cry out his praise, even at the gate, to the annoyance of its keeper. Dante, tongue in cheek, holds up Divine Providence with the recitation of his songs. And so, in Canto 11 of *Purgatorio* (again, a beginning, for in this place starts the "true purgatory") while a minor character recites:

> "La vostra nominanza è color d'erba
> che viene e va, e quei la discolora
> per cui ella esce della terra acerba."
>
> "Your fame is the color of grass
> which comes and goes, discolored by what
> drew it from the ground green."
> (*Purg.* 11:115)–17 [5]

The poet chimes, "Oh thank you for filling my breast with good humility and pushing down my big tumor, but . . . [that "but" resonating with Florentine panache] who were you talking of just now?" (*Purg.* 11:118–20). The canto is full of who is who in Florence, Giotto obscuring Cimabue.

---

5. Fame may be the "color of grass" but no fame has a sadder color as we may remember from *Inferno,* 3:35 than invisibility.

One cannot be purged of lust for fame in a literary work. Dante's appetite has the keenness of desire toward a mistress. Jilted in his political aspirations, Dante in his language characterizes Florence, a proud lady, now a whore. Even in Purgatory, he lusts for her applause, her rabble's. "La rabbia fiorentina, che superba / fu a quel tempo si com' ora è putta." "The Florentine rabble, as proud at that time as it now is prostitute" (*Purg.* 11:113–14).

That word "*superba*," proud, has been sounded before in *Inferno*, "là dove Michele / fé la vendetta del superbo strupo," "There where Michael/ made the vendetta on the proud adultery, (*Inf.* 7:11–12). But I prefer the English cognate, superb—"the superb adultery." Is there not admiration in Dante's description of Lucifer's revolt, as "*strupo*,"[6] a sexual betrayal, strumpetry? Who but Dante Alighieri has committed *strupo,* adultery, made it his raison d'etre? Who desires the "adulterous" love of Florence?

Smarrita, smarrita!

What if one were to transform that lust into love of God, to record the strumpetry of Florence and one's thirst for fame, one's adultery, in a chronicle as sacred as Scripture. Milton understood, hurried after his master, in the person of Lucifer, even in the Puritan world, fame, a spur to God. "Fame is the spur that the clear spirit doth raise / (That last infirmity of Noble mind)." Or is it an "infirmity"? A few lines down in the *Lycidas* just quoted, Milton resolves the question, as Dante will in his long climb up—resolves it by referring it to the eyes of the Creator.

> *Fame* is no plant that grows on mortal soil
> Nor in the glistering foil
> Set off to th' world, nor in broad rumor lies,
> But lives and spreds aloft by those pure eyes
> And perfet witness of all judging *Jove:*
> As he pronounces lastly on each deed,
> Of so much fame in Heav'n expect thy meed.

But what will the Holy One, remember of him, Alighieri? *Smarrita!* That vanity lingers. Dante can not disabuse himself of the notion of fame. Fame as an adulterer? Let it be. Outside of the church, fame is the one salvation. His skull tightens with horror as he stares on the anonymous, colorless souls. The worst fate is to be forgotten, invisible. For Dante, the least punishment is the most terrible, to be for-

---

6. John D. Sinclair translates *strupo* as "adultery," though Charles Singleton prefers the innocuous "rebellion" in his Princeton University Press edition.

gotten, to be, as Professor Clara Claiborne Park writes,[7] "Not yet *in* Hell—outside the gate. Not even worthy of hell, not worthy of mercy *or* judgment." That *"cieca vita,"* blind life, echoes of the master key, the *Nuova Vita,* "new life," forerunner of the *Commedia,* the *"nostra vita,"* "our life," a phrase that begins the latter, its first line, and also its secret title. Memory, even the blind worm, clings to its threads and so it winds on to man. Even Spinoza destroying the memory of myth, staring through telescope, microscope, grinding his lens to see abstraction, clings to that rope, as the scholar Harry Austryn Wolfson shows, clings to eternity through memory.[8] Somehow our actions, Spinoza says, will be remembered, recorded, even in the vast, impersonal universe. To be remembered is to live on, on, and on into eternity. That out of matter, aeons and aeons of dying matter, memory has emerged, staggers the imagination. "It strains credulity," exclaims the scientist.[9] Memory.

"Remember me!" cries Dante. Let it not all, my fear, lechery, be but a vanity.

Osip Mandelstam points out the importance of the steps in Dante.

Why? The steps are the way. In naming the sins, the sinners, remembering, excoriating, Dante is hoping to outstep Death, his tangled life. So the progression of the *Commedia* from the lurid fleshpots of the *Inferno* to the milder cries of *Purgatorio,* to the almost impossible, elevated language of *Paradiso;* Dante is straining harder and harder to elevate the act of sin. Beatrice, fleshless, formless, is a kind of music that he can worship but also assimilate into his flesh without violating again human taboo, adultery. Sad, comic dream!

Is this not the dream of the *Zohar?* Critics argue whether Beatrice stands for Jesus. If she is shot through with light from her unions with the First Lover of the

---

7. Notation of Professor Park on an early draft of this manuscript.

8. "He [Spinoza] presents his views on immortality not in opposition to those who maintain it in its traditional form but rather in opposition to those who in his own time and in his own city denied it altogether. To begin with, on the basis of his own philosophy, he could quite logically maintain that on the death of man neither his body nor his soul is absolutely destroyed, but as finite modes they both become reabsorbed into the infinite modes, namely, 'motion' and 'the absolutely infinite intellect,' of which they are respectively parts. Then, like Avicenna and Averroes and their followers in the past, he tries to show that the human mind, though in its origin it is only part of the absolutely infinite intellect, becomes individualized during the lifetime of man by its acquisition of knowledge of the type which he describes as the second and third of this three types of knowledge. Then this individualized human mind, on its reunion with the absolutely infinite intellect whence it originally came, somehow, in some inexplicable manner, retains its acquired indivduality. The human souls is thus immortal, or eternal, as he usually calls it, and its immortality is in a certain sense personal and individual" (Wolfson 1968, 422–23).

9. "But for life itself, for memory, to have emerged from out of the wasteland of degenerating matter—the raw fact that it did, strains credulity" (Bleibtreu 1968, 11).

Universe, the religious imagination of Dante striving through sexual union with his beloved after something more, trying to mate with the Creator, becomes clear.

It is the dreadful human comedy.

Take us back into you, we cry.

It is the common plea of *Commedia* and *Zohar,* through the family tree of Neoplatonism, derived perhaps from a few bare lines of ethics, a dream uttered as an aside by Socrates in the *Theaetetus.*[10]

10. Julius Guttmann makes reference to this in his *Philosophies of Judaism* (1973, 96). He also points out the radical change that Neoplatonism effected in Jewish philosophy.

"The new relationship [in the emerging thought of the 10th century, apart from the Kalam] on the part of the Islamic and Jewish Neoplatonists and Aristotelians was different not only in degree, but also in kind. Greek philosophy was no longer the source of particular doctrines only, but the systematic foundation of their thought. Even where they modified Greek ideas for religious reasons, the change applied to the system as such" (Guttman 1973, 95). This of course effected a much deeper kinship between the philosophers in the different religions. The touchstone is the common definition; "Philosophy is essentially a drawing near to God, as far as is possible for human beings" (Guttman 1973, 96). Although it is questionable whether either Dante or the author of the *Zohar* was aware of the source in Plato, it is worth examining. The words of Socrates in the *Theaetetus* have a curious circular movement. His "escape to the dwelling of the gods" turns out to be only a return to the earth and a life of righteous conduct. He goes from a multiplicity of gods, using conventional language, to the idea of a single God, and man's unique relationship to Him through ethical conduct, righteousness. He even gives to evil a kind of positive existence by stating the impossibility of the evil "impure" being received into the pure Hereafter. This last notion is perhaps the foundation of that education and purgation in the cosmologies of the other world that received such stunning literary form in the *Commedia* and *Zohar*. Socrates explains: "But it is impossible that evils should be done away with, Theodorus, for there must always be something opposed to the good: and they cannot have their place among the gods, but must inevitably hover about mortal nature and this earth. Therefore we ought to try to escape from earth to the dwelling of the gods as quickly as we can: and to escape is to become like God, so far as this is possible: and to become like God is to become righteous and holy and wise. But, indeed, my good friend, it is not at all easy to persuade people that the reason generally advanced for the pursuit of virtue and the avoidance of vice—namely, in order that a man may not seem bad and may seem good—is not the reason why the one should be practiced and the other not; that I think, is merely old wives' chatter, as the saying is. Let us give the true reason. God is in no wise and in no manner unrighteous, but utterly and perfectly righteous, and there is nothing so like him as that one of us who in turn becomes most nearly perfect in righteousness. It is herein that the true cleverness of a man is found and also his worthlessness and cowardice: for the knowledge of this is wisdom or true virtue, and ignorance of it is folly or manifest wickedness; and all other kinds of seeming cleverness and wisdom are paltry when they appear in public affairs and vulgar in the arts. Therefore by far the best thing for the unrighteous man and the man whose words or deeds are impious is not to grant that he is clever through knavery; for such men glory in that reproach, and think it means that they are not triflers, 'useless burdens upon the earth,' [Homer *Iliad* 18.104; *Odyssey* 20.379] but such as men should be who are to live safely in a state. So we must tell them the truth—that just because they do not think they are such as they are, they are so all the more truly; for they do not know

In the *Zohar,* the Hebrew document, without the constraints of courtly love, conventions, the call to the Female Presence of the single Unknown is clearer though less dramatic. Jewish apocrypha, under the influence of the rambling, genial talmudic style, while obsessed with numbers, is not so devoted to order, does not bother to construct Dante's artful edifice, 33 cantos, 3 books. The terror of masturbation rather than adultery stands at the center of the *Zohar.* Necrophilia is not an issue. The haunting voyage to a world beyond death for a forbidden act is the genesis of the *Commedia.* Dante's laughter is hellish, paradisaical, heretical. He defies popes, conventional church wisdom, to construct his own vision of Judgment, who sinned and who not.

Dante will make love to another man's wife.[11] He will make love to a corpse.

---

the penalty of unrighteousness, which is the thing they most ought to know. For it is not what they think it is—scourgings and death which they sometimes escape entirely when they have done wrong—but a penalty which is impossible to escape.

Theo: What penalty do you mean?

Soc: Two patterns my friend, are set up in the world, the divine, which is most blessed, and the godless, which is most wretched. But these men do not see that this is the case, and their silliness and extreme foolishness blind them to the fact that through their unrighteous acts they are made like the one and unlike the other. They therefore pay the penalty for this by living a life that conforms to the pattern they resemble; and if we tell them that, unless they depart from their 'cleverness' the blessed place that is pure of all things evil will not receive them after death, and here on earth they will always live the life like themselves—evil men associating with evil—when they hear this, they will be so confident in their unscrupulous cleverness that they will think our words the talk of fools" (Plato 1921, 127–31).

It is worth noting that Plato does not make knowledge alone the aim of the imitation of God, but righteousness and holiness as well. Elsewhere in his writing the virtue of knowledge, its acquisition, is the prime good of man, and evil is the absence of that knowledge. In the works of the early Neoplatonists, however, knowledge of God alone, became synonymous with imitation of Him. (See Guttman 1973, 97: "[T]he meaning of the religious ideal is completely changed when the communion with God is defined as the knowledge of truth, understood as systematic theoretical knowledge.") In Dante's thought, and the *Zohar*'s, identity with the Holy One is pursued through a woman, achieving a sensuous, even sensual, rather than a purely intellectual union. Wisdom and holiness, at least, are bound up, therefore, with ecstatic possession. In some ways, the thirteenth-century Neoplatonists return us to a Dionysian world, yet one tinged with prophecy, politics, God's attributes of holiness and righteousness in the Platonic system.

11. This issue is belabored with talk of the conventions of courtly love. What did society permit? Dante's Italy, according to his own testament, was a dangerous place for adultery. Francesca screaming, Paolo is dragged to his death in Rimini, the book of Lancelot scattered underfoot. This is not the smiling world of Boccaccio. (I note, however, that Thomas G. Bergin seems to think that Beatrice's husband would not have objected to the worship of his wife. "Her marriage would have been no bar to Dante's devotion to her. In fact, it would have been in harmony with the Provençal tradition of

Call that weeping corpse back from the dead and ask, for pity, a guide through Hell, Purgatory, *to* her: beg to be taken *by* her, sinless (somehow) into Heaven. These are the raw facts. Edward Dahlberg cried of Melville, Thoreau, "Where are the ladies?"[12] In Dante's *Commedia*, "Where is the husband?" And Alighieri's wife? It is double adultery. The Old Testament faces such violations without excuses. Moses is a murderer, David an adulterer. On Israel's harp sin plucks its plaintive music.

Dante's corrosive book is intent on constructing a Florentine gnosis of Heaven and Hell: one in which the church would find itself accommodated in a bizarre seating arrangement. Dante's self-portrait, self-mocking, touches blasphemy.

$\bullet$ $\bullet$ $\bullet$

I WAS ATTRACTED TO DANTE through the *Zohar* (the *Shining;* its title with the promise of illumination, if rumor of it reached him, would have made the sun-struck Tuscan [13] curious). Moses de Leon (1230–1305), the probable author of the *Zohar,* was born earlier than Dante. Did the Spanish Jew influence the younger Italian Catholic? Similar thoughts fill their pages. The *Zohar* redacts ideas and traditions about the afterlife that Dante surely would have known. Its Aramaic may be counterfeit, obscure, but the *Zohar* is the classic of Kabbalah, secret lore, creation dreams. Entangled in that light, its poetry shaped many imposing rabbinic minds in the wake of the thirteenth century. Dante Alighieri and Moses de Leon were both drawn to philosophy: besotted by the "wicked Aristotle."[14] Moses de Leon may have imbibed Greek philosophy through Maimonides (de Leon paid to have a volume of Maimonides' copied). Dante certainly was touched through Thomas Aquinas (who had read and was influenced by Maimonides).[15] Both poets attempted to make philosophy palpable. Rage fills the pages of the *Commedia* and the *Zohar,* a divine rage that is the will to be one with God, a female God,

courtly love, and would of course have been simply irrelevant in the later stages of his devotion, when the woman had all but vanished in the symbol" [Bergin 1965, 35]. I respectfully disagree.)

12. See *Can These Bones Live* for Dahlberg's denunciation of Puritan morals in the American novel, also the essay "Moby Dick, a Hamitic Dream," where he declaims, "In sixteen volumes by Melville, no woman is bedded, seduced or gulled, and, by heaven, that is gross deception" (Dahlberg 1967c, 191).

13. "He [Dante] was one of the chief proponents of the Neoplatonic sun symbolism" (Anderson 1980, 274). See also Anderson 403.

14. The quotation is from an epigram of Rabbi Joseph Soloveitchik, recalled from a lecture of his that I attended. "The rabbis counsel that in sexual matters we do not follow the Rambam [Maimonides], because there he learned from 'the wicked Aristotle.'"

15. See footnote 22 of this chapter for Aquinas's link to Maimonides.

the female aspect of God, the *Shechinah,* to Moses de Leon and the sages who preceded him. Dante summoned it in the form of Beatrice. Reading philosophy, what did Dante see? He testifies to it in the *Convivio,* the very gauze of her veil, "the stars appeared to be shadowed by some white mist" (Barbi 1966, 8).

All philosophy is an attempt to measure the body of God, which is the structure of the Universe. The measurement of the Body—it is a task where the wind of fantasy bends the laws of reason. *Shi'ur Komah* is one such text, how many parasangs are the whites of the Holy One's eyes? Measurement of the Almighty, His creation, the Universe, a serious task for Aristotle, among mystics is a source of comedy.[16] The sobriety of the philosopher who thinks to capture the ribs of the cosmos within a human brain is abandoned at the outset. Dante steps onto a stage built to the directions of Moses, Aristotle, Philo, Saint Augustine, and attempts in his own person to live out not the drama of poor broken Everyman, but the drama of man becoming God. Cosmic Comics!

Mysticism is a form of fiction, a surrender to poetic frenzy, to imagination. What can I *imagine* of the Holy One, not what do I *know.* But philosophy's imaginings are the grist for the mystics' voyage into the unknown.[17]

---

16. See Alfred Ivry's remark in a discussion of the uniqueness of Moses as a prophet on Maimonides' nervousness as he grew older about *shi'ur qomah [Shi'ur Komah],* for to him as a philosopher rather than as a poet, this text purporting to measure the human dimensions of the Unknown was less amusing than discomforting. "His statement in the *Commentary on the Mishnah* is the more radical, for there he claims explicitly that Moses is more dear to God than any other mortal that ever lived or that ever would live and that Moses actually attained the ranks of the angels, tearing down all physical barriers, dispensing with all but his intellectual faculty, having become pure intellect. . . . Maimonides stops himself at this point in his *Commentary on the Mishnah,* writing that he had intended to say much more on this topic, but that he would have had to enter into an extended discussion of difficult biblical passages and of difficult issues, including the existence and ranks of angels, depictions of angels and of the Creator Himself, and even of *shi'ur qomah,* the mystics' mythically proportioned embodiment of divine glory. Maimonides struck the sentence referring to *shi'ur qomah* from later recensions of the *Commentary on the Mishnah,* and it does not appear in the printed editions of the text. As we know from his correspondence, his attitude toward this mythical figure became decidedly negative" (Ivry 1995, 289).

17. As an architect of mystical worlds Dante must have known of the decision by Etienne Tempier, the bishop of Paris, in 1277 to reprimand those scholastics who were trying to ban speculation on the possibility of alternative universes. There is no question that Dante was treading the border of heresy in imagining Hell, Purgatory, and Heaven in such detail. They are in a sense "other" universes. It was Professor Seymour Feldman who first made me aware of Tempier's ruling in his notes to Gersonides' *The Wars of the Lord.*

"We have now raised the question of the plurality of universes, a topic that has become increasingly relevant in our space-travel age, but which was not unknown to our medieval ancestors. Indeed, the question was discussed by the ancient Greek cosmologists. In response to the atomist thinkers,

Beatrice may marry Jesus, blush, weep, and flow with love. But what may Dante do? Become a book, high in the empyrean. Upward he floats, entering her womb, exiting her ear. Upward to the wheel where desire and will are one, and he will be driven round in the sexual madness of the spheres, beyond Mary, Jesus,

---

such as Democritus who had suggested that there are other worlds beside our own, Aristotle argued that there is *only one universe,* 'outside' of which there is absolutely nothing, for our own world contains all the matter there is. [46 Aristotle *On the Heavens* 1.8–9.] . . . During the Middle Ages this cosmological question receded into the background as the main concern was with our own world's beginning. Perhaps because the Bible and the Koran were silent on the issue most medieval cosmological speculations ignored or denied the possibility of plural worlds. But the silence ended in the late thirteenth century, when in 1277 the Bishop of Paris issued a list of philosophical errors, among which was the Aristotelian dogma of the world's unicity. Why was this proposition now condemned? The Bishop of Paris regarded this thesis as an infringement upon God's omnipotence: if there can be only one world, this would imply that God is impotent. So anyone who really believes in divine omnipotence ought to be at least open to the possibility of plural worlds" (Feldman 1999, 206).

Feldman refers the reader to Steven Dick's *Plurality of Worlds,* where Tempier's ruling is examined in further detail.

"Aquinas followed the essentials of Aristotle's arguments against a plurality of worlds based on the doctrine of natural place. . . . He also agreed that there could be no matter outside our world. Neither elements nor Earths could exist outside our world 'since every earth would naturally be carried to this central one, wherever it was. . . . Aquinas found perfection in unity; one world constituted of everything that exists is perfect, whereas many worlds would not contain all sensible bodies, and therefore would each be imperfect. This definition of the perfection of the world—derived from Plato—held that it would be more in accord with God's omnipotence that he created a single perfect world than a great number of necessarily imperfect worlds. The unity of the world was the very reason for its goodness; division implied something lacking in goodness . . ." (Dick 1982, 26–27).

"Aquinas's attempts at reconciliation of reason and faith could not pacify the more hardline theologians who feared that reason might gain the upper hand. The conflict had grown so sharp by 1256 that only after papal intervention had Aquinas been allowed to deliver his inaugural lecture as a master of theology. The controversy came to a climax in 1277, only three years after Aquinas's death, when Etienne Tempier, the bishop of Paris, condemned 219 beliefs commonly held in the universities and which he considered heretical because they infringed on the power of God. Among those beliefs was 'that the First Cause cannot make many worlds.' The university masters, deeply religious and fearful of excommunication if they ignored a promulgation of the Church, were thenceforth forced to examine more critically the Aristotelian principles on which the impossibility of other worlds was based" (Dick 1982, 28).

The preceding passages illuminate perhaps some of the historical background of Dante's *Commedia.* There is a whiff of heresy in Dante throughout, despite his dependence on Aristotle and Aquinas (at this time still a controversial figure in the libraries of the church). I would say that the voyage of Ulysses to a real Purgatory, located in the world, speaks to the permission to speculate about "other worlds" that Etienne Tempier, the bishop of Paris, had made part of Catholic dogma. In imagining so vividly the spheres of Hell, Heaven, and Purgatory did not Dante go into both inner and outer space, exercising this new freedom of imagination that the bishop of Paris had granted? In the

male, and female to the single point of light that is the origin of the Universe. In
the *Zohar* that "brightness," or "shining," is the mysterious first flash of creation.
Isn't this the "brightness" that thrills Dante's "subtle spiritual" body? "Beyond that
point there is no knowable." "O somma luce che tanto ti levi / da' concetti mor-
tali," "O light Supreme which art lifted high / above mortal conceptions" (*Par.*
33:67–68).

What is that light? Is it palpable? What does it have to do with the search for
Beatrice?

Before going further, let me order. I am writing of different cosmologies,
Dante's and the *Zohar*'s, quoting the latter's only to instance the temptation of the
Hebrew universe for the Catholic poet.

Rome fell to Carthage, fell to the Canaanites some four hundred years after
Jesus the Nazarite, that spiritual son of Samson, set in popular motion ideas liable
to distortion. Out of Carthage came Augustine, deficient in Greek, misunderstanding the words of Jesus of Nazareth as quoted in the stories, according to the
scholar of religious philosophy Harry A. Wolfson.

> As to the necessity by which one sins, Augustine describes it by the term concu-
> piscence, which he identifies with sexual desire and considers it as the source of
> all sin. . . . There is no statement by any of the Fathers prior to Augustine in
> which the corruption transmitted by Adam to his descendants as a result of the
> fall is called concupiscence. . . . The reduction of all bad concupiscences to the
> concupiscence of sex and the identification of sexual concupiscence with the in-
> herited corruption is something new introduced by Augustine into Christian
> theology. . . . How Augustine arrived at the belief in the irresistibility of concu-
> piscence is explained by himself. Early in his life, he reminisces, even though in
> himself he did not find the power to overcome his sexual concupiscence, he still
> believed that continency was in our power. But a verse in the Latin translation of
> the *Wisdom of Solomon* convinced him that continency was not in the power of
> man. The verse in question (8:21) reads: *Et ut scivi quoniam aliter non possem esse*

---

voyage to the worlds beyond Dante joined the ranks of those curious about the possibility of God cre-
ating other universes. Ulysses makes a corporal voyage to the mountain, implying that the mountain
is not entirely constituted of spiritual matter. Dante, according to Benvenuto da Imola (whom I quote
in my final chapter), knew that he was inventing the voyage of Ulysses and "devised this on purpose."
I perceive the poet's laughter in this. Heresy in regard to the doctrine of Aquinas and Aristotle not
only brought Dante closer to the Catholic theology of the late thirteenth century, refusing to straight-
jacket the power of the Holy One; it made his comedy fellow to the wisdom in *The Book of Job* and
Isaiah.

continens, nisi Deus det, which was taken by Augustine to mean: "And as I knew that I could not otherwise be continent, except God gave (it)." If this is really what has led Augustine to the belief in the irresistibility of concupiscence, and it would seem to be so, for he quotes this verse twenty-odd times in his works in support of it, then this belief of his has its origin in a misunderstanding of the meaning of the verse. In the original Greek, the verse quite unmistakably refers to wisdom, which is mentioned previously, and it reads: "And as I knew that I could not otherwise obtain (egkratës) [it], except God gave [it]." This is undoubtedly what the Latin translation also meant, for in two other places it uses the term *continens* as a translation of the Greek (egkratës), namely in *Ecclesiasticus* 6:27–28, and 15:1, and in both these places there can be no doubt that the term *continens* is used in the sense of "obtaining" or "possessing." What happened here, then is that Augustine misunderstood the meaning of the term *continens,* taking it in the sense of "continent," and thus derived therefrom his belief in the powerlessness of man to abstain from sin. (Wolfson 1961, 164–67)

Thus begins the fearful drum roll in which sex is denounced, free will curtailed. Dante stop your ears! Listen instead to the songs of Provençe, the troubadours in whom is found "the first germ of the maxim that sexual love is virtue" (Vossler 1958, 1:301). Another critic who never read Talmud! Augustine goes from insufficient Greek to nonexistent Hebrew.

Every creature, since it is good, can be loved, both well and badly: well, that is, when order is preserved: badly when order is disturbed. If the Creator be truly loved, that is, if He himself, not aught else instead of Him which is not He, be loved, He cannot be loved badly. For even Love itself is to be loved in orderly wise, whereby what is to be loved is loved well. Therefore it seems to be that a brief and true definition of virtue is the *Order of Love:* on account of which in the holy canticle the Bride of Christ, the City of God, sings: *Set love in order in me.* (Augustine *De Civitate Dei* 15:22, quoted in Gardner 1968, 55)

Augustine is quoting the Song of Solomon, 2:4, in the Vulgate, *Ordinavit in me charitatem.* But the Hebrew Bible reads, "And his banner over me was love." The pennant of love, the flapping joy of Jerusalem is struck. Instead, Augustine hauls up the stiff ensign of the empire, arm rigid in salute.[18]

---

18. Albert Guerard, so often my guide, showed an imposing Dante scholar, his colleague, the manuscript of this text in an early draft. The latter wrote back that I was "insufferable" in my "treatment of Augustine." John Womack, professor of history at Harvard, to whom I submitted the manuscript before its final revision, also felt I had been unfair to the Catholic saint, particularly in not

Through that Empire so wide and so enduring and so renowned and glorious by
the virtues of such great men, to their labors the rewards which they sought was
given, and to us were examples set of needful admonition: that if, for the most
glorious City of God, we do not preserve such virtues as they for the glory of an

---

distinguishing between the young and the older Augustine. John Womack urged me several times to
read Peter Brown's book, *Augustine of Hippo.* When I finished this vivid evocation of Augustine and
his place in the Late Roman Empire, I realized that I had been unjust to a complex thinker. I have tried
to make some amends. Still, Harry Wolfson's critique of Augustine as a poor scholar of Greek is only
confirmed by Peter Brown. "Augustine found that Greek bored him to distraction at just the same
time as he had begun to 'revel' in the Latin classics. Augustine's failure to learn Greek was a momen-
tous casualty of the Late Roman educational system: he will become the only Latin philosopher in antiquity to be virtually ignorant of Greek. As a young man, he will set out, pathetically ill-equipped, on
a traditional philosopher's quest for Wisdom. A cultivated Greek audience would have treated this ex-
clusively Latin-speaking student from the university of Carthage as 'a dumb fool,' acquainted as he
was only 'with the opinions of Greek philosophers, or rather, with little snippets of these opinions,
picked up, here and there, from the Latin dialogues of Cicero'; not 'with those philosophical systems
as they stand, fully developed in Greek books'" (Brown 1999, 24).

Brown talks about how meticulous Augustine was as a bishop of Hippo in matters of detail. One
wonders about the saint's failure to have a colleague, competent in Greek, check the original sources
before making a statement so central to his theology; an error that according to Wolfson had a mo-
mentous effect. Brown's sympathetic portrait of Augustine sets the latter's realistic attitude toward
sexual life in the context of far more contemptuous attitudes in the church of the late fourth and early
fifth century. "[Augustine] was the contemporary of Jerome who spoke of marriage as a tangled
thornbush, good only to produce, in the form of children dedicated at an early age to the ascetic life,
the 'roses of new virgins'; of Gregory of Nyssa, whose gentle tone makes us forget the fact that he regarded sexuality with supreme lack of interest, as no more than an 'animal appendage to humankind's
original angelic' nature; and of Ambrose, who, when faced by married candidates to the episcopate,
expected his readers to agree without question that *voluptas,* sensuality alone, had driven Adam from
Paradise. Seen against that background, Augustine's preaching and written works represent, if anything, a call to moderation" (Brown 1999, 500). Still Brown clarifies just how much of a threat Augustine felt powerful sexual delight could be in his world to an ordered, Christian life. Order, and
authority, are the public preoccupations of the saint in *Augustine of Hippo.* Brown makes clear that
Augustine as a bishop used the threat of authority, the authority of the Roman state, against his religious opponents and sanctioned public religious coercion. Belief in the ultimate divine Authority and
that Authority's unpredictable gift of grace, which diminishes the scope of free will in human beings,
leads to Augustine's faith in predestination. What is the latter but an absolute, preordained order?
Seized in the moments of his letters when Augustine allows himself to doubt, the saint is a sympathetic, bedeviled thinker, rather than an autocratic bishop and self-assured theologian. Even Brown
will admit, however, that Augustine was "the first theorist of the Inquisition" (Brown 199, 236).

It struck me when Brown spoke about the revision under Aquinas and others, of Augustine's
reading of philosophy, that this revision by church theologians was probably one of the factors in lib-
erating Dante's sexual dreams. Augustine, however, speaks through Beatrice, and the drama of confusion with which Dante begins the *Commedia* may have been inspired by Augustine's boldness in

earthly city, we may be pierced with shame, and if we preserve them, may not be exalted with pride . . . even the Jews who slew Christ . . . were justly surrendered to their glory. (Augustine 5.18 quoted in Gardner 1968, 50)

"Wide . . . enduring . . . renowned . . . glorious," Augustine speaks the language of the Roman Empire. No wonder the *order* of love is so important.[19]

Did Augustine impose on the church a notion of order that could only be satisfied in a vision of empire? Thus apart from the donation of Constantine (that forged donation of power, wealth that Dante distrusted) was the struggle between temporal and spiritual ideas augmented. Whose "donation" was more awesome? For despite Dante's horror of a church empire, Dante's insistence on the rights of a secular realm, he is very much a child of Augustine. His Paradise is fixed. The heavenly trains run on time.

Contrast this to the heaven of the *Zohar*[20] filled with jealousies and angers,

---

presenting his own wrestling an all too human body in *The Confessions*. Did Augustine's fascination with the sexual life of Adam and Eve before the Fall touch Dante's startling portraits of an erotic Paradise, his hints about spiritual eroticism in the upper circles of Heaven?

19. On the question of free will, according to Wolfson, Augustine can not tolerate real freedom of choice in his universe. "Freedom thus to Augustine does not mean the choice to act one way or the other, for there is no such freedom; everything is determined to act only one way. Freedom is only relative, and it means to act according to one's own nature, without external compulsion. It is in this sense that man is free either to sin or to act righteously, for each man has a determinate nature either to sin or to act righteously" (Wolfson 1961, 175).

20. The *Zohar*'s whirling universe is particularly interesting in its self-evaluation of the work of the scholar/poet in the creation of cosmologies. Each true interpretation of the law creates a whole heaven and earth in itself, of which the angels are jealous. Each untrue interpretation hazards the emergence of a horrible New World of chaos.

"Our teachers have told us that at the moment when a man interprets a new meaning in the Torah, his idea ascends before the Holy One, blessed be He, and He takes it up and kisses it and crowns it with seventy crowns of graven and inscribed letters. When a new idea is formulated in the field of the esoteric wisdom it rises and rests on the head of the 'Zaddik, the life of the universe,' and then it flies off and traverses seventy thousand worlds until it rises to the 'Ancient of Days'. . . . And enters into the eighteen mystical worlds, about which we read, 'No eye has seen you, O God.' (Is. 64:3). . . . It flies up and down until it is made into a sky. . . .

"When the Torah was delivered to Moses, there appeared hosts of heavenly angels ready to consume him with their fiery breath, but the Holy One, Blessed be He, sheltered him. Similarly now when the new word rises and is crowned and presents itself before the Holy One, Blessed be He, He covers and protects that word, and also shelters the author of that word, so that the angels will not become aware of him and so be filled with jealousy, until that word is transformed into a new heaven and a new earth. [The Zohar ingeniously explains that this is the meaning of the verse from Isaiah 51:16, "In the shadow of my hand I covered you, to plant heavens and establish an earth." Of course the danger

hosts of angry angels and fleeing scholars, an empyrean of drama, struggle, and aspiration: a Babylonian vault of storm-tossed skies. This is the heaven of the Hebrews. A house of madness. Not even Maimonides, the most philosophic and ordered of rabbis building system upon system, could finally succumb to such a vision of order as obsessed Dante's teachers, Aquinas, Augustine, Richard of Victor, Jacopone da Todi. Jacopone cries out.

> Ordena questo amore, tu ch m'ami.
> Non è virtute senza ordene trovata. . . .
> Tutte le cose qual aggio ordenate
> Sì so facte con numero et mesura,
> Et al lor fine son tutte ordenate,
> Conservanse per orden tal valura. . . .
> Donqua co per calura
> Alma, tu sè empazita?
> For d'orden tu sè uscita:
>
> Order this love, you that love me
> No virtue is found without order
> All things which I have ordained
> Are made with number and measure
> And all are ordained to their end
> Preserving their worth through order. . . .
> How then though heat
> Have you gone crazy, Soul?
> You are out of order.
>   (Gardner 1968, 20–21)

Jacopone, Augustine, if you expect to be "amanza del primo amante" "beloved of the First Lover" (*Par.* 4:118), go crazy, *empazita*. Exactly. Maimonides would reply to you, "What is the proper measure of love? To love God with a great, overwhelming, extremely strong love, until his [your] soul is tied in the love of God. He is ravished always, *shogeh bah-tomid,* as if he were lovesick. His awareness

---

of false heavens exists as well.] When one who is a stranger to the mysteries of the Torah makes pseudo-discoveries, based on an incomplete understanding, that 'word' rises, and is met by the perverse One, the Demon of the false tongue, who emerges from the cavern of the great abyss and makes a leap of five hundred parasangs to receive that word. He takes it and returns with it to his cavern, and shapes it into a spurious heaven, which is called Tohu [chaos] . . ." (*Zohar* 5a).

never slips from his love of that woman [21] and he is always ravished in her when he sits and when he stands as well as when he is eating and drinking. More than that shall be the love of God in the heart of his lovers, that they are ravished always in her as we have been commanded, 'with all your heart and all your soul.' [Deut. 6:5]. And this is what Solomon said, 'Because I am love sick.' [Song of Songs 2:5]. All of the Song of Songs is a metaphor for this matter. . . .

"It is clear and known that love of God can not be tied to a person's heart until he's *shogeh bah-tomid,* ravished always in it and he leaves behind everything else in the world outside that love as we are commanded, 'with all your heart and all your soul.' " This is the wisdom of Moses Maimonides' "Hilchot Tshuvah" in the great codifier's *Mishnah Torah.* [22]

Shogeh. It is a three-letter root in Hebrew, shin, gimmel, hay, "to wander, go astray, err," but also, "to swerve, meander, reel or roll in drunkenness, to be intoxicated," and also, "to commit a sin of inadvertence." Savor its untranslatable ironies. There is even a pun possible for the word *shogeh* that means mad: *shin, gimmel, ayin,* is almost the same in pronunciation. A kind of madness touches this intoxicated state. That's what Maimonides understands the love of God as—anything but order—disorder, confusion, breakdown. Reeling and even sinning inadvertently; to experience the Holy One, Blessed be He, She, His Bride, the Shechinah, be always ravished, possessed, occupied, astray. [23] *Smarrita!* Dante's first cry in the *Commedia,* is the cry of his prophetic state.

21. What "woman"? It seems that Maimonides uses a woman as his way into the arms of the Holy One, Blessed be He. (The way is prepared of course by the use of Shechinah, the female presence of the Holy One in the Talmud and the *Bat Kol,* daughter of a voice, the remnant of prophecy which man may experience.) Neither Dante nor Moses de Leon would be indifferent to such hints.

22. For Dante's possible knowledge of Maimonides see Shlomo Pines's remarks in his, "Translator's introduction: The Philosophic Sources of The Guide of the Perplexed" (Maimonides 1963, lxi). Pines is discussing the appellation of Aristotle as "the chief of the Philosophers" in the *Guide.* "Moses, on the other hand is designated . . . 'Master of those who know,' an evidently higher rank. . . . The title might clearly have fitted the latter [Aristotle], to whom it is applied by Dante (*Divina Commedia, Inferno,* 4, 131) perhaps because of some recollection of the appellation used by Maimonides, which he might have encountered in a Latin translation of the *Guide.*"

23. King David, who left psalms entitled *shiggayon* [impulsive speech], is famous for his *mishiguss,* madness. Fleeing Saul, he runs away to the king of Gath. As the psalmist entered the city, he hears the retainers chatter, "Remember that famous Jewish song and dance, 'Saul has slain his thousands and David his ten thousands'? Isn't this that Dav. . . ?" Right away David starts to play the fool; a madman in the king's doorway, dribbling spit down his beard.

"What's the matter?" cries the king of Gath. "You see the man is *meshuggeh.* I don't have enough *mishigoyiim* in the house? I have to have him go *meshuggeh* before me?" (The rabbis speculate at

Savonarola, that Hebrew monk, will make the whole of Florence dance to David's, Maimonides' psalms, treading the order of Augustine, the order of the Medicis, into the dust of its squares.

> Non fu mai'l più bel solazzo,
> Più giocondo ne maggiore,
> Che per zelo e per amore
> Di Gesù, diventar pazzo.
> Ognun' gridi com' io grido,
> Sempre pazzo, pazzo, pazzo.
>
> Never was there greater solace,
> Fairer or more jocund,
> Than from zeal and love
> Of Jesus to go crazy.
> Everybody shout with me,
> Always crazy, crazy, crazy.
> (McCarthy 1963, 167)

Here is Dante in the middle. Dante is torn between Beatrice and Augustine. By identifying the object of his concupiscence with irresistible grace, he escapes from the clutches of Hell into the arms of his beloved. He leaves Augustine behind and goes up to see St. Francis, who is burning with love too, around and up, whirling.

Chaos and order, Hebrew and Hellenic. Dante the prophet, the erring servant, the lover—against Dante the philosopher, the imperialist. Fascist! Smarrita! The order of the poem against the chaos of his heart.

---

length on who those other crazy people, *mishigoyiim,* in the king's house could have been.) The cousinship between madness and prophecy, the apprehension of God, is close in the Bible. David and Saul, as receivers of the prophetic spirit, however, were practiced at receiving the spirit in a fit. See the description of the prophets dancing and of Saul's nakedness in the Book of Samuel.

CHAPTER FIVE

☉CEAN

DANTE'S CONFUSION, his *smarrita,* with which the *Inferno* begins, is manifold. His political life is in disarray, "tra li lazzi sorbi," "among the sour apples" (*Inf.* 15:65), and his romantic life is turning sour too. He goes back to his childhood sweetheart in the hope of redemption. Since Beatrice is dead, future adultery with her will be entirely a spiritual matter. The dread of it he can transform into a promise. He intends to seek in his will to make Beatrice "actual" again, an elevating virtue, to achieve a spiritual love.

Did he commit a further act, however, on earth that fills him with apprehension? Why give another sexual sin prominence in his poem? He has certainly thought about this other, and honesty compels him to face it before he can pass himself into Paradise. Too many of his masters have been of its persuasion. To think about sin, in the poet's world, to commit it "in the heart" is to share in it. For the Florentine—as a voyager in fantasy—there is no clear demarcation between the world of dreams and waking. Having written so convincingly of Hell, Dante was assumed by the children of Ravenna to have gone there.

His own sexual persona is torturing him. One must front the fear of sexual love between man and man for Dante. It is one of the issues of the *Inferno* where it rivals the guilt of adultery. It is no accident that Beatrice is absent from the first book and much of the second but for a flash in Virgil's memory. There is no place for her in the male *Inferno* or on the ascent of *Purgatorio* until Dante has struggled with the female in his nature.

> And Milton said: "I go to Eternal Death!"
>   Eternity shuddered
> For he took the outside course among the graves of the dead,
> A mournful shade. Eternity shudder'd at the image of eternal death
> Then on the verge of Beulah he beheld his own Shadow,
> A mournful form double, hermaphroditic, male & female
> In one wonderful body: and he enter'd into it

> In direful pain, for the dread shadow twenty-seven fold
> Reach'd to the depths of direst Hell & thence to Albion's land,
> Which is this earth of vegetation on which now I write
> （Blake, *Milton*, bk. 1, 16）

All this ocean in Dante—the waves, the passages of flight into that ocean all through the *Divine Comedy.* The island of Purgatory is placed so exactly in the path of the westering Ulysses, there can be no doubt that Dante, thumbing his Horace, knew where his *Aeneid* was tending.

> Us the encompassing Ocean awaits. Let us seek the Fields, the happy Fields, and the Islands of the Blest, where every year the land, unploughed, yields corn, and ever blooms the vine unpruned, and buds the shoot of the never-failing olive: the dark fig graces its native tree: honey flows from the hollow oak: from the lofty hill, with plashing foot, lightly leaps the fountain. There the goats come unbidden to the milking-pail, and the willing flock brings swelling udders home: nor does the bear at eventide growl 'round the sheepfold, nor the ground swell high with vipers. . . . Hither came no ship of pine with straining Argo's oarsmen . . . no Sidonian mariners hither turned their spars, nor Ulysses' toiling crew. No murrain blights the flock; no planet's blazing fury scorches the herd. Jupiter set apart these shores for a righteous folk, ever since with bronze he dimmed the luster of the Golden Age. With bronze and then with iron did he harden the ages, from which a happy escape is offered to the righteous, if my prophecy be heeded. （Horace 1964, 405–7）

Troy had burned. For Dante, Florence was burning. Rome burned. It was time for the valiant to set out. A scant fifty years before, the Mongols had ridden into Europe as the scourge of the Apocalypse. All around him Dante saw a collapsing world. Franciscan friars as well as the Polo brothers had brought back descriptions of the terrain of these demons. But what are their terrors, wonders, dog-faced, ox-footed men, to the horrors of the *Inferno,* the penances of *Purgatorio?* Insofar as *Paradiso* is concerned—Dante teases—it is you, the reader, who is in danger of being "*smarriti,*" bewildered.

> O you who in a little bark
> desirous to hear, have followed
> behind my keel, which sings upon its way
> turn to see again those shores of yours
> do not put forth on the deep, for perhaps

losing me, you would be left *bewildered.*
Minerva breathes, Apollo conducts me
and nine Muses show me the Bears.
(*Par.* 2:1–9)

Dante does not wish to stir from the travels of his own conscience. Yet science obsesses him, the geography of the stars, the precise positions of sun, moon, planetary bodies. Imagining them circle his travelers, he creates a model of the universe, of Hell and Heaven. So the Jewish mystics wrote of *Shi'ur Komah,* measurement of God, the Holy One, Blessed be He's body.

Rabbi Yishmael said: "What is the measure of the Holy One, Blessed be He, who is hidden from all creatures? The sole of His feet fills the whole world, as it is said (Is. 66:1) *The heaven is my throne, and the earth is my foot-stool.* The height of each sole is three ten thousand thousands of parasangs. . . . From the sole of His feet to His ankles one thousand ten thousands and five hundred parasangs, and the same for His left." *Shi'ur Komah* 1976, 25)

But the measurements are infinite, impossible, only serve to make the human body quake, grown faint, swoon into surrender before the Unknowable dimension. Now *body* is all to this Florentine, both as philosopher, narrator, and lover. Philosophy also sought to measure the body of the Holy One, Blessed be He, His universe through the compass and rulers of Greek and Arabic terminology; emanations, attributes in the centuries preceding Dante. The philosophers begin with the Unmoved Mover and go down toward the microcosm. Dante is with the mystics, moving upward, not to explain or measure, but to become one with that Unknown. His sins he leaves below on earth, and further down, in Hell.

He goes down through the ocean, following Ulysses. (I regard the twenty-sixth canto as a flashback, which allows us an insight into Dante's own descent to the entryway of Hell.) In very sight of Purgatory, Hell gaped for the Greek. Now Dante comes up from the *Inferno* to the beach of that island, which Ulysses will forever miss.

On the isle of Purgatory, a gilded mountain cone piercing the sky, the poet moves toward the stars, toward the uncharted Universe, through circles of love outside the boundaries, adulterous, heretical, hermaphrodite love. Of all those circles, he will enter the scalding penance of his own personal door to Heaven from the circuit of the hermaphrodite and bestial lovers, in a searing confession.

Smarrita.

My cheeks burn. The sin he has to answer to Beatrice for is sealed in *La Vita Nuova*. He has betrayed her body.

But his own body? Before he can receive forgiveness from her lips, entrance into Paradise, he must ask pardon for the dream that lies between him and his teachers.

It begins in Hell, in the circle of the Sodomites. "*Qual maraviglia!*" "How marvelous!" (*Inf.* 15:24). A shiver of recognition goes through Dante.

"Siete voi qui?" "Are you here?" (*Inf.* 15:30), he asks as Brunetto Latini, in the *bolgia* [pit] of the homosexuals, presses his hem. What does the response mean—horror or mock horror? Despite Brunetto's "baked features," the pleasure, the laughter implicit in the irony of delight in Hell "How marvelous!" dispels the gloom. Its enthusiasm, to use the imagery of fruit that Dante will introduce in the same breath, is almost overripe, a parody of female charm. His teacher, Brunetto, accosts and acclaims him. Is it pity, respect, or attraction that makes Dante wish to sit beside him? Brunetto's laughter and Dante's will be at one at the end of the canto.

Here I must make the first motion of refutation to the scholar who denies the obvious dalliance between Dante and Brunetto in this scene and its sexual implications. He discourages our belief in the plain meaning of the text in order to advance the thesis that an *intellectual* unnaturalness is meant.[1] Now that may be so, but the details of Brunetto's physical presence impart to the scene its comedy. From his first cry, "How marvelous!" we hear, we see, Dante's master caper before us: "ché tra li lazzi sorbi / si disconvien fruttar al dolce fico," "for among the sour apples/ it is not suitable for the sweet fig to fruit" (*Inf.* 15:65–66). Is there a confidence whispered into Dante's ear with that honeyed compliment, "sweet fig"?

If there is any question that "*dolce fico,*" "sweet fig," is carrying the connotation of a male organ, the thumb between the fingers, it is answered in the twenty-fifth canto, its first lines. The rabid Vanni Fucci pricks his thumbs at heaven. "Al fine de le sue parole il ladro / le mane alzò con amendue le fiche, / gridando: 'Togli, Dio, ch'a te le squadro!' " "At the end of his words, the thief, / lifted his hands with both the figs / crying, 'Take that God, for I at you I square them.' " For Vanni the *fig* is a gesture of futile *machismo* and blasphemy. In Brunetto's case, however, *fig* smacks of sly suggestion. Dante *skips* beside Brunetto in Hell. The pupil has echoed his master's voice uncannily and even sketched in a raised eyebrow. Dante flirts with the temptation of Latini's magnetism, flattery, insouciance—it is the spirit of this fifteenth canto. One of the critics has noted the puckering of the brows among the knot of ogling men out of which Brunetto bursts and pointed

---

1. See Richard Kay's remarks in *Dante's Swift and Strong.*

out that the lilt over the eye is more than curiosity. "Ci riguardava come suol da sera / guardare uno altro sotto nuova luna; / e sì ver' noi agguzavan le ciglia / come 'l vecchio sartor fa ne la cruna." "Regarded me as men at dusk / stare at one another under a new moon, and so towards us knit their eyebrows / as an old tailor in the eye of a needle" (*Inf.* 15:18–21). *Aguzzavan,* knit, is carrying the connotations of tightening, bunching, sharpening, pointing, exciting. I bend my eyebrow to imitate the tailor, and sense the back alleys of Florence. Even scorched looks in this context are suggestive of a kind of rouging. "I will sit with you," Dante offers.

"No, no," Brunetto cries. "i 'ti verrò a' panni." "I will go at thy skirt" (*Inf.* 15:40). There is teasing in this image from Latini's lip. Recall their first moment: "che mi prese / per lo lembo e gridò: 'Qual maraviglia!'" "he pressed me by the hem and cried 'How marvelous!'" (*Inf.* 15:23–24). In the light of this, there may be some apprehension in Dante's remark that he is "afraid to descend" to Brunetto's level. When Dante first sees the troop of men in which his teacher circles, he uses an expression that renders his self-consciousness, "Così adocchiato da cotal famiglia," "Thus ogled by that family" (*Inf.* 15:22). One can also translate *famiglia* as entourage, but the ambivalence is clear in the English cognate, family. Whose family—Dante's?

There is the final detail that runs into the next canto. A footnote in the Sinclair translation reveals that the race at Verona for the green cloth was run in the nude (*Inf.* 1972a, 199). In the sixteenth canto the oiled and naked bodies *"nudi e unti"* of the three distinguished Florentines before whom Virgil counsels Dante to show deep respect appear. If they are identified as sodomites, it is with ambivalence, no less than that implied in the constant reiteration of "son" by Brunetto to Dante, and the latter's cry to him that he has always held a "dear and kind paternal image" of his teacher. There is a parody of sexual exhibitionism in these images of nakedness, the nude Brunetto running the race, the nude bodies of the Florentine gentlemen wheeling, a nude ending and a nude beginning, which suggests less scorn than sympathy. (In the *Purgatorio* this same sense of parody and theater will return in the very circles where Dante's sexual identity will be at issue.) One cannot escape the sense of high spirits in Hell. Brunetto gains a kind of victory at the end of his canto.[2] He appears to Dante as a winner. Green is the messianic color and the color of Beatrice's robe. Is Brunetto's *Tesor* that he bids Dante remember an attempt by Brunetto to cover himself? This allusion is far-fetched, but note again the stress on nakedness and a possible drapery in the final sprint of the fifteenth canto.

2. Reading later in *Purgatorio* (*Purg.* 24:94–97), of Forese Donati's footrace, his rush to honor and first place, one cannot help but remember this burst of speed from Brunetto, though Forese is given the dignity of a horseman's gallop.

Poi si rivolse, e parve di coloro
che corrono a Verona il drappo verde
per la campagna: e parve di costoro
quelli che vince, no colui che perde.

Then he turned round and seemed of those men
who run at Verona for the green cloth
through the field, and appeared of those
the one who wins, not the man who loses.
(*Inf.* 15:121–24)

This is not the heavy-handed fun of Malebolge. The laughing and spoofing lines are pointed. Dante is holding out to his old master against all possibility, a thin gauze of green hope. He may yet cover his shame.

The comedy betrays the poet's self-concern. It is not Brunetto's perversion, intellectual or bodily, that has brought him to this level. The act of male sexual love is pardoned plainly enough in *Purgatorio,* where all or most of Dante's *famiglia* of poets seem to be sharers in it. Could it be that Brunetto's mincing implies a certain impenitence? What is peculiar, however, is that Dante seems to share his teacher's insouciance. He, Dante, may also squirm to victory.

The fifteenth canto ends with this image of "covering." In the sixteenth Dante opposes to it an act of uncovering. His "superiors" (as Virgil makes clear) wheel before him nude. Dante unloosens the friar's cord, the belt of male chastity. To this lure Fraud immediately comes swimming. Dante once thought to defeat the leopard of lust, his adulterous passion, and others perhaps as well, with religious vows, but the belt is only a bait for hypocrisy. Perhaps, as scholars suggest, other unnatural behavior is meant as well. It is clear that the cord of chastity for Dante is *the* lifeline of hypocrisy. It is "coiled and knotted," around the loins of Guido da Montefeltro, lower down, "fui cordigliero, / credendomi, sì cinto, fare ammenda," "I was corded, / thinking, thus cinched, to make amends" (*Inf.* 27:67–68). Sexual, political, religious hypocrisy, the cord writhes in the tail of Geryon. Guido in like fashion, betraying his vows to serve God, not man, is wound round in a burlesque in the belt of Minos's tail, "A Minòs mi portò; e quelli attorse / otto volte la coda al dosso duro: / e poi che per gran rabbia la si morse." "To Minos he carried me / who coiled eight times the tail around his hard back / and then with great rage, biting it" (*Inf.* 27:124–26).

Anticipating Guido, Dante loosens his cord in the circle of the homosexuals. He casts it off after seeing the damage. "Ahimè, che piaghe vidi ne' lor membri, / ricenti e vecchie, da le fiamme incese! / Ancor men duol pur ch'i' me ne rimembri."

"Ah me, what sores I saw in their members, / recent and old, burnt in by the flames. / It still hurts me, when I remember them" (*Inf.* 16:10–12). Even at the desk, writing, he winces in his own member. "Ah me!" Is he only remembering or is he self-accusing? If he names so many as believers in male love, it is not in spite, certainly. The pain goes to his own sexual organ.

Why is it so important?

Dante as a poet of heterosexual love wants to come to union with Beatrice as Divine Presence, with a body made holy according to biblical text. Therefore the bisexuality of the poets, that fantasy that carries one not only into the arms of one's beloved but into very imagination of her, must be purified, scalded. He immerses himself in the boiling fire of *Purgatorio* just as an iron pot is lowered into scalding waters to become clean for the Paschal season.

Some ambivalence remains. The *"maraviglia"* sounds when the poet's belt is restored to him in the beginning of his ascent in *Purgatorio*. (And hearing it, I cannot but think of Brunetto's cry of recognition, joy.) It is no longer the friar's cord with which the leopard of lust is feigned to be caught, a belt of abstinence, but a smooth rush, a sprig of eternity, a green plant of Eden. As the angel bids:

> Ricinghe
> d'un giunco schietto e che li lavi 'l viso
> sì ch'ogni sucidume quindi stinghe;

> Retie him
> with a smooth reed and wash his face so
> that every obscenity fades from this moment.
> (*Purg.* 1:94–96)

And so Virgil does, at the edge of the lonely plain, desert shore, and great sea:

> Quivi mi cinse sì com' altrui piacque:
> oh maraviglia! ché qual elli scelse
> l'umile pianta, cotal si rinacque
> subitamente là onde l'avelse.

> There he girt me, as the other requested:
> oh marvelous! for such was the
> humble plant he chose, another such sprang
> immediately there where he plucked it.
> (*Purg.* 1:133–36)

Dante passes King David, who is attired thus, "humble . . . girt up" (*Purg.*
10:65). Dante and David are bound up in one another, David and the leopard with
the gay hide. Adorned with the emblem of his love for Beatrice, for woman, Dante
comes to the cantos of his great sin after pride of fame, anger—lust for his own
body. All who live in fantasy have stared into the pool of Narcissus, put their lips to
its waters. Seed, seminal seed—from *Purgatorio*'s twenty-fourth canto the air will
be murky with spores. Self-love and self-abuse—the crime of angels and men in
the *Zohar,* brings on the Flood. A scalded cherub appears before Dante directly
after the Florentine boasts in response to praise of his poetry:

> "I' mi son un che, quando
> Amor mi spira, noto, e a quel modo
> ch'e' ditta dentro vo significando."

> "I am one who, when
> Love breathes in me, note—and in the way
> it speaks within—go set it down."
> (*Purg.* 24:52–54)

How pure is that breath of love within him? Look forward to the rebuke of
Beatrice. "*Male seme*—evil seed!" she hurls in Dante's face. He knows what she
means, and it is not the genealogies of Fiesole. Now the portent of the purification
appears, the terrible bath of fire shines in the angel's face.

> Drizzai la testa per veder chi fossi;
> e già mai non si videro in fornace
> vetri or metalli sì lucenti e rossi.

> I lifted my head to see who it was;
> and never was there seen in furnace
> glass or metal so red and glowing.
> (*Purg.* 24:136–38)

It would be too painful to advance another step, if the promise of Eden did
not loom behind the screen of fire. Dante *feels* the "breath of ambrosia,"[3] the

---

3. In *Purgatorio,* canto 24, line 150 he refers to "*d'ambrosia l'orezza* the odor of ambrosia." Although Dante establishes the fragrance of May, he is careful not to say that the odor actually comes to
his nose. Here his hunger, thirst, anticipation of satisfaction, even through smell, is stressed. It is in the
Garden that there will be a riot of sniffing, drinking, and eating. And it is there that the exclamation of

smells of May. He cannot taste them. It is the heat; from the sexual heat (note that "impregnated") of Purgatory, hotter than the fires of Hell, rise zephyrs that strike again and again:

> Tutta impreganata da l'erba e da' fiori;
> tal mi senti' un vento dar per mezza
> la fronte.

> All impregnated with herbs and flowers;
> such a breeze I felt beat in the midst
> of my brow.
> (*Purg.* 24:147–49)

They fan the forehead of the poet, inflame his limbs on the way to the Garden. There in a mist of seed under the wet green branches, he will blaze with a painless heat. Body will be all air and fire, pure ecstasy, smell. Now, because his body is the vessel of his longing for union with the Divine, this *male seme*, evil seed, must be burnt away. Beatrice, in Dante's eyes, is a form of what becomes the Female Presence of God in the *Zohar*, the *Shechinah*. But anyone so fascinated by the Female Presence of God must be tempted to assume the form of such a divinity. And Dante details his terror as he comes to give himself up to God as female. He bears the stain of his own indulgences—*male seme*. The *Zohar* sees seed as blood on one's hands—calls self-abuse worse than murder. Dante screams in dread of what his dreams, his sexual bliss, has drawn him near. So Milton, as he begins his recovery of Paradise, prays to an androgynous Spirit, who "with mighty wings outspread / Dove-like sat'st brooding on the vast Abyss." And in the next breath makes this cosmic hen, rooster—"And mad'st it pregnant" (*Paradise Lost,* 1:20–22).[4]

Dante's temptation—"*Qual maraviglia!*" The fires of Purgatory are there to burn away his self-abuse, dalliance with other ladies, the stains of evil seed. So the emphasis on body in these cantos before his entrance to the Garden. Dante's cor-

---

the angel, that the love of taste ought not to kindle too much desire, will receive a partial reply. See *Purgatorio* 31:127–29. The sexual implications of taste echo not only in the original image but also in the reply of the thirty-first canto. Sinclair quotes *Ecclus.*, 24, 21, "They that eat me shall yet be hungry, / And they that drink me shall yet be thirsty," as proof that it refers to wisdom. In the Talmud, however, appetite that in satisfying itself creates more appetite, refers to the sexual. See in my chapter, "Dante and King David," the quotation from *The Babylonian Talmud, Sanhedrin* 107a.

4. Professor Clara Clairborne Park in my manuscript notes the parallel "as with Milton's angels, total, they mix."

poral nature is pointed out again and again. He is to suffer in a real body now and later—presumably after his death—in a spiritual one.

Forese Donati appears, cheeks pale and sunken. Hunger is palpable to these spirits. Dante is careful to emphasize the pinch of famine in the hollows of their eye sockets. The twenty-third canto, with its skeletons driven on by the odor of an apple, of water "so wasted that the bones inform the flesh," is followed by the twenty-fourth, where the ambrosia of Eden is wafted to Dante's temples, the bone of his brow, even as the bony figure of Ubaldin dalla Pila is nibbling on vacancy. Body! Body! The cantos before and after, line after line, beat out a preoccupation with bones. It is the riddle the narrative addresses in the dry, apparently boring speech of Statius in the twenty-fifth, lecturing formally on the nature of the body of the soul: "ecco qui Stazio; e io lui chiamo e prego / che sia or sanator dele tue piage," "behold, here is Statius; and I call on him and pray / now that he will be the healer of your wounds" (*Purg.* 25:29–30). Why does Virgil use that peculiar locution, "healer of your wounds"? What wound, *piaga*?

The *piaga* is revealed at the end of the canto, its last line.

> E questo modo credo che lor basti
> per tutto il tempo che 'l foco li abbruscia:
> con tal cura conviene e con tai pasti
> che la piaga da sezzo si ricuscia.
>
> And this manner lasts them I believe
> all through the time the fire scorches then;
> with such a cure and with such food it is necessary
> that the wound of the breach be sewn up.
> (*Purg.* 25:136–39)

The context makes the wound clear. The bank is shooting fire. Dante is beginning to shake in his boots: "e io temëa 'l foco / quinci, e quindi temeva cader giuso," "I feared the flames / here and I feared, on the other hand to fall below" (*Purg.* 25:116–17). It is no joke. They are, as he says, "venuto a l'ultima tortura." "Arrived at the last turning" (*Purg.* 25:109). A pun—they are arrived at the last "torture" too, and the flame is only too palpable. Dante has to go into it, and he doesn't scruple to tell you he is terrified. Not only the flames, but the company frighten him. He is standing on a terrace full of bestial sinners dominated by the image of Pasiphae. (Pasiphae is the Queen of Crete who fell in love with a sacred white bull. She persuaded the artificer, Daedalus, to fashion a hollow cow of wood into which she crept. Uncovering her private part over the slot for a vagina in the idol,

Pasiphae received there the pumping seed of a bull of the field maddened by Neptune.) "Nela vaca entra Pasife / perché 'l torello a sua lussuria corra," "Into the cow enters Pasiphae / so that the bull may run to her lust" (*Purg.* 26:41–42). From this breach of nature is born a monster, the Minotaur. In such a context, doubt what *piaga* must be sown up—what *"piaga da sezzo,"* "wound of the breach," can be?

It is the anus or vagina, an orifice abused in bestiality. The image of a wound or breach that will finally be sewn up, knit together, suggests before the canto that it introduces, the twenty-sixth, where the circle of hermaphrodites will scream, "*Regina,*" "Queen" (*Purg.* 26:78) in Caesar's ears, that the wound of sex, vagina, anus, will be at last closed up. Does the poet imply that the joys of sex will be diffused in Paradise through the whole body chastely? The translator Sinclair uses "heal" for *ricuscia* as if to balance the original *sanator,* healer, which appeared with wound, *piaga,* at the beginning of the canto. But the word *ricucia* clearly means re-sewn. It recalls the image of the eyebrows of the circle of homosexuals in Hell, "knit ... as an old tailor in the eye of a needle." It seems to imply that on earth, sexual life is imperfect through its very nature, experienced through a wound or breach. What is clear is that this wound must be stitched with fire before one enters Paradise.

What is Dante confessing to? In *La Vita Nuova* I suggested that Dante used a long-winded philosophical disquisition to cover an admission. He disguised intercourse with Beatrice, covering the bed with the fresh leaves of a treatise on the "vulgar" tongue. Now in Purgatory he fears the fire for his own "wound," *"piaga,"* even while Statius drones on about the nature of spiritual bodies. Yet this lecture is of the utmost importance to Dante—the reason he has endured the *Inferno,* and is willing to endure the flames of *Purgatorio.* He has come in search of the body of Beatrice. The question of its substance is crucial to him.[5] At this all-important moment Dante cannot truly concentrate. He is forced to think about his own body and the approaching trial he faces. What he wants to know is—will it hurt?

Virgil divines this. Answering Dante's question at the beginning of the twenty-fifth canto about the nature of hunger in souls who have no substance, Virgil understands that the flame ahead is troubling his charge. Virgil's remark about Meleager, "consumed in the consuming of a brand," is however, hardly reassuring. Dante goes into a kind of shock before the flames. He remembers vividly the sight of charred bodies:

5. Again, this question of body, reality, or substance in the spiritual and the real world is the animating question of the *Commedia.* And it is also the question, as Ivry shows, that bedevils Maimonides, in trying to explain the unique experience of Moses with the Unknown. See note 16 of my first chapter, where I quote the passage in which Maimonides tries to explain the "voice" that Moses heard.

In su le man commesse mi protesi
guardando il foco e imaginando forte
umani corpi già veduti accesi.

Above I stretched out, clasped hands
staring at the fire, imagining strongly
human corpses I had seen burnt.
(*Purg.* 27:16–18)

In this light, I understand why Virgil drops his explanation after trying to defuse its effect by talking about a glimmer in the mirror. It is no comfort for Dante Alighieri, who faces immersion in fire, to hear that Meleager's life ended when the firebrand that stood for his body was returned to the flames. Virgil's unfitness to guide Dante becomes apparent for the first time. "Having thus prepared his disciple's mind," says a usually reliable guide to the *Commedia*, "Virgil leaves the real explanation to Statius."[6] Virgil has hardly prepared Dante. He has frightened him. Even Statius's sermon is abruptly terminated by their arrival before the bank shooting flames. Statius's remarks, their significance obscure, seem more abstract than they are.[7] The reader who is in sympathy with Dante must feel his mounting terror. The poet can hardly think of Beatrice's body while he is in such apprehension over what awaits his own.

Dante trembles at the lip of doctrine for a drink of fire—"*calor del sol.*" It is not Statius so much as Thomas Aquinas pouring. The "state of souls after death" (*Epist.*, x)—the whole of the *Commedia*'s intent as expressed by Dante to his patron Can Grande, vicar general of Verona, is to illuminate this subject. There is a significant departure of the student Dante from his master, Thomas. Cut from the flesh, the soul arrives at death. The Grandgent and Singleton edition notes, "Statius describes the acquisition by the soul of an aerial body. . . . In this invention

---

6. See Grandgent and Singleton in their notes (*Commedia*, 531).

7. Dante uses Statius rather awkwardly from the perspective of the poem's dramatic tension, to try to explain the riddle of the body in the afterlife. This, as I have already remarked is one of the most pressing questions of Dante's journey—what body will Dante carry, when he returns after his death, to the spheres of the worlds of Hell, Purgatory and Paradise? "As soon as space circumscribes it / the informative virtue radiates around / just so as in the living members. / And as the air when very moist / through another's rays which it reflects / becomes adorned with diverse colors / so the neighboring air here is put / into a form, stamped within it / by the power of the soul which stopped, / and then like the flame that follows / the fire there, wherever, it shifts / the spirit follows its new form. / Since it has its appearance from this, / it is called shade, and forms by this organs / for every sense even to sight. / By this we make tears and sighs / that throughout the mountain you may have heard" (*Purg.* 25:88–105).

Dante seems to run counter to St. Thomas who denies [*Summa contra Gentiles*, 2.90: *Summa Theologiae*, Prima Qu. 51, Art. 2] that angels and devils can shape for themselves bodies of condensed air" (*Commedia*, 533).

Dante's speculation is part of the Neoplatonic background of medieval philosophy. Maimonides worries on the subject. "Some physical phenomenon . . . manifests itself at the time of the prophetic experience. Such a phenomenon is described by him as being created by God out of some 'substance' which is less material than the Aristotelian fifth substance out of which the celestial spheres consist but which is not of the same grade of immateriality as God" (Wolfson 1977, 114). It figures as the poetic "stuff" of his great rival and predecessor, Judah ha-Levi.[8] The whole universe of the *Zohar* is made of this Neoplatonic "stuff," swirling, dancing, bodying forth the dreams of the sages. It seems as if the bodies, the building blocks of Dante Alighieri's world, are made of the same sparkling quartz—the immaterial Neoplatonic. Dante goes a step further. He endows the substance of his world, its bodies, with feeling. This is the "wine," warm and blushful, of Statius. (And it seems that the mystery of the Eucharist and worship of the Sun god are coloring these images.)

> Guarda il calor del sol che si fa vino
> giunto a l'omor che de la vite cola.

8. Harry Wolfson, speaking of the universe of the Jewish poet, Judah ha-Levi, born in Toledo, 1086, tells us that this conception was drawn from Aristotle's *Meterologica*. The passage demonstrates curious parallels with Dante's image of the body of the celestial souls as expressed by Statius. "'Spiritual forms' . . . appear to the prophets" during their prophetic experience. These 'spiritual forms' arise by the divine will out of this 'subtle spiritual substance,' called Holy Spirit, by means of a 'ray of divine light ' or a 'divine light ' which acts upon the Holy Spirit, after the analogy of the action of the rays of sunlight upon the clouds which produce the colors of the rainbow . . . where the ray of sunlight is not identical with the sun and the rainbow is not identical with the ray of sunlight, so also in the case God and the ray of divine light and spiritual forms, the ray of light is not identical with the essence of God. . . . The 'Holy Spirit' or 'the subtle spiritual substance' corresponds to the clouds in the phenomenon of the rainbow. The 'spiritual forms' are thus the result of the action of the ray of the divine light upon the Holy Spirit, the latter being related to the former as an active principle to a passive principle, or as form to matter.

"Now this conception of Hallevi [sic], that there is a 'subtle spiritual substance' which is acted upon by Divine Light as its form, reflects a Neoplatonic view. Hallevi's 'subtle spiritual substance' corresponds to that divine (θεια) or intelligible (νοητη) matter (υλη) or substance (ουσια) of which Plotinus speaks. Similarly Hallevi's Divine Light corresponds to that light (φῶς) which according to Plotinus, proceeds from God and illuminates the intelligible matter and which with reference to that matter is called reason (logos) by which is meant form (ειδος). This Neoplatonic conception of an intelligible matter of which the form is spoken of as light was widespread in Arabic philosophy" (Wolfson 1977, 87–89).

. . .

Regard the heat of the sun which makes itself wine
joined to the juice which drips from the vine.
(*Purg.* 25:77–78)

The body of the shade may be "immaterial," but it feels. The discussion of the corporal nature of the spirit's body after death emphasizes not only the real hunger and wasting that Dante has seen, but more important, the real pain of the burning that the bodies of the bestial must undergo. It is the shadow flesh of the sinners that will be punished in fire. And that burning is a kind of baking. So the phrase *"con tai pasti,"* "with such food," at the end of the canto. The sun makes the juice of the vine into wine. So the heat of the burning will ferment the spiritual "perfect blood" of the dead to the divine blood, the wine of the Divine. The fire is cure and bread, *"cura"* and *"pasti"* at once. The soul must suffer but it is being transubstantiated.

Appetite, hunger, these are the questions of the cantos before the entrance into Paradise. What do you want to eat? Your body has changed, so has your appetite. Human lust must be left behind. Desire the fare of divinity! The meal of the Eucharist is being set. Through a scorching sun under the dripping blood of the Catholic messiah, Dante will enter Eden. And the elements of divine wine, *"sole,"* "sun" and *"sangue,"* "blood," appear again.

Sì come quando i primi raggi vibra
là dove il suo fattor lo sangue sparse,
cadendo Ibero sotto l'alta Libra,
e l'onde in Gange da nona rïarse,
sì stave il sole;

So—as when its first rays strike
there where its Maker shed his blood,
Ebero falling under the high Scales
and the waves in the Ganges scorched by noon,
so stood the sun.
(*Purg.* 27:1–5)

Dante bears a double burden in his ascent and purification. He is not shadow flesh. While there may be some ambiguity about the nature of Dante's body further on in *Paradiso*, the narrator takes pains to assure us that he is traveling not in a spiritual, but in a real body. "'Colui non par corpo fittizio'" "'This man doesn't seem fictitious flesh,' " (*Purg.* 26:12), one of the bestial shades remarks in the canto before the burning. A few lines on, the thought is emphasized again, "non son rimase acerbe né mature / le membra mie di là, ma son qui meco / col sangue suo e con le sue giunture." "My members are not green or ripe, / left below, but are with me here / with their blood and with their joints" (*Purg.* 26:55–57). It is not until the very end in *Purgatorio,* in an image that brings together the open frond of the plant that he has tied around his waist with the dream of a new body, absolved from his sins against himself and Beatrice—a body awash in her sensual gifts—that we may question whether he is traveling in flesh or fantasy.

> I returned from the holiest waves
> Remade—as new plants
> Renewed with new leaves,
> Pure and disposed to go up to the stars.
> (*Purg.* 33:142–145)

Dante in his purgation will become more than flesh burnt or spirit seared and sanctified. As a living man he is in double jeopardy, and his entrance to the bower of bliss is fearful. (In a reading that borders on the callous, Dorothy Sayers has suggested that his hesitation and Virgil's blandishments to go into the fire are funny (Sayers 1954, 164–65). There is laughter but its source is deep fear.

Before the flames the *Zohar* and Dante part company. Hebrew imagination does not relish dreams of holocaust. It smacks of Moloch and the burning of babies. And Dante, even as he is brought to his confession, agonizes through the canto before his cruel baptism, distracted by the fire.

In the entryway to Eden, a wine-drunk sun burning on his right, Dante's body glowing in flame, just in the midst of the *ultima,* that is the ultimate turning, the vestibule of Paradise, the twenty-sixth canto—he sees a parody of spiritualized love.

On their tiptoes, the sexual sinners kiss and nuzzle each other. I am treading the most ambivalent of circles in Dante's winding after the threading of Paolo and Francesca's bolgia in Hell. It is the salon of the purgatorial poets. Dante goes about in a ballet of discretionary lust while the bestial, the hermaphrodite, bellow in penance around him. Here is that laughter the critic looked for at the moment when Dante's flesh took fire. Here everything is parody, comedy, exquisite manners in tension with forbidden appetite. Dante's very body is theatrical. It casts a shadow like a lantern in a play, "più rovente / parer la fiamma;" "makes the flame appear / more scorching" (*Purg.* 26:7–8). These penitent spirits, at least, are well aware of artifice, and it makes them bold, seeing but a flicker, to remark, "This man doesn't seem fictitious flesh." Of course there is a leering irony in this remark.

Dante's body, which is real, creates an artificial effect. Real flesh in a circle full of flesh abusers is a temptation. "My members are not green or ripe left below, / but are with me here, with their blood and with their joints" (*Purg.* 26:55–57). Is there a sexual lilt in that, "sue giunture," "their joints"? To what purpose does Dante drop into the comedy of the following image if not to smile and slightly disparage?

> Lì veggio d'ogne parte farsi presta
> ciascun' ombra e basciarsi una con una
> sanza restar, contente a brieve festa;
> così per entro loro schiera bruna
> s'ammusa l'una con l'altra formica,
> forse a spïar lor via e lor fortuna.
>
> I see there on either side each shade
> make haste, and kiss one with another
> without stopping, content with brief welcome;
> Thus within their dark band
> one ant nuzzles another
> perhaps to espy the way and their fortunes
>   (*Purg.* 26:31–36)

The kiss of the spirits is the tender nosing of ants. Something strikes Dante as funny. It is the parody of a fable—Kafka's fable. Even in their penitence, something of the sadness of the modern *Metamorphosis* sticks to this *"schiera,"* "band, troop, file." They are like insects. The commentators are bewildered here as Guido Guinizzelli comes from the group that cries of forbidden lust, of fornication with beasts, and identifies himself. No, no, it can't be.[9] Another puzzles, "What reason Dante had for putting these two poets [Guinizzelli and Arnaut Daniel] among the penitents of lust we do not know, unless it be that among the writings of both are poems of amatory passion without measure or restraint, etc."[10] How plain can a poet be? Guinizzelli comes up to Virgil, Statius, Dante, states, "Nostro peccato fu ermafrodito," "Our sin was hermaphrodite" (*Purg.* 26:82).

Guido Guinizzelli is no closet sinner. He is frank and though not knowing Dante, Guinizzelli adds (Note the personal *"te,"* "thou"):

9. In the Grandgent edition, revised by Singleton, the introduction to this canto remarks: "Among those whose offense was not contrary to nature is Guido Guinicelli [Guinizzelli] of Bologna. . . . Like Arnaut Daniel, he is doubtless consigned to this circle on the general ground that he was a sincere poet of love" (*Commedia*, 541).

10. This is John D. Sinclair in his notes to the *Purgatorio* (*Purg.* 1972c, 347).

"Beato te, che de le nostre marche. . . .
per morir meglio, esperïenza imbarche!"

"Blessed are you, who from our boundaries. . . .
to die better, takes on experience!"
(*Purg.* 26:73, 75)

It is a very different voice than that of Brunetto Latini, whose "marvelous" made him seem to almost caper in the flames of hell. Guido warns Dante to watch his own step, to repent, to begin, "ben dolermi prima ch'a lo stremo," "afflicting myself well before the last extreme" (*Purg.* 26:93).

But—but—something is funny all the same. What "experience"? Dante briefly nuzzles his master. He reveals more in the image he uses to detail the loving exchange between them when Guido uncovers his identity.

Quali ne la tristizia di Ligurgo
si fer due figli a riveder la madre,
tal mi fec' io, ma non a tanto insurgo,
quand' io odo nomar sé stesso, il padre
mio e de li altri miei miglior.

Such—in Lycurgus's wretchedness as
became the two sons seeing again their mother,
so I became, but not with such great wildness,
when I heard naming himself, the father
of me and of others, my betters.
(*Purg.* 26:94–98)

It is a hermaphrodite image. Guido first appears as Alighieri's "mother," and only afterward his "father." [11] What better echo to the line, "Nostro peccato fu ermafrodito"? Dante honors *"nostro peccato,"* and leaves his own homosexual terror in the shade. He stares long and hard. He is fed with staring, "di riguardar pasciuto fui" (*Purg.* 26:103). He "eats" Guinizzelli with his eyes. The remark from the preceding canto echoes in the line, "With such food it is necessary that the wound of the breach be sewn up."

11. This recalls an equally puzzling moment in *Hamlet,* when the young prince taunts Claudius by calling him, "dear mother" (4.3). While Hamlet gives an explanation to the puzzled Claudius, who corrects him with, "Thy loving father, Hamlet," talking about father and mother being one flesh, it may indeed reflect the prince's ambivalence about himself and his identity.

Appetite? The look he throws at Guido can be inferred from the latter's, "Why do you show yourself in speech and look to hold me so dear?" They exchange, *"caro,"* "dear," [12] with one another, Dante under the guise of praising the very ink that holds Guinizzelli's speech. It is almost reassuring to hear from the latter in a moment, that in the world of *Purgatorio,* the power to sin "is no longer ours" (*Purg.* 26:132). For Dante is bearing his "blood" and "joints" in the circle.

Is it only fear of the fire that keeps Dante from touching Guinizzelli?[13] Sanitized male affection? What is one to think of Jesus in this company on Guinizzelli's lips, "Christo abate del collegio," "Christ, abbot of the college" (*Purg.* 26:129), in the *"chiostro,"* "cloister," where Dante is permitted to go? A reference to Jesus as head of the all-male abbey is peculiar in the context of hermaphrodite repentance. Dante's imagery reaches beyond what he is prepared to admit. And it grants an indulgence to Guinizzelli from the flames—a bath in cool water for an exit.

> Poi, forse per dar luogo altrui secondo
> che presso avea, disparve per lo foco,
> come per l'acqua il pesce andando al fondo.

> Then, perhaps to give another a place
> who pressed him, he vanished through the flame
> as a fish through the water going to the bottom.
>   (*Purg.* 26:133–35)

"Through metaphor to reconcile," sings the poet, Williams. Water and fire—Arnaut Daniel, his great Provençal predecessor, gives Dante a final verse "forget me not." Arnaut, "que plore e vau cantar," "who weeps and goes singing" (*Purg.* 26:142). Given the example, Dante must plunge into the contradiction, embracing while shrinking from the "foco che li affina," "fire that refines them" (*Purg.* 26:148).

Dante is before the wall of flame that is the trial of the saved, fire and baptismal water at once! But the poet is going to no cloister. It is the ladies who are waiting for him.

"Christo abate del collegio."

"Had Jesus married the illuminated prostitute, Magdalene, he would have

---

12. See their exchange (*Purg.* 26:110–11). "Che è cagion per che dimostri / nel dire e nel guardare d'avermi caro." To which Dante replies, "Li dolci detti vostri, / che, quanto durerà l'uso moderno / faranno cari ancori i loro incostri."

13. See the following lines (*Purg.* 26:100–102). "I went a long time staring at him / yet not, for the flame, did I come closer."

forsaken the Acts, the overthrowing of the tables of the pigeon and money-vendors, and the Bleeding Cross and given man as inheritance an imperishable generation of gentle little children or Galilean verse" (Dahlberg 1967b, 129).

The worship of the Holy One, the Unknown, in the form of a man's body, as flesh dead that one strives to union with, remains strange to Israel. It is precisely in the Florence of Dante where representations like Cimambue's were appearing that R. W. Southern's observation in *The Making of the Middle Ages* holds true, speaking of "representations of the Crucifixion in art. To a Jew these must have always been offensive, but they became doubly so when the Savior was depicted with an intensity of human feeling [in the words of Gilbert Crispin's Jewish disputant] 'as a wretched man nailed to the Cross, hideous even to behold'" (Southern 1964, 237).[14]

The *Divine Comedy,* the great human poem of Christian Europe in its pages casts light on the image that Peter, Paul, Augustine, Aquinas, willed to the peoples of that land mass, its far-flung archipelagoes. Devotion to a man mortified, lowered from a wooden cross. Dante takes their image, lies with and flips it. In its embrace, Dante discovers himself in bed with his adolescent sweetheart, Beatrice. In this he has written the *Megillah*[15] of Jesus and made what the rabbis call the Purim flip, the erotic masquerade.

Others had chosen to worship divinity through the mother of Jesus, Mary. Some of this, mingled with an "illuminated" Mary Magdalene, shines in Dante's dreams. The ancient Sophia, Wisdom, is diffused in the portrait as well. But at last, it is Beatrice, Beatrice Portinari, scolding, flirting, to whom Dante rises. Dante's devotion to her is his first heresy. (Even if the thesis of the scholar Richard Kay is correct, that Dante called Brunetto, Arnaut, Guinizzelli sodomites only to point to their heresy, it is hard to escape Dante's identification with them. Through the circle of the latter two, he exits *Purgatorio*'s refining fires for Eden.)

Dante treats the dilemma of his city's religion by worshipping through Beatrice a man's naked form stretched on a tree, limbs gray with the cold of the grave. He transformed this into a man's love for a woman by addressing himself to the cool, melancholy limbs of a young lady—one who gave him all.

14. The first footnote on the same page cites the source of Southern's quotation, "'as a wretched man. . . .' 1. The phrase is used by the Jewish disputant in Gilbert Crispin's *Disputatio Judaei cum Christiano,* P. L. vol. 159, 1034."

15. The *Megillah* or *Scroll of Esther,* filled with intimations of sexuality, delighted and discomforted the rabbis. It is read on Purim, a day on which a Jew is commanded by the Talmud to be drunk through excess of joy and to attain such bliss as to see the whole of existence—not distinguishing between the villain of the story, Haman, and its hero, Mordechai, good and evil confounded. The Purim masquerade and its theatrics was especially popular in the streets of Italy in the centuries that followed Dante's.

Sì udirai come in contraria parte
mover dovieti mia carne sepolta.
Mai non t'appresentò natura o arte
piacer, quanto le belle membra in ch'io
rinchiusa fui, e che so' 'n terra sparte;

So shall you hear how in the opposite way
my buried flesh should have moved you.
Never did nature or art present you
with a pleasure equal to the beautiful limbs in which I
was enclosed, and they are scattered in earth.
                    (*Purg.* 31:47–51)

Dante, in what woman's body shall we meet? Alive and quick, that is your cloister, your school, your study.

CHAPTER SIX

Dante and King David

I WISH TO TELL THE TALE of Dante and King David.

Florence is a city in love with David; the handsome youth rises from the bulk of a flawed stone in its public square—through which the minions of Dante's puritan successor, the monk Savonarola, danced to a hymn which sang that for love of God, "Go crazy! Everybody cry as I do, always crazy, crazy, crazy!"

David and madness? David dancing in madness; so taught the teacher of Aquinas, Dante's teacher, Moses Maimonides: "What is the proper measure of love? To love God with a great, overwhelming, extremely strong love, until his soul is tied in the love of God. He is ravished always, *shogeh bah-tomid,* as if he were lovesick."

Dante opposes his *smarrita,* confusion, to order, hierarchy. Catholic hierarchy, Augustine. There is a close parallel between *smarrita,* madness, ravishment. Maimonides identifies the deliberate seeking of this disordered, confused state as the path to experiencing ravishment by God, *shogeh-bah-tomid,* 'love of God can not be tied to a person's heart until he's always ravished in it and he leaves behind everything else in the world."

Where did I receive my first direction for the stargazing chart of this fiction? It was in the most sacred of chambers, the *shiir,* or genius of the Lithuanian firmament of rabbinics, Rabbi Joseph Soloveitchik, lecturing toward the hour of midnight to a room of two hundred souls, Saturday night, at the Maimonides Institute in Brookline, Massachusetts.

Imagine over the white and black beards of the rabbis, the clean shaven jaws of the old *Baalaabatiim,* the businessmen who ran the synagogues of Roxbury and Dorchester, in their eighties now, the young beardless students of the Hebrew schools, the sprinkling of women at the tables on the right; over the Bibles, Talmuds, Codes, books open down the length of the long room, nodding; rose the

Rav, his silver beard shadowed by a powerful nose like a rod over hoarfrost, calling out in the midst of a complicated dialectic, "Shogeh . . . like David's sin with Bathsheba, it was committed out of an excess love of God."

Did anyone else hear it? Around me the faces were stolid, unexpressive. And Rav Soloveitchik moved on to other matters. I wandered about after he had risen, left the room. I asked, "Did you hear? 'Shogeh. . . ,'" but was met with irritated looks. Some stared at me as if I was crazy. No one could enlighten me.

I sought other commentators. Rabbi Ben Zion Gold spent an evening, two, turning his circular bookshelf until from lexicon to commentary, we found the beginning of the riddle. In Brooklyn with Rabbi Meir Fund I found another reference to it in the work of Maimonides, the medieval commentator who was one of the most important influences in the Rav's life.

In the lexicons there is a difference between two *shogehs,* one spelled with the letter *hay,* the other with the letter *ayin,* the former meaning disorder, the latter craziness. The words seem to have an affinity for each other. Did Immanuel of Rome know this? Did Dante know his Jewish imitator, Immanuel, who would write a Hebrew version of the *Commedia?*

I saw Immanuel and Dante Alighieri sunk together in a dire circle of Dante's own imagining of Hell. "Are we here forever?" asks the Florentine.

"King David will rescue us," his Jewish friend replies.

Condemned for sexual flattery, their excuse will come from David's defense, the dangerous doctrine of deliberate sin. Dante and Immanuel will gather the sparks of texts that promise that the sin of the erotic was but an overspill of ardent joy in the Unknown, Holy One, Blessed be He.

◆   ◆   ◆

THE TENDER THRILL of the Mexican merchants as they lift the dead body of the god from the grave and begin to make love to it—give it life, the heart of a living being. They are dreaming through the ecstatic dances not of the boy before them whom they will murder, but the shining body of the bird-man who will come alive in their arms, the angel. This is the ancient horror that lives in the religion of Osiris. New World and Old, the dismembered deity is lovingly reassembled.

I go no further. I have a horror of dead flesh. I do not think death a tender or sweet thing. It is sour, and I cry with my forebears, "How can I praise you from the grave?"

Under the vast machinery of the *Commedia* are Hebrew secrets. The Florentine will not rest easy. It nags at him, the questions of election to Heaven, why some are to be exalted more than others, and the iron rule of exclusion of the pious nonbelievers. Why must Virgil be left behind? In the thirty-second canto, at the very last circling in the sky, he is troubling St. Bernard with the question like a balky schoolboy, "Or dubbi tu, e dubitando sili," "Now you are perplexed and silent in your perplexity" (*Par.* 32:49). Bernard promises to untie the hard knot, "in che ti stringon li pensier sottili," "in which your subtle thoughts are binding you" (*Par.* 32:51). But it is useless. Virgil has tried. Beatrice has tried; the great eagle of Divine Justice has harangued him. Dante listens to Bernard and does not reply. Recall the fatal *squeeze* in Hell. Francesca describes Lancelot's adultery, "come amor lo strinse," "how love squeezed him" (*Inf.* 5:128). Adultery and democracy are the two silent heresies Dante has brought from his city. (With the subtlety of the Florentine politician, he inquires of Piccarda consigned to a lower circle of Heaven, "Ma dimmi: voi che siete qui felici, / desiderate voi più alto loco, / per più vedere e per più farvi amici?" "But tell me, who are happy here, / do you desire a higher place, / in order to see more and make yourself more dear?" (*Par.* 3:64–66). Again and again he has raised it—the question of hierarchy, order, the justice of consigning to Hell those who are good but do not believe—and no one can satisfy him. Has Dante heard from his friend Immanuel of Rome, the talmudic dictum, "A pious gentile is equal to the high priest"?[1] A part of him accepts that those who do not believe in the dogma of the church cannot ascend, but the host of believing pickpockets, murderers, that crew, "ingrata, mobile, e retrosa," "ungrateful, shifting, and stiff-necked" (*Par.* 32:132), that has fed on manna in Florence—what right do they have to the eternal light above? The laughter of the Jews is in his ears. He begs the world to stop it.

> Se male cupidigia altro vi grida
> uomini siate, e non pecore matte,
> sì che 'l Giudeo di voi tra voi non rida!
>
> If evil greed cry something else to you
> be men, not insane sheep
> so that the Jew at you—among you—does not laugh!
> (*Par.* 5:79–81)

Too late. Dante is writing a comedy. Who laughs hardest at the insane sheep of Italy—Dante and Beatrice? Laughter is something he cannot deny. For the *Commedia* began with laughter, self-laughter. Physician heal thyself. He will heal himself with a spiritual adultery.

Who will laugh with him?

---

1. See the *Babylonian Talmud*, Baba Kamma 38a; Sanhedrin 59a.

David the King! At the gates of Hell, in the first canto of the *Inferno,* Dante encounters a leopard. A singular leopard with a spotted hide, a gay hide, light on its feet, even playful, constantly before his face as if sporting. The commentators note that it is the beast of Jeremiah. "Run *to and fro through the streets of Jerusalem* and see now, and know" (Jer. 5:1). Through the alleys of the holy city by the mountain it comes padding. "Wherefore a lion out of the forest shall slay them, and a wolf of the evenings shall spoil them, a leopard shall watch over their cities; everyone that goeth out thence shall be torn in pieces" (Jer. 5:6).

Why?

"Because their transgressions are many, and their backslidings are increased."

What "transgressions" and what "backslidings"?

The prophet knows, Dante knows:

"How shall I pardon thee for this? Thy children have forsaken me, and sworn by them that are no gods. When I had fed them to the full, they then committed adultery, and assembled themselves by troops in the harlots' houses. They were as fed horses [sexually excited] in the morning: Every one neighed after his neighbor's wife" (Jer. 5:7–8).

What was the prophet looking for running, "to and fro through the streets of Jerusalem"?

"A man who will do justice and seek truth" (Jer. 5:1).

Can Dante answer to this description and yet commit the sin of adultery?

A terrible neigh rises from the streets of Florence, Jerusalem, "stinks in the eye" of the Holy One.

Is there anyone who has straddled the contradiction, sought truth, and executed judgment, despite the sin of adultery?

The cry goes up from the cobbles, "David the King! *Dovid ha-melech.*"

Dante knows why the leopard minces with him, keeps him off the mountain. The others, lion and wolf, will slay him, but the leopard is his watch.

At the very gates of Hell, we meet the adulterers, Paolo and Francesca, hear their story. An unsympathetic commentator points a stern moral. "Writing and reading romantic fiction is almost as bad as yielding to romantic love" (Poggioli 1965, 76). This judgment on a poet who owed his inspiration to the very springs of the romance in poetry and prose makes one wonder what the critic imagines he is reading—the tract of a frustrated cleric? Dante faints at the story of Paolo and Francesca. He falls like "a dead man" in their circle of Hell. It *is* his story. He is the writer whose poetry, whose themes, are meant to seduce. His is a tale of adultery as well—and his love, Beatrice, is as commanding as poor Francesca, more so. The one drags her partner into Hell; the other will draw her lover, Alighieri, up to Heaven. Irony within irony, but the critic, who deftly draws the curtain on the naked action of the canto in which the adultery is confessed, lowers the boom at the last moment on his own head.

> The real kiss of Paolo and Francesca follows the imaginary kiss of Lancelot and Guinevere, as an image reflecting its object in a perspective similar and different at the same time. In brief, the seduction scene fulfills within the entire episode the function of a play within a play: more properly, of a romance within a romance. This creates an effect of parody, or, if we prefer to use a less negative term, something akin to what in modern times has been called "romantic irony," which in this case operates in an antiromantic sense. This means that the two romances, one of which may be likened to a frame, and the other to the picture enclosed therein, react reciprocally in such a way as to annihilate each other. (Poggioli 1965, 76)

> For a while, at the close of the canto, Dante the character becomes thus the equal of Paolo, and even of Lancelot, who for a while seems to swoon himself, while talking with the Queen of his still unrewarded love. In this brief moment, Dante himself is but a creature of pathos, a victim of pity and self-pity, like Paolo and Lancelot. Dante the poet stops short of the ridiculous, but it is only the timely fall of the curtain which saves the final scene of the episode from an unexpected caricatural effect. (Poggioli 1965, 74)

Great knight and prince, both become pathetic in their servitude to love, and Dante too. The scene may fall short of caricature but not of comedy. Who else is wounded so? It is the divine disease. "David the King, *Dovid ha-melech!*"

Rising on the stairs of Purgatory, Dante freezes for a moment before a tableau.

> Lì precedeva al benedetto vaso,
> trescando alzato, l'umile salmista,
> e più e men che re era in quel caso.
> Di contra, effigiata ad una vista
> d'un gran palazzo, Micòl ammirava
> si comde donna dispettosa e trista.

> There preceding the blessed vessel
> capering, girt up, the humble psalmist
> and more and less a king was at that moment.
> Opposite, figured at a window
> of a grand palace, Michal looked on
> like a woman full of scorn and sullen.
>
> (*Purg.* 10:64–69)

David at his moment of ecstasy, of ravishment, is both more and less than a king. To his wife, Michal, looking on, with the eye of a critic, he is a caricature, a poor creature in his underwear, a joke that demeans her among her handmaidens.

Only Dante understands—what is kingship at such a moment? *"In quel caso,"* "in this case," for he, too, is a "humble psalmist," and he wants ravishment, prophecy. "Shiggayon le-Dovid. Shiggayon bah-tomid." The madness of David, to be ravished always. I tasted its honeycomb a few pages before. What is David to Dante? A moment on a staircase? It is David who is the source of hope, the first light of his poetry, as he announces from the pinnacle of Purgatory.

> Da molte stelle mi vien questa luce:
> ma quei la distillò nel mio cor pria
> che fu sommo cantor del sommo duce
> "Sperino in te," nella sua tëodia
> dice, "color che sanno il nome tuo":
> a chi nol sa, s'elli ha la fede mia?

> From many stars this light comes to me
> But he distilled it within my heart first
> who was the supreme singer of the Supreme Leader
> "Let them hope in thee" in his sacred song
> he says, "They who know thy name."
> And who does not know, who has my faith?
> (*Par.* 25:70–75)

What is the hope of the poet as poet? Can it aspire higher than to be "sommo cantor del sommo duce," "supreme singer of the Supreme"? This poet, David's song, is linked as Dante's is, to adultery. In the thirty-second canto of *Paradiso,* but one away from the final gyre in the sky, Dante cries out his atonement in David's name, under the skirts of David's great grandmother, Ruth. "Colei / che fu bisava al cantor che per doglia / del fallo disse 'Misere mei,'" "She / who was great-grandmother to the singer who for pain / of his sin, cried, 'Have mercy on me'" (*Par.* 32:10–12).[2] Can it be plainer? Psalm 51: "A Psalm of David when Nathan the prophet came unto him, after he had gone in to Bathsheba." What is Dante's hope? That the miracle of David's hope, that he will be washed and made whiter than snow, that his lips, despite, despite adultery, will open and speak that praise.

Ha! Here is madness. Here *Shiggayon le-Dovid. Shiggayon,* disorder, anarchy.

---

2. Dante's reluctance to name Ruth directly as he does the biblical matriarchs only points to the anxiety of his confession at this moment.

Dante's very movement, a circular descent and ascent shows his condition, reeling through a vortex, spinning in fear. Dante dreamed that if he could go up in turns of light, he could unite himself at least with that female spirit to whom he had been singing all his life, a spirit that would embrace Beatrice, the lady at the window, the stone-hearted lady, Dominic, Saint Francis, male, female, in the "immense sea of being," milk and seed of that female shudder of bliss that the Jews called the *Shechinah,* and sectarians assign to Mary, wife of Joseph of raw, quarrelsome Nazareth. Every one of that sect's mystics kick against that town as they strive to get free of an overcrowded Galilean hilltop, its low, smoking rooftops, mean gossip, step off into the Empyrean.

Milk streams through the cantos of my Paradise, but I will come with pails later. Order, hierarchy, a sort of fascism gives a deadly luster to the marble tiers of the other *Paradiso,* a Victor Immanuel monument, crowning the poem with the weight of a mausoleum in the highest heavens.

Against this is Dante the Hebrew, the surrogate of David who inhabits the universe of the *Zohar,* an astronomer's heaven full of starbursts and looming black holes where balance is relative. It is a universe seen from a hill named Zion by the walls of David's city.

Where did Dante acquire the courage to see this sky—in which, swirling around the hierarchies of Augustine, Benedict, and their rigidities, is the notion of *shiggayon,* the holy sin?

Immanuel of Rome might have whispered the secret of Talmud in his ear.

> Amor non lesse ma l'avemaria
> Amor non temme mai legge ne fede
> Amor é un cor, che non ode né vede
> e non sa mai che misura si sia.

> Love never read the Avemaria
> Love never held with the law or faith
> Love is a heart that does not hear or see
> And never knows what limit may be.[3]

Immanuel it was who sang in Hebrew, "If I were not ashamed before God, and did not fear the holy people of Israel, I would build altars to the goddess of love: I would fall on my knees before beautiful women and kiss the dust before their

---

3. Author's translation: the Hebrew can be found in *The Cantos of Immanuel of Rome* (Immanuel of Rome 1957, 559).

feet."[4] Through Immanuel, or their bosom friend, Cino da Pistoia, somehow, Dante has heard of King David as holy fool. Have Dante and Immanuel sat together pressing the grapes that blush, perfect and purple, together with other poets of "the sweet new style" at the court of the Scaligeri in Verona; or caroused in some mountain fast, a tower high in the Apennines, an upper room overlooking the rush of mountain streams down to the sea, by a field of vines breaking their branches under the weight of the grapes, the clusters? "Oh please, let your breasts be like clusters."

Dante hears the Jewish lyricist expound golden heresies. Immanuel is the disciple of opposites, like Dante, of romantic Kabbalah and the rationalist, Maimonides. Wine soaks the hems of their cloaks and the breadknives clatter off the table. The puckish Immanuel rises to declaim: "David sinned to do God a favor. Not to make God look bad! Normally you associate service with the utmost of sincerity, but here it is associated with the utmost of insincerity, in order to please." The eyes of the Tuscan lift up. As Immanuel babbles, Dante's head begins to spin.

"David was the clown before God. And even though he is in pain when he stands before the King, David does his act in order to make the King laugh."

The sweet new laughter fills the room.

"You don't believe me, Dante? Listen to what the rabbis overheard. David begging—'Master of the Universe, test me!'

"'You won't be able to withstand the test.'

"'I sinned,' David says afterward, 'in order that You may be upheld in Your words. For if it were not so, if I were not to sin, my words would have been the truth, and Your words in vain. I am sinning, therefore, so Your words will be the truth"' (*Talmud, Megillah*, 14b).

"He was a clown, and he clowned with adultery. He did a handspring over Bathsheba. Hear!" Immanuel's eyes are gleaming. The hierarchies tumble upside down before them. "'*Your priests will robe themselves in justice and your pious [Chassidim] will sing.*' Psalm 132:9. Notice anything strange? There is a flip here. What do the sages, let their memory be a blessing, say? 'From this we learn now that if someone invites the King, he should alter his actions in order to bring joy to the King.' How is it that King David did this? Normally the ones that are considered to be the jesters of the King are the Levites. They sing for joy before him. But David flipped it that the jesters of the King should be the priests, the kohanim.

---

4. From *The Cantos*, Makama 8, p. 58, as cited in *A History of Jewish Literature* (Zinburg 1972, 2:209).

"The gist of it is, you serve God through a reversal of what's normal. You disorder the order, doing a flip before him. David flipped the priests into the jesters of the King."

The polite laughter of the sweet new style fills the room. Where has Immanuel his authority? "My dear friend," he replies. "These stories antedate your Messiah. Our 'Dovid' was a prophet, which is both more and less than a king. Like his father-in-law, Saul, David threw himself naked and raving in the street. His wife Abigail was a seer too. She prophesied the sin of Bathsheba (*Talmud, Megillah* 14b). David walked three parasangs in pitch dark by the light of her thigh. Here!" Immanuel lifts up a scroll from his table and reads.

Rab Judah said in Rab's name, "One should never (intentionally) bring himself to the test, since David king of Israel did so, and fell." He said unto Him. "Sovereign of the Universe! Why do we say (in prayer) 'The God of Abraham, the God of Isaac, and the God of Jacob, but not the God of David?' "

He replied, "They were 'tried' by me, but you were not."

"Sovereign of the Universe," replied David, "examine and try me—as it is written: *Examine me, O Lord, and try me.*" Ps. 26:2.

He answered, "I will test you and yet I'll give you an edge. For I didn't inform *them* how I was going to try them, but I'm telling *you* that I will try you in a matter of adultery."

Right away! "And it came to pass in an eveningtide, that David arose off his bed, etc." (2 Sam. 11:2). R. Johanan said, "He changed his night couch for a day couch (he made love by day instead of night, in order to be free of lust during the day) but he forgot the law. In man there is a small organ that satisfies him in his hunger but makes him hunger when satisfied.

"And he walked upon the roof of the king's house: And from the roof he saw a woman washing herself: And the woman was very beautiful to look upon" (2 Sam. 11:2). Now Bathsheba was cleansing her hair behind a screen when Satan appeared in the shape of a bird; David shot an arrow at it, which broke the screen. She stood revealed.

Immediately! "David sent and asked after the woman. One said, 'Is this not Bathsheba the daughter of Eliam, the wife of Uriah the Hittite?' And David sent messengers, and took her, and she came to him, and lay with him, for she was purified from her uncleanliness. And she returned to her house" (2 Sam. 11:3–4).

Thus it is written, "You have tried my heart, you have visited me in the night, you have probed and shall find nothing; I am purposed nothing shall transgress my lips" (Ps. 17:3).

David cried, "Would that a bridle had fallen into the mouth of my enemy (myself) that I had not spoken thus" (*Talmud, Sanhedrin,* 107a).

"Gentlemen," whispers Immanuel of Rome. Two other poets, Cino da Pistoia and Bosone da Gubbio have entered the room and joined Dante at the table. "There is a pun in Hebrew between the word 'purpose' and 'bridle.' It points with a joke, the purpose of the passage, to emphasize the impulsive speech of King David. It was a byword of his poetry, and so the phrase that introduces Psalm 7 is '*Shiggayon l'Dovid,*' 'the impulsive speech of David which he sang to God about the words of Cush, the Benjamite—beautiful black King Saul' (Ps. 7:1). Some rabbis assume that *Shiggayon l'Dovid* is just a harp note to instruct the singer at the beginning of Psalm 7 and Habakkuk 3. It is a harp note for madness! Both passages urge the Holy One to judge the singer and his nation. But—judgment in the sense of the singer coming close—He whom He loves, He drives mad. Remember Maimonides—Be always ravished, wandering, confused, overstepping, even sinning. *Shogeh ba-tomid!*

"This is the madness of David, a love that brought Saul and Jonathan to death, Bathsheba to evil, that David sang, 'tore his soul like a lion, ripping it to pieces'" (Ps. 7:3) until he cried, 'Tread down my life upon the earth and lay my honor in the dust'" (Ps. 7:6). It is a ravishing, *Shiggayon,* a plea for the Holy One to take David up in anger, 'Get up, O Lord in your anger . . . judge me!' (Ps. 7:7,9). And the explanation of this is to be found in the verses of Habakkuk which begin, 'A prayer of Habakkuk the prophet upon Shigionoth. . . . When I heard my belly trembled, my lips quivered at the voice; rottenness entered my bones, and I trembled in myself, that I might rest in the day of trouble; when he comes up into the people, he will invade them with His troops. . . . Yet I will rejoice in the Lord, I will joy in the God of my salvation. The Lord God is my strength, and he will make my feet like hinds' feet and he will make me to walk upon my high places. To the chief singer on my stringed instruments' (Hab. 3:1,16,18–19).

"'Play upon me, O Lord.' To understand this music, we must listen to the sages on Psalm 7. They hear the echo of *shiggayon, shigionoth* in the phrase of Job 12, 16, '*shogeg umashgeh,* the deceived and the deceivers.' What does the phrase *shogeg umashgeh* mean? According to R. Simeon ben Lakish it means 'prophets and their prophecies.' According to R. Johanan, it means 'the madman and the madness.' At the last moment, the sages rescue it and claim it means 'occupation with the Law.'"

Dante retrieves a crust of bread from the floor. He dips into a puddle of spilled wine on the table. "And even this linguistic turn takes them into erotic byways. For it is in Psalm 7 that David utters fatal words, 'His mischief shall return upon his own head.' Poor David, he cried out again and again to be excused from his own prophecy, madness, occupation. 'Do not fetch up against me words spoken impulsively as though they had been spoken deliberately.' And later, 'Master of the universe, forgive and pardon me for all the impulsive acts (*sheggiot*) I committed.' And David excused himself to God, pleading: 'Who can understand his impulsive acts [sheggiot]? Clear me from hidden faults!' (Ps. 19:13).

"But this prophecy, this wandering ravishment is the true road—for David's impulsive speech brings him ecstasy. The rabbis declare this subtly when they decide that *shogeg umashgeh* means 'occupation with the Law.' According to Psalm 7, David has been struck on the skull, his life trod into the dust, his honor lies there too—he is a sinner. He has prophesied impulsively but he was right—without it he could not have come to the last line of his psalm. Dear compatriots, suffer a Hebrew lesson! Proverbs 5, 18, and 19. 'Let your fountain be blessed: And rejoice with the wife of your youth. Let her be as the loving hind and pleasant roe: Let her breasts satisfy you at all times: And be ravished always with her love. *Tishgeh ba-tomid,* be ravished always with her love,' reads the final phrase.

"Squeeze the grapes of Samuel h. Nahmani, the Talmud of Babylon, Erubin, 'Why were the words of the Law compared to a hind?' (For so the sages interpret 'the wife of your youth' equating a man's grasp of the Law, with his embrace of his wife. 'To tell you that as the hind has a tight cunt and is loved by its mate at all times as at the hour of their first embrace, so it is with the words of the Law. They are loved by those who study them at all times just as in the hour when they first entered them. 'And a graceful roe'? Because the Law bestows grace upon those who study it. 'Her breasts will satisfy you at all times.' Why were the words of the Law compared to a breast? As with a breast, however often the child sucks it, so often does he find milk in it, so it is with the words of the Law. As often as a man studies them, so often does he find relish in them. 'With her love will you be ravished always.'

" '*Tishgeh ba-tomid,* be thou ravished always!' Now we know where Maimonides derives *shogeh ba-tomid* as the image of love of God. But we are not through with Proverbs 5. You know the repetitions of the sweet new style. You must hear them in Hebrew. At the very end of the fifth chapter of Proverbs, there is a pun. In verse 19, we heard, *tishgeh.* We hear it again in verse 20. 'And why my son, will you be ravished with a strange woman, and embrace the breast of a stranger?' Again *tishgeh,* the word for ravished. What is the fate of the poor fool who sins on a strange girl's tits? Verse 23, the last line sums it up. '*In the greatness of his folly, he shall go astray, wander.*' The word for 'go astray' is *yishgeh,* the third person of *tishgeh.* To be ravished, one must wander, go astray. Maimonides understood in the greatness of his wisdom that man must straddle that contradiction. And this was the very impulse of King David!"

Dante swallows his soaking gout—its taste as sweet as honey cake. Immanuel sings, "Through Bathsheba, adultery, David really came to love, to know the Holy One, Blessed be He, She!"

"This is a joke," Cino says. "You are fooling us."

"Exactly," Immanuel cries, "That's what David was—a comedian. And so, in the joyous week of the Harvest Festival, on Hoshanah Rabba, we Jews pray, 'God save us for the sake of the clown who danced with song.'"

Dante steals out of the room with beating heart. He is saved. He has hope. Hebrew will take him in Beatrice's arms up to the Catholic Heaven.

"How did you hope to come here?" Saint James inquires, years later, in the heights of Paradise.

"He first distilled it within my heart / who was the supreme singer of the Supreme Lord" (*Par.* 25:71–72), Dante answers, invoking King David.

John, James, Peter burst into laughter. The apostles *are* Jews. Round and round they go, flaming in "the laughter of the Jews." Poor Dante can't see Beatrice in the splash of bright sparks.

Why are they laughing so loud?

They know what Dante Alighieri is really hoping for.

CHAPTER SEVEN

Πude in Paradise

I INTENDED TO SPEAK OF HERESY.

The laughter of the Hebrews interrupts me, Babylonian tub-thumping, the sly cat's grin of the Middle Kingdom, David's handstand on a holy mountain.

Dante warns his contemporaries from the lips of Beatrice—"beware the laughter of the Jews."

Look back into the dark of the way we came before looking forward. Otherwise, as the poet warns, the eye can barely sustain the bursting novas, stars—the final rounds of Paradise.

To the laughter of her peers, James, Peter, John, Beatrice blushes and smiles.

That smile, erotic flash, is the first motion of a spiritual universe. Long before Dante has come to this height, the poet sang

> Quel ch'ella par quando un poco sorride,
> non si pò dicer né tenere a mente,
> sì è novo miracolo e gentile.

> What she is like as she smiles a bit
> one can not speak or hold it in the mind
> so new and gentle a miracle it is.
> (*Vita*, 21)

This is the state of angelic bliss, without conception of past or future, wholly in the present which Dante sings of as he bears the full beams of Beatrice's smile in Paradise. He turns from the mirrors of the saints, irradiated with Primal Love. Hot with the sweetness of love (*Par.* 29:140–41), he glories in his inadequacy before its surge.

> La bellezza ch' io vidi si trasmoda
> non pur di là da noi, ma certo io credo

che solo il suo fattor tutta la goda.
Da questo passo vinto mi concedo
più che già mai da punto di suo tema
soprato fosse comico o tragedo:
ché, come sole in viso che più trema,
così lo rimembrar del dolce riso
la mente mia da me medesmo scema.

The beauty, which I saw, so exceeds
not only what is ours, but indeed I believe
only its Maker enjoys it all.
At this pass, I concede myself vanquished
more than ever by point of his theme
comic or tragic poet was overwhelmed
so that as the sun in the most wavering sight
thus the remembrance of the sweet smile
my mind of its very self deprives.
                    (*Par.* 30:19–27)

From the very first smile at the age of nine to this moment, Dante has followed her.

Dal primo giorno ch' i' vidi il suo viso
in questa vita, infino a questa vista
non me'è il seguire al mio cantar preciso;
ma or convien che mio seguir desista
più dietro a sua bellezza, poetando,
come a l'ultimo suo ciascuno artista.

From the first day that I saw her face
in this life, until this sight
the pursuit of my song has not been cut off;
but now must my pursuit desist,
from following her beauty in my poetry
as with every artist at his ultimate.
                    (*Par.* 30:28–33)

Will this be *l'ultimo,* the limit of Dante's pursuit, that dazzled present moment of her smile burning off the mirrors of the Primal Light? Not for the child of Aquinas who understands that matter has appetite?

Why is she smiling?

Recall the crowds that go after her in the streets of Florence, begging for a hello, inspired by her greeting. Recall the healing balm of her smile to the injured poet. Must it live, after her death, only in memory? And when he feels it again as light, heat, what does it promise?

Recall the words in Hell, "Il disïato riso," "the desired, the longed-for smile," the key to adultery, on the lips of Guinivere, on the lips of Francesca, "tutto tremante," "all trembling." Dante is swooning, falling with the cadence of a corpse, those lips twisting, "la bocca mi bacciò tutto tremante," "my mouth he kissed all trembling," the sun is trembling in the eye as he remembers the same smile, "il disïato riso," depriving his mind of reason, "del dolce riso, La mente mia di se medesmo scema."

Desire, love, and the smile—he walked these tortured miles only for her smiles! Tramping through Hell, Purgatory, Paradise? Does her smile imply something? The scholar Poggioli sees it, but cannot bear the flash of laughter. He demurs even as he plumbs the psychology of Francesca and reveals, unwittingly, the guilt of Dante.

(The presence of two adulterers at the door of Dante's descent into Hell, a Hell populated by figures he has known, not only the characters of his reading, cannot be accidental. Dante's faint before Paolo and Francesca implies how much fear is in his sympathy. Has he been lured to the descent only to be faced with his own guilt and incarcerated? Dante could not, in honesty, begin the journey to Beatrice without having to front their common adultery. Why should he be spared, and these two, Paolo and Francesca, be punished? He will argue that he sinned for the sake of Heaven, a higher love, knowledge of the Unknown.)

For Dante has not only committed (or dreamed) adultery, he has written to seduce—not just the living, but in Beatrice's case—the dead. I read Poggioli wondering what decorum forbid him to draw obvious conclusions:

> Lust and adultery replace for a moment passion and love: a cry of nature breaks forever the mirror of illusion and the veil of self-deceit.
>
> The proof of this is evident in the two statements by which Francesca concludes her tale, each being enclosed in a single line. The first is but an exclamation, ambiguous and significant at the same time. Its clear purpose is the acknowledgement, on Francesca's part, of the role which the reading of that famous medieval romance played in their life, as well as the recognition that that role was identical with the one played by Gallehaut in the story they read not too wisely but too well. The ambiguity lies in the mixed tone of the phrase, conveying a double sense of regret for all the bliss and evil of which that hour was the seed: "*Galeotto fu il libro e chi lo scrisse,* Gallehaut was the book and he who wrote it."

By equating the effect of the reading with the action performed by Galle-haut, by identifying the unknown author of the romance with Gallehaut himself, who still preserves a graceful dignity despite the vileness of his services, Francesca treats the book and its author as if she would like to accuse and to absolve them at the same time. She cannot forget the beauty of the story and the glamour of the characters, since that beauty and that glamour still reflect a kind of redeeming light on the sin they committed at the example of Lancelot and Guinevere. While on one side, Francesca tries to emphasize in her story all the aspects that may en-noble her experience, she has still too much sense of responsibility to lay more than part of their guilt on others than Paolo and herself. She knows that she has been more sinning than sinned against, hence she dares not call the romance and its writer by the ugly name of panderers. The reader feels nothing more need be added, yet Francesca has something more to say. Strangely enough, she feels it necessary to allude to what happened after the reading had aroused and bared to them their own "dubious desires." To be sure, the allusion is merely negative in character and takes the form of another reference to the book which they forgot and discarded as soon as it had led them to their first kiss, "'Quel giorno piu non vi leggemmo avante, That day we read no more therein.'"

At first sight, the final words of Francesca (since these are her final words) seem to be superfluous, and even to lack propriety: they may even sound impu-dent, or at least too complacent, even more than merely unnecessary. What is Francesca's purpose in telling Dante that they did not read in that book any fur-ther? Why unveil so deviously, as well as so brutally, those intimate secrets which even a lost woman prefers to keep hidden? Only a harlot, devoid of the last shred not only of modesty, but even of self-respect, would go so far as to speak of her fall in such cynical terms. (1965, 63–64)

Off Poggioli goes on a tangent now, to try to show us the phrase—"That day we read no more," implies that the couple came back to read again on subsequent afternoons to recapture "idealizing and sublimating illusions" (psychological jar-gon, which betrays Poggioli's nervousness). As if this takes the sting out of the book dropping from their laps, the body of Dante in the shadows; the three drop-ping in a swoon of delight and death, tangled in each other.

"Quali columbi, dal disio chiamate," "As doves called by desire" (*Inf.* 5:82), their souls came to Dante, Francesca and Paolo's. He is the *"dolce nido,"* "sweet nest." I will not yet speak of the full purport of the "nest," but it is clear that the "nest" is the womb of adulterous love. He boasts in *Paradiso* that he has come from "del bel nido di Lida," and Francesca and Paolo come, "Con l'ali alzate e ferme al dolce nido," "With wings poised and firm to the sweet nest," as Dante prepares for his ravishment and faint before their story. (Echoing of course, their faint, fall, into love, as they hear a story, signaled by the dropping book, hearing their own fall in the romance of Lancelot and Guinevere.) In the twenty-sixth canto of the *Inferno,* the same ambiguity overcomes the poet, and the key again is the call by "desire" which brings Dante in joy, terror, close to fainting. "Dal disio chiamate" of Francesca is echoed by "'vedi che del disio ver le mi piego!'" "'thou seest how I bend toward them with desire!'" The poet leans toward the forbidden, the flame of Ulysses and Diomedes, forbidden knowledge and yet Virgil answers, "Your prayer deserves praise." Dante's desire is good! though Dante himself has admitted to almost falling into the abyss, stretching toward it a moment ago. "[S]ì che s'io non avessi un ronchion preso, / caduto sarei giù sanz'esser urto." "So that if I hadn't taken hold of a nearby rock, / I would have fallen below without being pushed"(*Inf.* 26:44–5). No push is needed. That *caduto* has been heard before, and precisely in Francesca's canto, "E caddi come corpo morto cade" (*Inf.* 5:142).

The doctrine of subsuming sin in love has brought him to this second dangerous tryst, trial, deep in the *Inferno.* Dante faces the figure of Ulysses, who has been punished for sailing to the very island that Dante will tread, the brown mountain of Purgatory; Dante's question sounds in Ulysses' speech to his men. Ulysses has been punished for seeking knowledge. Why? Somehow, and Dante's ambivalence sounds in his vagueness, he has sought it impiously without the aid of Heaven.[1]

This is a canto where Dante again, fears himself, his own sympathy. "Then it grieved me and I now grieve again / when I direct my mind to what I saw / and curb my genius more than is my wont" (*Inf.* 26:19–21). One more step of sympathy and he is over the abyss. Here it is death to faint. The wind of his own soul is blowing, the sound of sighs, murmuring and tossing. "Lo maggior corno de la fiamma antica / cominciò a crollarsi mormorando / pur come quella cui vento affatica," "The greater horn of the ancient flame, / began to toss, murmuring / as if it were tormented by the wind"(*Inf.* 26:85–87). That wind has been heard before. Wind blown souls! "Sì tosto come il vento a noi li piega, / mossi la voce: 'O anime affannate, / venite a noi parlar, s'altri nol niega!'" "As soon as the wind bent them

---

1. The impiety is deliberately pointed up by the ironic repetition of oars and wings in the appearance of the guiding white angel in *Purgatorio.* Ulysses declares in the *Inferno,* "De' remi facemmo ali al folle volo," "We made of the oars, wings for the mad flight" (*Inf.* 26:125). In *Purgatorio,* Dante says of the angel, "Vedi che sdenga li argomenti umani, / sì che remo non vuol nè altro velo / che l'ali sue tra liti sì lontani," "See how he scorns the instruments of humans / so that for oar he wishes not nor sail other / than his wings between shores so distant" (*Purg.* 2:31–33). The notion of seeking "virtue and knowledge" is undercut by the cynical laughter of "my little speech," in which the adventurer reflects ironically on his oration.

to us, / I raised my voice, 'O winded spirits, / come and speak to us, if none forbid it!' " (*Inf.* 5:79–81).

"I bend with desire." And he who bent toward the *"disïato riso"*? The lovers who knew the torment of *"dubbiosi disiri"*? Dante's fall at the end of the fifth canto, his almost fall in the twenty-sixth, Virgil's abstention from interference, rebuke, the sense of flame flickering—the cantos recall each other and "none forbids" the intercourse of Dante with these sinners.

"Con l'ali alzate e ferme al dolce nido," "With wings poised and firm to the sweet nest." What nest?

"The passion I had to gain experience of the world and of man." What experience?

It is to the unspoken lines of Paolo's sexual delight[2] that Dante falls like a corpse into horror. He has come for the body of Beatrice. The smile, "il disïato riso, la bocca tutto tremante," "the mouth all trembling" which Paolo has kissed, these are but foretastes. He has come for the "dolce nido," the sweet nest. "Dolci pensier, dolcezza," drips from the lines of Dante throughout his encounter with Francesca. He wants to know (to "know" in Hebrew is a synonym for copulation), to be ravished by the Divine Presence.

"Down, down," Dante drops through Hell. "Brother," Muhammad greets him with as the poet's thoughts swirl, caught on a ridge of Heresy. "'Ma tu chi se' che 'n su lo scoglio muse, / forse per indugiar d'ire a la pena / ch'è giudicata in su le tue accuse?' " " ' But who are you musing on the ridge, / perhaps to delay going to your punishment, / which has been judged upon your accusations?' " (*Inf.* 28:43–45).

Virgil denies it. "Death does not touch him, nor the least guilt bring him here to be tormented" (*Inf.* 28:46–48). But Dante is silent. What does Virgil know? Dante's grief and anguish in the *Inferno* is not guiltless. Virgil will not step with the Tuscan before the frown of Beatrice. Virgil does not guess at the curiosity of the poet on the chance of bodily resurrection. Virgil's pagan mind knows of divine adultery among the gods, not the common man's hope for ecstasy in the Hereafter.

The inevitable question of the lover who has been cheated by death of his beloved occurs to Dante. He knows he will meet Beatrice in the realm of death, but what exactly does that reunion promise? How much of her body can he expect to touch? The grounding of the metaphysical in the earthly, or play of sex, is comic.

2. The moment contains at least three levels of irony: Francesca's next line, which we never hear, would speak of the details of their erotic play: but the memory provokes tears from Paolo. Dante, in their midst, faints. He faints not only from emotion but to make good his promise that his poetry "non corra che virtó nol guidi," "will not run where virtue will not guide it" (*Inf.* 26:22). The faint speaks for him silently—speaks of terror and eroticism at once.

The question, though answered, is never resolved. It keeps returning when the metaphysics of Statius, Beatrice, and others ought to have settled it. Indeed the question—What can I enjoy of you?—is part of the romantic dalliance between Dante and Beatrice. They circle each other, exchanging glances, vows, on their way upward. The poet reveals the jealousy of his youthful mistress in the lines. The imagery is almost forced: Dante's spine frozen like "the back of Italy, blown and packed by Slavonic winds." [3] But the scene in Eden also prepares us to accept a notion (of all lovers) as fact: that a glance from the beloved's eyes, of anger, of passion, has the power to make one melt or freeze. Without this demonstration of the physical power of the intangible—sight—the drama of *Paradiso*, Dante and Beatrice's lovemaking through voice and sight would not be credible.

How palpable Beatrice makes her body in Eden has already been seen. How green and ripe the members he has sung. How angry she is, how slow to show that smile until her lover has bathed his face in tears and begged forgiveness, drunk forgetfulness, stopped flirting with the other female graces of the Garden—refreshed, reborn, turning a literal new leaf, "rinovellate di novella fronda," "renewed with new leaves," vegetable image, "rifatto sì come piante novelle," "remade like new plants" (*Purg.* 33:144, 143). The leaf, fig leaf, around his middle, that plant he had plucked at the bottom of the Mount of Purgatory, waving his frond, goes up with him to the stars.

That would be the end of it, *the ultimate,* for the rest of the sweet new stylists, but not for Dante. What is Paradise?

Laughter of Dante, Beatrice, David the King—love is Paradise. Dante is going to take the troubadours at their word and sing of sex in the highest Heaven. The composer of the *Commedia* is determined to touch his mistress, to "know" her. Mounting the stairs of Paradise, the lovers, Alighieri, Portinari, circle each other in the steps of a Provençal courtship, the strum of innuendoes, gentle rebukes, side glances, affectionate outbursts, between lines that act as blinds.

Dante took inspiration from Provence, Languedoc, seed plot of Kabbalah, mysticism, poetry.

We find in the troubadours of Provence the first germ of the maxim that sexual love is virtue. And just as in the development of the problem of nobility a distinction has to be first made between aristocracy of blood and nobility of character, so in the question of love a preliminary division is made into sensuous and su-

---

3. Dante has aged well beyond Beatrice at the time of their reunion. She speaks as a very young woman to an older man. She is frozen at the moment of her death while he ages as he writes, ages even in the composition of the cantos, coming to the gates of Paradise.

persensuous love. Were the troubadours the first to bring a spiritual element into passion? According to them it was the intellectual and sentimental element that constituted the very essence of love itself. The churl in whom this element is lacking is unfitted for true service of woman.

To the extent that this spiritual element was more or less emphasized in relation to natural impulse, a higher or lower type of love was attained. Courtly society was best aware of the means by which an aesthetic and sentimental enhancement of sexual love is assured; namely, by setting as many obstacles as possible between desire and fruition. Unhindered intimacy, wedded life, can never lead to love, but only to friendship. True love is—even for Dante!—outside of wedlock. All such restraining emotions as jealousy, fear, defiance, and above all, coyness, are a welcome spice in love-service, and are to be diligently sought after and, if need be, artificially created.

Love becomes an art, and its sentimental ennoblement soon leads to the distinction between mixed and pure love, so the French chaplain assures us, extends to the kiss, the embrace, "et verecundum amantis nudae contactum, extremo praetermisso solatio: nam illud pure amare volentibus exercere non licet." (Vossler 1958, 301)[4]

Dante has already passed the limits of the priest's regard. After all, how far can the church stretch its sanctification and give *solatio?* The scattered pages of Lancelot and Guinivere, the leaves, mask the trembling, awkward, nude bodies. The poet of Paolo and Francesca, Ulysses, Count Ugolino, cannot have repressed the utmost appetite, the "final solace."

The Paradise of the Catholic philosophers, however, poses problems for this solace. Alighieri and Portinari are not in their proper bodies. How shall they have intercourse? Without bodies? It is not talk but touch, touch pointed, touch exalted, touch made spiritual even as it eroticizes, enhanced by philosophy—but finally touch, unavoidably that most lovers want. These two are no exception. Why prolong the song thirty-three cantos on, if there is no touching in Paradise?

Dante has been cautious to bring real flesh, his flesh, "questa vera carne che 'l seconda," "this true flesh which seconds him,"(*Purg.* 23:123) into Purgatory. He has insisted that it is no dream. Yet flesh is impermissible in Paradise until the Last Judgment. And dream is all we have of Paradise.[5] Dante may go up but under con-

---

4. The Latin is quoted from Andreas, *De Amore* (ed. Trojel, Hauniae, 1892), p. 182 seqq. "And actual contact with the naked lover, the final solace left out, for it is not permitted to those who wish to love purely" (Translated by Frederick Goldin).

5. Whereas dream, even in *Purgatorio* is dangerous, allowing the sexual importuning of the Siren to rise to consciousness, something to be guarded against, dream in *Paradiso* is a form of true knowl-

ditions that hobble his courtship, his hope of yet another *superba strupa,* exalted adultery. It is all well and good to admire Beatrice high in the Empyrean, but isn't there a way to touch her, take her under a bush? Is there no cover, foliage, *freschetta,* in the clouds?

It is no trip for conventional troubadours. Beatrice will make the Empyrean ruddy with the "lineaments of gratified desire."

The substance of Beatrice in Paradise has been dogging the poet's thoughts in Purgatory. To Virgil he can say nothing. The Mantuan so knowledgeable in courtesy is a neophyte in metaphysics. It is with Statius that the subject is broached.[6] Dante is puzzled, awkward, *verecundum,* filled with the wish to fly, yet feeling not like a dove—the emblem of Francesca, the Apostles, but as an infant stork that cannot rise from the nest, "il cicognin che leva l'ala" (*Purg.* 25:10). Virgil tries to answer but his powers of metaphor are inadequate, and he turns to Statius with a phrase charged as I observed, with sexual significance, "sanator de le tue piage," "healer of thy wounds" (*Purg.* 25:30).

Statius unfolds the Neoplatonic doctrine of the soul taking a substantial body again from light. This prepares us for the solution of corporal love in Paradise. It is light that has substance, light in which touch is manifest, light, then sound, odor: so the components of physical love in the Empyrean will be smell, hearing (language or words), and sight (vision).

At first it seems hopeless, and indeed the images strain to serve the ardor of Beatrice and Dante, for Beatrice's eyes must play the profound sexual role. They strike with physical force, ravishing, blinding. They smite—the invitation through the eyes—that is what is left of touch. It is not surprising to find that they "strike" Dante so when he first meets Beatrice's gaze in *Purgatorio.*

> Tosto che ne la vista mi percosse
> l'alta virtù che già m'avea trafitto
> prima ch'io fuor di püerizia fosse.

---

edge. So in canto 29:82–83 "Sì che là giù, non dormendo, si sogna / credendo e non credendo dicer vero," "So that down there, not sleeping / as they dream, believing or not believing that they speak truth," seem to indicate that inspiration may come in true dreams, fantasies received in the bosom of sleep. Saint Bernard in the final moments of Dante's gaze into the mystery of Primal Love tells him, "'L tempo fugge che t'assona.'" "'The time flies that holds thee sleeping.'" (*Par.* 32:139), giving us to understand that at least this leg of the journey has been such a true dream.

6. The context, Dante's fear of the approaching purification by fire, obscures the purpose of his questions. It seems as if he is asking about his own body. But that, as we are told, is real flesh. It is Beatrice's body that is under discussion (and of course the other shades' bodies). The promise of her body as presence beyond the wall of flame is the spur to get him through it.

. . .

> As soon as within my sight struck
> the lofty virtue which has already transfixed me
> before I was out of childhood.
> (*Purg.* 30:40–42)

Percosse![7] It struck, smote through her veil, gaze (*percosse,* so palpable, the sound of music in it, *trafitto,* transfixing, crucifying him) makes him tremble, piercing through the cloth, her veil, though he has with his own eyes no more knowledge but the hidden sight of "d'antico amor sentì la gran potenza," "of old love feeling the great power" (*Purg.* 30:39).

As the veil falls and she commands him to stare, driven back as by force, he fixes sight on the water, the grass. He tastes bitterness through his whole body. He freezes, his spine like "lo dosso d'Italia si congela, / soffiata e stretta da li venti schiavi," "the back of Italy is frozen, blown and packed by the Slavic winds" (*Purg.* 30:86–87). Here is wind, spirit, but again palpable, felt.

Through her look Dante can feel his shame, feel the great power of his old love. And it is only when Beatrice has made him understand that he can so far feel her that she complains that she has "shown her young eyes to him," "mostrando li occhi giovanetti a lui" (*Purg.* 30:122). She signals an organ he may expect favor from again. The eye is a metaphor for touch throughout *Paradiso.* But now, Dante shivers in Eden. What, will she never smile?

NOT UNTIL THE MEMORY OF HIS INFIDELITY HAS STUNG HIM SO AND (How many? There is the *"novo augelletto,"* "young chick" [*Purg.* 31:61], a *"pargoletta,"* "young girl" [*Purg.* 31:59] that "vanita con sì breve uso" [*Purg.* 31:60], implying a quick jerk in the pants, details she mercifully withholds, and her phrase, two or three shots of the arrow, has an amused ring [even in wrath Beatrice cannot help but smile at Alighieri in pursuit of the young fryers of Italy]) HAS TURNED HATEFUL ("tutte altre cose qual me torse / più nel suo amor, più mi si fé nemica," "of all other things, whatever turned me before / most to its love, now made itself most hateful" [*Purg.* 31:86–87], so that "ch'io caddi vinto," "I fell vanquished" [*Purg.* 31:89]), DOES BEATRICE SEND HER HANDMAIDENS TO HANDLE HIM. *"Tiemmi, tiemmi!"* "Hold me, Hold me!" (*Purg.* 31:93). This intimacy would have been dangerous before. ("Hold me" is the cry of the enamored lady, Matilda, with whom he briefly dallied at the entrance to the Garden, "the lady whom I found alone" [*Purg.*

---

7. Compare (*Purg.* 33:18), "When with her eyes she smote (*percosse*) my eyes and with tranquil appearance said, 'Come more quickly.'" Even when "tranquil," *"tranquillo,"* her eyes have a percussion as they light on her lover.

31:92]. Dante cannot help remembering even as he is about to enter her fair arms and be ducked.) Now *"La bella donna"* (*Purg.* 31:100) and Dante may go naked, dance, since he has sung, "Under her [Beatrice's] veil, and beyond the river, she did seem to vanquish (*vincer*) even her former self, to vanquish (*vincer*) as she did others when she was here" (*Purg.* 31:82–84). To vanquish, surpass, overcome—and the call comes from the nymphs who are stars to the dripping Dante. "Do not hoard your gaze / you have placed before you the emeralds / whence love once shot his arms at thee" (*Purg.* 31:115–17).

And to his mistress, they call, "Turn Beatrice, turn your holy eyes . . . to your faithful / that to see thee, has shown so many steps! / for our grace, do him the grace to unveil / to unveil your mouth, so he may see / the second beauty which thou hides" (*Purg.* 31:133–38). Dante is burning. "Mille disiri più che fiamma caldi / strinsermi li occhi a li occhi rilucenti," "A thousand desires hotter than flame / pressed my eyes to the glittering eyes" (*Purg.* 31:118–19). In that "pressed me," *"strinsermi,"* I can but hear the echo of Francesca's Lancelot whom love "presses," "'Lancialotto come amore lo strinse'" (*Inf.* 5:128). The eye eats. "Mentre che piena di stupore e lieta / l'anima mia gustava di quel cibo / che, saziando, di sé, di sé asseta," "While full of stupor and happiness, / my soul ate of that food / which satisfying with itself, makes itself hungry" *Purg.* 31:127–29). As in the Talmud, "There is a small organ in man which satisfies him when in hunger and makes him hunger when he is satisfied."

Here Beatrice turns and Dante cries, "I'm going crazy," *"Mente ingombra"* (*Purg.* 31:142).

"Lo santo riso," "the holy smile" and if there is any doubt that it is one and the same joy, entanglement, squeeze, the poet felt in Florence, the image dispels it, "lo santo riso / a sé traéli con l'antica rete!" "the holy smile drew them to itself with the old net!" (*Purg.* 32:5–6). Net as an image suggests traps, ploys, a gladiator, the victim in a lover's duel. These lines contain another hint. This stare of Dante into the eyes of Beatrice is "fissi e attenti / a disbramarsi la decenne sete, / che li altri sense m'eran tutti spenti" "so fixed and intent / to quench their ten year's drought / that the other senses were all spent in me" (*Purg.* 32:1–3).

Dante feels, touches, eats, joys in that heat, receives the embrace of Beatrice through the eyes. All other senses are "spent" at this moment and this suggests sex, even seed. Instead of fainting, he goes blind. It is now the metaphor of ravishment rather than confusion, *smarrito.*[8] Ecstasy in Paradise is light, sight. He is over-

---

8. See the *Purgatorio,* canto 16, where the blindness and the gloom of Hell are equated, lines 10–12, and the phrase *"per non smarrirsi"* predictably occurs in line 11 in the dramatic metaphor of a blind man fearing confusion.

whelmed at first. *"Troppo fiso!"* "Too fixed!" (*Purg.* 32:9) cry the nymphs, stars, as his sight goes.

When it returns, he is dazzled with visions, dreams, to which Beatrice's apostrophe, "non parli più com' om che sogna," "Speak no more as a man who dreams" (*Purg.* 33:33), must be ironic since she is the vehicle of them. The first smile in Eden is unbearable and blinds the gazer, but the second, sly, amused, gives us a foretaste of what awaits Dante in Paradise.

"Why don't I understand you?" he complains in the last gyre of Purgatory. "Ma perché tanto sovra mia veduta / vostra parola disïata vola, / che più la perde quanto più s'aiuta?" "Why so far over my head / do your longed for words fly / that I lose them the more I follow?" (*Purg.* 33:82–84).

"So you can see just how far your behavior was below the way you ought to have flown," jibes Beatrice. She cannot resist teasing.

"Non mi recorda. . . ," answers Dante. "I don't remember. Did I do something to make us drift apart? My conscience doesn't prick."

Here Beatrice smiles, the real smile, not the *santo riso,* but the old smile of that net, tender and bemused at once. What an innocent! What an infant! Dante colors with pleasure as she picks up his words, repeating them, "'E se tu ricordar non te ne puoi' / sorridendo rispuose," "'If you can't remember,' she answered smiling, 'Recall now how you drank this day of Lethe.'" Your very forgetfulness ought to make you understand that a sin was washed away. "Your longing went wandering." And then, listen to the laughter, "'Veramente oramai saranno nude / le mie parole, quanto converrassi / quelle scovrire a la tua vista rude.'" "'Truly, from this moment my words will be nude, / so much as is necessary to discover them to your rude sight'" (*Purg.* 33:91, 94–102).

"Parole nude" and *"Vista rude,"* these are the cymbals of love. "Words nude, sight rude!"

"Paradise."

CHAPTER EIGHT

A Mother's Milk

THE MILK OF PARADISE, a drop in Coleridge's opium vision of the heavens, *Kubla Khan,* is a stream through the cantos of Paradise. Except for the sudden cry of pathos for his mother's flesh (the end of the line falls on mommies and gives us the bleat of the infant), Dante remains silent about his mother. Her position was usurped by Beatrice.[1] (This sheds some light on the strange dignity with which he invests Beatrice at the age of nine.) If Dante Alighieri suffered two unspeakable losses, his mother at the age of five, six, then his mistress in his early twenties—one can understand his poem's tension between the maternal and the erotic.

The discussion of bodily metaphysics is deliberately abstract. It is easy to forget that the lovers are talking about their ability to touch each other. The nature of Dante's listening to his mistress drew Osip Mandelstam's attention. Dante sits happily imbibing theological and metaphysical lessons from his tutor, Beatrice. (Few male lovers are so blessed.) This ideal of platonic love is almost comic in its extremity, drawn from the adoration of the mistress in Provençal poetry, the versification of Moors and Jews on the Iberian peninsula, the cult of Mary, Neoplatonism's will to rise toward ideal beauty.

As "spiritual" teacher, Beatrice, however, has the attribute of jealousy. Dante forgets his indiscretions in Eden but not Beatrice. Indiscretion or betrayal is excused, though, when it is the betrayal of a vow that would have been perilous to fulfill. From the height of Paradise the poem seems to look back at the world of *La Vita Nuova,* measuring the dangers of its sentimentality and his lover's vows unto death.

---

1. Dante's mother died when he was five or six years old. "His father then remarried. The poet's stepmother was Lapa di Chiarissimo Cialuffi. It is known that Dante had a half-brother Francesco, and a half-sister, Tana or Gaetana. He also had a full sister. Her name has not been preserved" (Chubb 1966, 53).

Dante draws Beatrice "in relief," separates her thoughts from his. Beatrice is no friend to the Jews. One observes that Dante does not acquiesce in her judgments. He maintains independence as to his politics and theology. In the seventh canto, bearing the number of the Hebrew Sabbath, the gates are inscribed in Hebrew and Dante becomes most playful, speaking of Beatrice as a girl, dropping her name in code, as if he were dallying with her in Florence.

(In canto 14, twice seven, the figure of Solomon appears and the subject is the body, its restoration to actual flesh on the Day of Judgment. The laughter of this canto is emphasized by the pathos of the one that follows, where blindness, despair, strike him high in the circles of Paradise. His rescue comes not from Beatrice, but from the ancient, gross father of mankind. It is a joke of a cosmic eroticizer.)

• • •

PARADISO! Beatrice is holding Dante Alighieri from its first canto in *"l'antica rete."* She is the Beatrice Dante knew in the halls and courtyards of Florence. Never in *La Vita Nuova* did he allow her to be familiar with him. Where in the streets of Tuscany, Dante sung of an etherealized creature, in *Paradiso,* paradoxically, Beatrice becomes flesh and blood. She calls her lover "dull"; "Tu stesso ti fai grosso," "you make yourself dull" (*Par.* 1:88), scolds, sighs, gives him a technical description of the universe. We sit with Dante through a lecture on art, metallurgy, optics. Beatrice Portinari's family was well known for its connoisseurship. Her father endowed the hospital in Florence with art. Is it an echo of some conversation the untutored Dante had at his mistress's skirt? Osip Mandelstam points out the Florentine's awkwardness, that he is a *raznocinec,*[2] an intellectual not of noble birth, that he must constantly be tutored in correct behavior by Virgil. This is a harsh, class-conscious judgment. That soft laugh of Beatrice, a cough which res-

---

2. See "Talking about Dante," where the Russian poet Osip Mandelstam remarks: "Dante is a poor man. Dante is an internal *raznocinec* [an intellectual not of noble birth] of an ancient Roman line. Not courtesy but something completely opposite is characteristic of him. One has to be a blind mole not to notice that throughout the *Divina Commedia* Dante does not know how to behave, he does not know how to act, what to say, how to make a bow. . . . The inner anxiety and the heavy, troubled awkwardness which attend every step of the unself-confident man, the man whose upbringing is inadequate, who does not know what application to make of his inner experience, or how to objectify it in etiquette, the tortured and outcast man—it is these qualities which give the poem all its charm, all its drama, and they create its background, its psychological ground.

"If Dante were to be sent out alone, without his *dolce padre,* without Virgil, a scandal would inevitably erupt in the very beginning, and we should not have a journey among torments and remarkable sights but the most grotesque buffoonery" (Mandelstam 1971, 72–73).

onates in the poet's ear, tolling like the warning of sin in the romance of Lancelot and Guinevere (note that in Dante *pride* not *adultery* occasions it) comes as he attempts to make much of his family lineage. So it is true that Dante realizes his absurd position in asserting patents of nobility. But it is not a drama of manners, the *Commedia*. When Dante's confidence deserts him, he is less awkward than childlike. Beatrice does tease him, but not so much for being a boor as for being ignorant, untutored, childish. That Beatrice condescends to Dante is unmistakable. But it is a maternal condescension.

> "Do not marvel that I smile,"
> She said to me, "at your childish thought. . . .
> since upon the truth it yet does not trust its foot
> but turns you round as is its wont, on vacancy."
> (*Par.* 3:25–28)

Dante accepts her condescension gratefully, even seeks it. "Quel sol che pria d'amor mi scaldò 'l petto / di bella verità m'avea scoverto / provando e riprovando, il dolce aspetto," "That sun which first scalded my breast with love, of beautiful truth, has discovered to me / proving and refuting, its sweet aspect" (*Par.* 3:1–3). Why is the scolding sweet? Because it allows him to accept her love as a child. Beatrice will be mother, lover, savior to him. This indeed makes possible the peculiar religious exaltation of his lust. The *"superba strupa"* is both a proud and an exalted adultery. Dante uses the word *"superbo"* first with its tainted, sinful connotation, then with its holy one.[3] He flies at the end of the *Commedia*, upward, guided by Saint Bernard, who also longs for breasts, the divine milk of Mary. The sin of adultery has been transformed in the worship of the Divine Presence that lies upon their ladies' breasts, streaming "the milk of Paradise." This was the dairy of Co-

---

3. The ambivalent use of the word in the course of the *Commedia* encapsulates the whole of its drama. Twice it is used to signify the sin of Lucifer, in the *Inferno*, 7:12, and in *Paradiso*, 19:46. Yet it also describes the face of the mother from whom the child takes a rebuke, "Così la madre al figlio par superba," "as the mother to the child seems elevated" (*Purg.*, 30:79). Finally at the end of *Paradiso*, when Beatrice tells Dante that his vision is not yet, *"tanto superbe,"* "exalted enough," just before the "climactic" vision of the rose, *superba*, reveals its cryptogram. The meanings of "exalted," and "adulterous," are squeezed together into a milk, spermal and maternal, the milk of Paradise.

Dante reaches out at this point with a directness that borders on the vulgar to Beatrice's tit for inspiration. "Non è fantin che sì subito rua / col volto verso il latte, se si svegli/ molto tardato da l'usanza sua, / come fec' io," "No infant falls on the instant with its face toward the milk, if it wakes long after its usage, as I did" (*Par.*, 30:82–85).

leridge.[4] For Dante, who lost his mother at five or six, the Eden of suckling at the breast and motherhood may be synonymous. The milk of Paradise promises a return to infancy and the original personal Eden.

Dante's courtship begins in the first canto of *Paradiso.* Its characteristic notes will be played over and over, Beatrice's condescension, her mother's milk, laughter, the instruction of *"materia sorda,"* "dull material," and the glimmering under the cover of instruction. How telling the phrase (*Par.,* 1:95), "le sorrise parolette brevi," "the smile of her brief words," for Beatrice's smile promises Eros.

What gives complexity to the courtship of the *Paradiso* are the two strands that loop the pole of Love, striping it, the gaudy red of erotic joy and the pure white of mother's milk. "See where *Beatrice's* breasts stream in the firmament!" to paraphrase Marlowe. The omnipresent image of mother and child is not the conventional Holy Family portrait of Mother and Infant Savior, but courtly Mother and beloved, "delirious child."

> Ond' ella, appresso d'un pïo sospiro
> li occhi drizzò ver me con quel sembiante
> che madre fa sovra figlio deliro.

> Therefore she, after a sigh of pity
> turned her eyes toward me with that look
> which a mother gives to a delirious child.
> (*Par.* 1:100–102)

The awkwardness of the love before his lady shades imperceptibly into the bleating of an infant at his mother's breast. This play of emotions in Dante's face cannot but draw the indulgent, amused smile of his beloved. Poggioli has testified to Dante's daring in presenting Paolo.

No poet went as far as Dante in this reduction to a cipher of the masculine partner of a great passion. Considered alone, Paolo, a bleak pale creature, whose only action is weeping, pales nearly to a vanishing point. Love changes man into a woman's shadow, and this is true of Paolo not only as the ghost he now is, but as the man he once was. Francesca projects the memory of herself even before the

---

4. See the "Kubla Khan" of Samuel Taylor Coleridge where the poet's final vision is of himself, so smitten with poetic inspiration that he became a whirling figure in a magical circle, going up, one feels, to the heavens. "And close your eyes with holy dread, / For he on honey-dew hath fed, / And drunk the milk of Paradise."

time of her fatal affair, but evokes her lover only during the moment of their sin. And, unconsciously, she fixes him forever in a vision of passive pusillanimity. At least in appearance she describes him the very moment he acted like a man: when he took the initiative, as he was supposed to do, and kissed her on her mouth. Yet Francesca finds it fit to remember that even in that instant of daring he was trembling in every fiber of his body, like a leaf. . . . Paolo perhaps trembled because he was afraid: of woman and love, or of death and of sin. (Poggioli 1965, 73)

Dante shows successive sides of himself, boasting that few can follow his inspiration, calling for Apollo to deck him in laurel, then fleeing into the skirts of Beatrice, crying for his "mamma." In the latter moments, he is not shy to present himself as a creature of masculine abasement. But not for the sake of appearing a "cipher." Nor is Paolo one.

The power of woman winds through the great horn of Dante's poetry. Poggioli does not hear it. The pull between mother and lover in Beatrice, her sexual ardor, threatens to overwhelm Dante. In the *Paradiso,* she appears as mother when he cannot bear her appetite as partner. In the twenty-second canto, he runs to her as a frightened babe, and she warns that her full smile and song would have destroyed him.

> Oppresso di stupore, a la mia guida
> mi volsi, come parvol che ricorre
> sempre colà dove più si confida;
> e quella, come madre che soccorre
> sùbito al figlio palido e anelo
> con la sua voce, che 'l suol ben disporre,
> mi disse: "Non sai tu che tu se' in cielo?
> e non sai tu che 'l cielo é tutto santo,
> e ciò che ci si fa vien da buon zelo?
> Come t'avrebbe trasmutato il canto,
> e io ridendo, mo pensar lo puoi. . . .
> poscia che 'l grido t' ha mosso contanto."

> Overwhelmed, with stupor, to my guide
> I turned like a little one who runs back
> always, there, where he most confides
> and she, as a mother who gives succor
> quickly to the pale and breathless child
> with her own voice which sets him aright

said to me, "Do you not know that you are in heaven?
And do you know that heaven is all holy
and that whatever is done here comes from sound zeal?
How the song would have transmuted you
and I by smiling, now you can comprehend
since the cry has so much moved you."
(*Par.* 22:1–12)

The threat of that smile, its burning, is real. Beatrice has warned him in the twenty-first canto, just before this, making the danger of a fiery transmutation, primal sunstroke, clear.

E quella non ridea: ma "Si io ridessi"
mi comenciò "tu ti faresti quale
fu Semelè quando di cener fessi:
ché la bellezza mia, che per le scale
de l'etterno palazzo più s'accende,
com' hai veduto, quanto più si sale,
se non si temperasse, tanto splende,
che 'l tuo mortal podere, al suo fulgore,
sarebbe fronda che trono scoscende."

And when she did not smile, but "If I were to smile,"
she began, "You would become such as
was Semele when she turned to ashes
since my beauty, which is on the stairs
of the eternal palace is kindled the more
as you have seen, the more it ascends,
if it were not tempered, so great is its brightness
that your mortal powers, at its flash
would be a frond that thunder cleaves."
(*Par.* 21:4–12)[5]

What tempers the heat of her smile? Milk, in a cooling draught a few lines on.

---

5. The peculiar nature of the simile calls attention to itself. Why use a thunderbolt to cleave a frond? But that frond is the leaf that Dante has bound around his middle at the start of Purgatory, the frond that has been renewed just before the *Paradiso,* a frond that replaced the belt of chastity, the hypocrisy he has cast from his monkish robes to the monster Fraud. It is a frond stirring under the garments of Adam. The smile of love in the sphere of monks and contemplatives involves Dante in a paradox. He withdraws from mortal erotica, to prepare for immortal eroticism.

"Luce divina sopra me s'appunta,
penetrando per questa in ch'io m'inventro,
la cui virtù, col mio veder congiunta,
mi leva sopra me tanto, ch'i veggio
la somma essenze della quale è munta."

"Divine light above so focuses upon me
penetrating through this in which I am wombed
whose virtue, joined with my sight
so lifts me above myself, that I see
the Highest Essence from which I am milked."
(*Par.* 21:83–87)

Saint Peter Damian has had a nip too.

The experience of woman, the female spirit (as James Joyce in the footnote on Shakespeare and Anne Hathaway in *Ulysses* points out) seem to be common among those poets to whom the ecstasy of poetry has come down with that measure that I would call "prophetic." Thus they are *oppresso di stupore,* that untranslatable phrase, almost "oppressed, tumbled over," by the stuporous clap of Divine love, made female by the Divine, the *Shechinah,* in its *percosse,* percussion upon their person.

The poet showers images of milk, breasts, the puling of the infant in *Paradiso*. But before Beatrice will open her breasts for Dante (remember the small-minded scorn of Forese Donati in *Purgatorio* toward the "donne fiorentine, / l'andar mostrando con le poppe il petto," "the Florentine ladies / who go showing with their breasts the paps" [*Purg.* 23:101–2]), she has a score to settle. What of the vows, his oaths, to her? He has broken them.

But I am anticipating. Dante's chronology means that I can know, hope, only so much at a time. In the first and second cantos of *Paradiso*, as he enters the realm of the blessed, the poet attends to those questions that are consuming him. What is his substance? How does he ascend?

In Beatrice's beauty, Dante sees his happiness. "[S]ì lieta come bella," "as happy as she was beautiful." He stares at her; they flash together in an ecstatic mounting.

Beatrice in suso, e io in lei guardava
e forse in tanto in quanto un quadrel posa
e vola e da la noce si dischiava,
giunto mi vidi ove mirabil cosa
mi torse il viso a sé.

. . .

Beatrice above, and I on her, staring
and perhaps in the time that a bolt stays
and flies and from the notch discharges
I saw myself come where a marvelous thing
turned my sight to itself.
(*Par.* 2:22–26)

Beatrice's happiness shines on Dante, joins him in a flash. She turns and lectures on the most important topic of *Paradiso*. "come nostra natura e Dio s'unio," "how our nature and God are unified" (*Par.* 2:42). The union of bodies, Beatrice's, Dante's, cannot be demonstrated, yet he knows, feels it must be so. Eros and metaphysics join. I can echo with Dante, "S'io era corpo, e qui non si concepe / com'una dimensione altra patio, / ch'esser convien se corpo in corpo repe," "If I was body, and here we can not conceive, how one dimension endures another, / as must be if body creeps into body" (*Par.* 2:37–39). The union of bodies creeping into one another, the cry of the eel napped in the paste? In the sphere of the moon, the imagination of a Divinity's union with man will serve as the metaphor of the union of solid bodies, "com' acqua recepe / raggio di luce permanendo unita," "as water receives, a ray of light remaining whole" (*Par.* 2:35–36), so will Dante and Beatrice sail into the bulk of the moon. The formative principle of light and dark, of the world, of the moon, of the spheres, is the smile on his mistress' lips and the sparkle in her eye.[6] Not density and rarity, Dante has Beatrice explain, make up the Universe, but the brilliance of a lover's smile. Forget the solid bodies of the earth, cautions Beatrice, here even the spots on the moon are light, or lack of it.

"S'io era corpo," "if I were body. . ." Am I body? Am I solid? Is Beatrice solid? This is no peccadillo. This is the pathos of the comedy. Dante has come for Beatrice. As her light scalds, warms his face, he feels she is almost in grasp.

Is it possible, Beatrice corporal in Heaven? Dante will dally with this hope through most of his winding in Paradise. In his courtship, it is his secret. "May I enter you here?" he asks. Beatrice answers, "Yes, yes, as light, as happiness." Dante's unspoken question is, Have I really had your body? "S'io era corpo."

The answer waits at a further gyre.

Canto 3 does not take up directly the theme of body but that of inconstancy. Having introduced him to the consummation of light, why is Beatrice so sharp

---

6. "Per la natura onde deriva / la virtù mista per lo corpo luce / come letizia per pupilla viva." "By the joyous nature whence it derives, the mixed virtue through the body shines, as joy through a living pupil" (*Par.* 2:142–44).

with Dante? She lays aside the interpenetrating of bodies on the moon: "il voto," "the vow" is her theme. Before he has a right to bask in light, Dante must be teased and lectured on the subject of fidelity. The canto begins with reproof and refutation warming the breast of the poet. Under the guise of a lecture on substance, reality, she pricks his conscience again. She repeats her complaint from *Purgatorio.* How could you? How could you do what you did after I offered my young eyes, my young body, to you? How empty, what emptiness those vows to worship me. The waters of Lethe[7] may wash away the sin, but Beatrice is too human to let the subject pass. She has been hurt, and that pain echoes in her smiles still and her remarks. You are worried about what is real and what is not? Look at you, she laughs. What do you know of reality, poor child? The dream of me was more real than the bodies of all those young chicks you put in my place. Here you stare away from the real to vacancy.

> "Non ti maravigliar perch'io sorrida,"
> mi disse, "appresso il tuo püeril coto,
> poi sopra 'l vero ancor lo piè non fida
> ma te rivolve, come suole, a vòto:
> vere sustanze con ciò che tu vedi
> qui rilegate per manco di voto."

> "Do not marvel that I smile,"
> she said to me, "At your childish thought
> since upon the truth it yet does not trust its foot
> but turns you round, as is its wont, on vacancy.
> True bodies are what you see
> here relegated for failure of vows."
>   (*Par.* 3:25–30)

Why this curious business of punning on *vòto* and *voto,* vacancy and vows? For three cantos the word will return, obsessively, to the characters' lips. Piccarda Donati has been put in the "slowest of spheres," and she repeats the pun of Beatrice.

> "E questa sorte che par giù cotanto
> però n'è data, perché fuor negletti
> li nostri voti, e vòti in alcun canto."
>   . . .

---

7. See the process in *Purgatorio,* canto 31, and the reference again in canto 33, line 96.

"And this the lot which appears so low
is given us because our vows were
neglected, and vacant in some part."
(*Par.* 3:55–57)

Before you worry about *the substance,* Dante, of my *body,* how about the *substance* of your *vows?* They were vacant. Beatrice chides and Piccarda warns, vows in Heaven are reality. Dante, alas, is a little deaf. He is *"materia sorda,"* "dull material," as Beatrice wryly observed in *Paradiso's* first canto. He doesn't hear the rebuke. Instead he sees that Piccarda is looking very pretty in Paradise. A cavalier, he ignores her pun and answers, "'Ne' mirabili aspetti / vostri risplende non so che divino / che vi trasmuta da' primi concetti"; "In your wondrous aspects, / I don't know, something divine / which transforms you from our former impressions'" (*Par.* 3:58–60). Little Piccarda looks like "a well created creature" made to taste the sweetness, *"dolcezza,"* of Paradise. Twice she smiles, first coyly, "pronta e con occhi ridenti," "eager and with smiling eyes" (*Par.* 3:42). Then when he asks if she wouldn't like to take a spin to a higher sphere, where the pace is faster, "Pria sorrise un poco; / da indi mi rispuose tanto lieta, / ch'arder parea d'amor nel primo foco"; "First she smiled a little: / then she replied to me with such happiness/ that she seemed to burn in the first fire of love" (*Par.* 3:67–69).[8]

Does Beatrice resent it? When Dante looks back at her from the smile of Piccarda, Beatrice is so brilliant he can't bear to look. She has turned up the candlepower. "My sight which followed her as long / as it was possible, when it lost her / drew to the goal of greater desire / and to Beatrice turned itself totally / but she blazed in my look so / that at first my sight could not suffer it / which made me slower to question her" (*Par.* 3:124–30). This sexual teasing goes on from the *Purgatorio* into *Paradiso,* a lingering of the Provençal on the poet's lyre. Something in that sudden blaze of Beatrice makes the poet nervous, "a dimandar più tardo," "slow to question her." The fact that he uses the expression in turning back, after following Piccarda, "che tanto lei seguio quanto possibil fu," "as long as possible," saying that she, Beatrice, is the "segno di maggior disio," "goal of greater desire," is suspicious. Not only does he fail to understand Beatrice's pun on vow and vacancy. He shows how fickle he is by flirting with Piccarda.

Wonder after this, that the next canto begins with a discussion of divided will. There is something distasteful, not "kosher" in the image of a *"liber'uomo,"* "free

---

8. These lines have a distinct echo of the erotic shepherdess evoked by Dante's friend, Guido Cavalcanti, in the poem quoted in a previous chapter.

man," who is caught between two foods, "*intra due cibi*," equally tempting (*Par.* 4:1–3). "'Io veggio ben come ti tira / uno e altro disio,'" "' I see well how you are drawn, / by one, then another desire,'" says Beatrice. What became of your vows to me? You who have given yourself to so many?

Piccarda in her dalliance has given Dante an excuse. Beatrice reads his thoughts. She is the stern creature of a will that cannot be wrenched aside, "come natura face in foco, / se mille volte violenza il torza," "as nature does in fire, / though violence wrench it a thousand times aside" (*Par.* 4:77–78). However, there is another will, an "absolute will" which, though one's behavior may not show it, still remains secretly constant. That's me, says Dante, "I'm the boy whose only joy was loving you." Since both Piccarda and Beatrice speak the truth, suddenly the holy stream burbles forth and "puose in pace uno e altro disio," "put in peace one and then the other desire" (*Par.* 4:117). Is not all human love a distraction from the Divine? And Dante can truthfully say that in all these ladies he has only been pursuing Beatrice.

In the next canto Dante will make the admission, "Io che pur da mia natura / trasmutabile son per tutte giuse!" "I who am of my nature / subject to every kind of shift!" (*Par.* 5:98–99). Fickle, transmutable. All through the *Commedia,* Dante is nervous about his place. Perhaps he can get a seat in Limbo among the pagan philosophers, perhaps in Hell with an old teacher. Muhammad claims him as a brother. In *Purgatorio* he lingers in a dozen spots. Now at the entrance to the gyres of Heaven, he whose vows have been so consistently lacking, falling short, "manco di voto. . . . voti in alcun canto," "vacant in one way or another," surely he will be confined to this slowest of the spheres. Piccarda certainly looks more attractive than he remembers. Here she blazes with the first fire of love. But Beatrice has something better for Dante Alighieri. If only her child, her dull pupil, will hear.

He does. The echo of Beatrice's, Piccarda's, words, sound in his own. He asks the right question.

> "Io vo' saper se l'uom può sodisfarvi
> ai voti manchi sì con altri beni
> ch'a la vostra statera non sien parvi."
>
> "I wish to know if a man can satisfy you so
> or vows unfulfilled with other good deeds
> that in your scale they will not seem too little."
> (*Par.* 4:136–38)

At last the *"voti manchi"* are admitted to his consciousness. Can't I make it up with some other good, sweets, *"altri beni"*? And the reply?

> Beatrice mi guardò con li occhi pieni
> di faville d'amor cosi divini,
> che, vinta, mia virtute diè le reni,
> e quasi mi perdei con li occhi chini.
>
> Beatrice looked at me with eyes full
> of the sparks of love and so divine
> that, overcome, my power gave up the reins
> and I almost lost myself with eyes bent down.
>   (*Par.* 4:139–42)

He seems to bend, fall, *vinta,* vanquished, the percussion of those eyes tumbling him into stupor. His is that death in life one seeks, exalted, *strupo,* by the fall. (And this erotic faint echoes, "I fell like a dead body falls," his famous cry of the fifth canto of the *Inferno.*)

He not only asks the right question, he pays the correct compliment. "'O amanza del primo amante, o diva,'" "'O beloved of the First Lover, o divine one'"(*Par.* 4:118). It turns Beatrice's face ruby. She glows, sparks, as Dante rushes on to promise making things up. (But has he not pricked her too? After all, Beatrice has been sporting with the Almighty. Aristotle's Unmoved Mover has donned in Dante the costume of a lover, is out and about spinning, dallying in Ptolemy's spheres. Aristotle's Mover does not move after the First Push.) Hasn't Dante hinted that he has lost out to the Holy One in *La Vita Nuova?* Here the Deity appears not as the beneficent, older and wiser rival, but the very First Gallant of the Universe. What is Paradise but a sharing of love? Can Beatrice really begrudge Dante a side-glance at Piccarda? Aren't they all involved in the game? Beatrice gives him confirmation of his courtly teasing in the very next canto as she hands him this excuse.

> I see well how already there shines
> in your intelligence the eternal light
> which seen, alone and always, kindles love:
> and if some other thing seduced your love
> it is nothing but some trace of this
> badly understood, which shines through there.
>   (*Par.* 5:7–12)

All of Dante's seductions were just "badly understood" traces of the single Divine light. Evil is only a misunderstood form of good in the poet.[9] Your side glances, your failings in your vows, those eyes tumbling into one stupor after another were but the imperfect seeking of my light, cries Beatrice, my reflected glory of the *"prima amante,"* "First Lover."

Now Beatrice should let the matter of vows go. But she doesn't. She goes on harping in canto 5 about perverse vows, until Dante, as we have heard, admits to his fickle character. There is more to these vows, this vacancy than just Dante's bad behavior as a faithful lover.

> Non prendan li mortali il voto a ciancia;
> siate fedeli, e a ciò far non bieci,
> come Ieptè a la sua prima mancia;
> cui più si convenia dicer, "Mal feci,"
> che, servando, far peggio:
>
> Let mortals not take the vow as a game
> Be faithful, but in so doing, squint not
> as Jephthah in his first gift
> who would have better said, "I did ill,"
> than keeping it, to do worse:
>   (*Par.* 5:64–68)

This is a chapter about "not taking the vow as a game." It is also about the unreasonable, perverse vow. Squint not! Beatrice, whose eyes are blazing with Divine Love, with some humor refers to the reflection of a vow to the Divine that is perverse as "squint-eyed." Yet in that same breath she warns, beware the laughter of the Jews.

A few lines earlier she has spoken of the Hebrews too. "Però necessitato fu a li Ebrei / pur l'offerere, ancor ch'alcuna offerta / si permutasse, come saver dei." "Therefore it was still incumbent on Hebrews to offer, though the thing offered might be changed, as you should know" (*Par.* 5:49–51). The Jews, free will, and fulfillment of vows are mingling in Dante's head. (In cantos 5, 6, and 7 they will be mentioned again and again.) "L'alto valor del voto," "the high worth of the vow"

---

9. See *Midrash Rabbah* 1977, 9:7, "Is the evil inclination very good? Yes, for if it were not for the evil inclination, man would not build a house, or take a wife, or beget a child, or engage in business." Nahman of Bratslav, quoted by Martin Buber (1965, 39; quoted at Glatzer 1946, 108): "Without the evil urge there is no perfect service."

(*Par.* 5:26). The compact between God and man implied in the vow can never be annulled, except by being kept, fulfilled, "Quest' ultima già mai non si cancella / se non servata," "this last may never be canceled / except by being kept" (*Par.* 5:46–47). Yet the Hebrews were allowed to change the way that they fulfilled their vows, their sacrifices. Beware that these wise, sly creatures laugh not at you, "che 'l Giudeo di voi tra voi non rida!" "that the Jew among you, laugh not!" (*Par.* 5:81). Why? What vow would they laugh at you for keeping? "Non fate com' agnel che lascia il latte," "Be not like the lamb that leaves the milk" (*Par.* 5:82). What does Beatrice mean by showing her breast to Dante at this moment. "Be men not sheep," she has exclaimed a moment ago. Don't run from my breast like a baby. "Semplice e lascivio / seco medesmo a suo piacer combatte!" "who silly and lascivious / for his pleasure fights with himself" (*Par.* 5:83–84).

These are the pieces of the puzzle. Dante steps for a moment aside from his reverie and makes plain that we are to pay attention by making us conscious of his position as narrator. "Cosi Beatrice a me com' ïo scrivo; / poi si rivolse tutta disïante / a quella parte ove 'l mondo é più vivo." "Thus Beatrice to me, just as I write. / Then she turned all desire, / to that part where the world shines most" (*Par.* 5:85–87). And as they shoot into the second sphere, Dante reports:

> Quivi la donna mia vid' io sì lieta,
> come nel lume di quel ciel si mise,
> che più lucente se ne fé 'l pianeta.
> E se la stella si cambiò e rise
> qual mi fec' io che pur da mia natura
> trasmutabile son per tutte giuse!
>
> Here my lady I saw so happy
> when she passed within the light of that heaven,
> that the planet itself became more brilliant for it.
> And if the star changed and laughed
> what did it do to me, I who am of my very nature
> subject to every kind of shift!
>   (*Par.* 5:94–99)

Suddenly Dante is teasing again. Has he recovered from his scolding, since his downcast eyes rise and he jokes about himself, his mistress? The very planet is smiling with Beatrice's smile. By the end of the canto, Dante is in such high spirits that he threatens to turn on the reader and leave him hanging.

> Think, reader, if that which I here begin
> did not proceed, how you would have
> an anguished craving to know more.
> (*Par.* 5:109–11)

How did the "delirious child," the whipped schoolboy get so cocky? For a moment his melancholy is dispelled.

Has some perverse vow of his been lifted? Is it like that of Jephthah, whom he mentions, a pledge of murder? Did he not promise to follow his lady untimely into death? Dante Alighieri, in *La Vita Nuova,* moaned, Death, come, I find you sweet, hurry up, Death, Death, come get me, *"Moia, moia,"* cry the stones in sympathy.

Has Dante kept this pledge, his implicit vow of suicide to Beatrice? (This trip, to the other world, speaks to his promise, but does not fulfill the "letter" of the vow.)

Does it trouble him, now, face to face with her? Is this what she means by shaking, *"manco di voto,"* "failure of vows," at him, on the first level of Paradise? She offered her young body—does that mean he should have removed himself from temptation forthwith. He promised it. In this canto, Beatrice signals her forgiveness. No, such a vow is *"ciancia,"* "nonsense," a sport, a game. To fulfill it, keep it in its letter, like Jephthah or Agamemnon, would be perverse, squint-eyed. You should never have made it, but to fulfill it is worse. Do not make yourself ridiculous, especially in the eyes of the Jews in the matter of vows? Why the Jews?

Ostensibly, the lines refer to the scorn of the Jew watching his Christian neighbors take on vows with a light heart, knowing that the easy availability of pardons from unscrupulous ecclesiastics will afford them a facile annulment. The context suggests to me something more—especially as we have the echo of the Hebrews and vows from just a few lines before. "Therefore it was still incumbent on Hebrews to offer, though the thing offered might be changed, as you should know." The distinction is being drawn between the details in which a vow is fulfilled and the vow itself. Beware the laughter of the Jew before the vow to suicide, in making and in breaking it. The matter of the vow—suicide—was a mistake but its intention, to follow Beatrice always, *that* can never be annulled. Beatrice glows with desire now to draw Dante up to the greater light. His vow will be fulfilled in another way, just as the offerings of the Hebrew took a different form.

The Jewish smile, however, troubles Dante. Once the Hebrews have been invoked in his similes, their judgment, their vows, begin to haunt his lines. It is the Jew who will not follow the aspirant to the role of Messiah. It is the Jew who finds death bitter in every respect, counting out the hours to a demonstration of Messiah as Salvation on the earth. It is the Jew who wants God or His Messiah in the world of here and now. It is the Jew who will laugh loudest if Dante, turning "like a feather in every wind" (*Par.* 5:74) sports with vows to death and turns away from the sweet mother's milk of the female breast and the breast of the Divine. Justinian will announce in the next canto that Titus, the Roman emperor, has done vengeance on the Jews for the vengeance they were instruments of against the ancient sin of Adam. "Poscia con Tito a far vendetta corse / de la vendetta del peccato antico." "Afterwards with Titus it ran to make a vendetta / on the vendetta for the ancient sin" (*Par.* 6:92–93). But the formulation, "vengeance on the vengeance" is perhaps ironic. It is the language of knights, of the Crusader's tales of derring-do. In the sweeter melodies of the *Commedia* it sounds crude, unlettered. I wonder if Dante is not sharing the bitter smile of the Jews at the *"mala cupidigia,"* "evil cupidity" (*Par.* 5:79) of those knights with vengeance on their shields who began their quest for the Holy Land by burning and looting the Jewish quarters throughout Europe.

Read Dante in his silences. What is he thinking but dares not say? Beatrice reveals it to us inadvertently, the drift of his heretical mind.

> Però d'un atto uscir cose diverse:
> ch'a Dio ed a' Giudei piacque una morte;
> per lei tremò la terra e 'l ciel s'aperse.
> Non ti dee oramai parer più forte,
> quando si dice che giusta vendetta
> poscia vengiata fu da giusta corte.

> Thereupon from one act came diverse effects
> a death rejoicing both God and the Jews,
> the earth quaked from it and the sky opened.
> No longer should it seem to you very hard
> when it is said that a just vendetta
> afterwards was avenged by a just court.
> (*Par.* 7:46–51)

Has it seemed *"più forte,"* "very hard" to Dante that this vendetta that Justinian mentioned a canto back should be practiced on the Jews?[10] The same double

---

10. How sharp the difference between Dante Alighieri and his putative teacher, Thomas Aquinas, is on this issue can be gauged by the quotation from the latter's letter to the duchess of Brabant (Belgium) "who had consulted him about the morality of confiscating the property of the Jews, which was done everywhere. In his reply St. Thomas says, 'It would be licit, according to law, to hold

play almost, *"vendetta"* and *"vengiata,"* that we heard from the Roman emperor, Titus—what is Beatrice telling us? What secret sympathy is this in canto 7 where Dante would speak the language of the Jews?

I look in the seventh gyre to its gates. They are inscribed in Hebrew.

> "Osanna, sanctus Deus sabaòth,
> superillustrans claritate tua
> felices ignes horum malacòth!"

> "Hosanna, holy God of Sabaoth
> illuminating brilliantly with your light
> the happy fires of these kingdoms!"
>   (*Par.* 7:1–3)

They are but the pathetic shards of Hebrew, the Tuscan's *"Osanna . . . Sabaoth . . . malacoth,"* but he is not ashamed to place them at the entry of his seventh round. Lift up your heads, o ye gates, for Dante wishes to come into you speaking Hebrew. For it is to be the sabbatical canto. The poetry skips and leaps on holiday.

> Io dubitava, e dicea "Dille, dille!"
> fra me: "dille," dicea "a la mia donna
> che mi diseta con le dolci stille."
> Ma quella reverenza che s'indonna
> di tutto me, pur per Be e per ice,
> mi richinava come l'uom ch'assonna.

> I was wavering, and said, "Speak to her, speak to her!"
> within me, "Speak to her," I said, "to my lady
> who quenches me with the sweet drops."
> But that reverence which so masters

---

the Jews, because of their crime [deicide], in perpetual slavery, and therefore the princes may regard the possessions of the Jews as belonging to the state; nonetheless, they should use them with a certain moderation and not deprive the Jews of those things necessary to life. . . . I consider that the punishment must be greater for a Jew and for any usurer than for another culprit, particularly since it is known that the money taken from him does not belong to him. One can also add to the fine another penalty, lest it not appear to suffice for his punishment that he be deprived of the money owed by him to another' ('De Regimine Judaeorum,' sec. 2, *Opuscula omnia*, ed. J. Perrier, Paris, vol.1, page 213–14, see also A. P. D'Entreves, *Aquinas, Selected Political Writings* [Oxford, 1959], pp. 84ff." (Haberman 1979, 188).

all of me, just through Be and through ice,
again bent me down as a man who sleeps.
(*Par.* 7:10–15)

The tripping of the *ds*, willy dilly, dallying with his *donna*, the *indonna* pun on
mastery, domination and *donna*, the scrambling of *Be* and *ice*, for Beatrice's nickname, all provoke not only laughter but the most carefree moment of the *Commedia*. Here the fall into the faint of joy, of sleep, is wholly happy. The thud of a corpse
does not distract one. In the seventh, sabbatical circling, under the smiles of the
Jews, Beatrice's nipples dribble of the sweet new style, to this heretical compliment:

> Poco sufferse me cotal Beatrice
> e cominciò, raggiandomi d'un riso
> tal, che nel foco faria l'uom felice:
>
> A bit Beatrice suffered me thus
> then began, shining with a smile
> such, that in the fire, would make man happy:
> (*Par.* 7:16–18)

Dante, even in the fire of Hell, would her smile make you happy? Are you
thinking of Hell even here? Has the notion of a "just vengeance" sunk you to that
depth, even as her smile makes you merry? Are you with the Jews?

The canto is a lecture on the necessity of Jesus and his act of redemption, both
for the original sin of Adam and Eve, and for the crucifixion of Jesus. In particular
it is a criticism of the Jewish refusal to acknowledge Jesus. It is Beatrice's lecture,
however, not Dante's. It is a lecture on the Divine bounty and Beatrice's bounty. I
distinguish because Divine goodness, unlike Beatrice's, burns without envy, according to the Florentine. It is a form of self-sacrifice, not compounded with revenge, *livore.*

> La Divina bontà che da sé sperne
> ogni livore, ardendo in sé sfavilla
> sì che dispiega le bellezze etterne.
>
> The divine goodness that from itself spurns
> all spite, burning in its very sparkling
> so that it spreads out its eternal beauties.
> (*Par.* 7:64–66)

Not so Beatrice's *bonta,* goodness. She plays once more on the word *vòta,* here in its sense of emptiness rather than vow, though the connotation rings in our ear. Sin steals man's freedom and light.

> e in sua dignità mai non rivene
> se non rïempie, dove colpa vòta
> contra mal dilettar con giuste pene.

> and he never returns to his dignity
> if he does not fill up, where the fault makes a void
> with just penalty against evil delight.
> (*Par.* 7:82–84)

What *"mal dilettar"* is going through her mind? *"Vostra natura,"* she scolds Dante, speaking of original sin in Paradise. But does she not share that nature too? She means us to recall his confession of *"mia natura"* in canto 5, "I who am of my nature, / subject to ever kind of shift." But Dante, like all men, in Beatrice's vision could never give satisfaction. "Nor could man within his limits, ever give satisfaction." The argument is hinging, however, not only on Divine Bounty but on Beatrice's. Without her grace, Dante could never have won forgiveness or given satisfaction.

Such is the argument of courtly romance. Beatrice, however, is only an aspect, as she admits, of something beyond her. Here the *Commedia* touches Kabbalah, its extension of Neoplatonism, the notion of man and woman, their erotic coupling, as a means to the original unity of the human being and God. If Beatrice can forgive, spurn envy, vengeance, spite from her, it is because beyond those images of motherhood, those dripping breasts by which Dante is holding on to salvation, is Divine Unity.

> "Ma vostra vita sanza mezzo spira
> la somma beninanza, e la innamora
> di sé sì che poi sempre la disira.
> E quinci puoi argomentare ancora
> vostra resurrezion, se tu ripensi
> come l'umana carne fessi allora
> che li primi parenti intrambo fensi."

> "But without an intermediary your life
> the Highest Beneficence breathes forth

of Himself so that it desires him ever after.
And from this you can also argue
your resurrection, if you recall
how the human flesh was made so, when
the first parents both were so made."
                    (*Par.* 7:142–48)

You are desired through the *Shechinah,* the Divine Female Presence by the Ancient, the Holy One who breathed you from Himself into existence. And this argues your resurrection. The seventh canto closes with hope for the body, the bodies of Adam and Eve, breathed from the dust of the ground into life. This canto of paradox ends with the invocation of the Divine Love that, restoring one to its mysterious bosom, restores one also, at that moment, to the body, individual and unique.

The smile of Beatrice, the Jews, burning on my face, I am ready to fly up through *Paradiso* image by image, obsession by obsession after Dante, drawn up by the body of his mistress.

CHAPTER NINE

Holy Number

DANTE DOUBLES SEVEN upon seven—the fourteenth canto—and makes substance again his argument. As Saint Thomas falls silent, Beatrice calls out to the spirits.

> "A costui fa mestieri, e nol vi dice
> né con la voce né pensando ancora,
> d'un altro vero andare a la radice.
> Diteli se la luce onde s'infiora
> vostra sustanza, rimarrà con voi
> etternalmente sì com'ell' è ora;
> e se rimane, dite come, poi
> che sarete visiblili rifatti,
> esser porà ch'al veder non vi nòi."

> "This man has a need and does not tell you
> either with voice, or yet by thought,
> to go to the root of another truth.
> Tell him if the light in which your substance
> flowers, bedecked, remains with you
> eternally as it is now;
> and if it remains, tell how, when
> you are made visible again
> it can be that it will not harm you to see."
> (*Par.* 14:10–18)

The question seems almost trivial. Will you be too bright for each other's sight, restored to real bodies? Yet Beatrice asks the question with pleasure, "It pleased," "*piacque*" (*Par.* 14:9) Beatrice to begin. The pleasurable flash is because it is the query of the lover in the *Commedia*'s Heaven. Will I get my body back? Will

I retain the light in which my body flowers? And the reader is meant to retain that unusual image, *infiora*.

It pleases Beatrice to ask, and the voice of the most extreme pleasure, playfully referred to as "modest," replies. But before it breathes, the circle of spirits takes up a courtly dance, a roundelay.

> Come, da più letizia pinti e tratti,
> a la fïata quei che vanno a rota
> levan la voce e rallegrano li atti,
> così, al'orazion pronta e divota,
> li santi cerchi mostrar nova gioia
> nel torneare e ne la mira nota.

> As when thrust and drawn by increasing joy
> those who go in circle lift their voices
> from time to time and rejoice their steps,
> so, to the immediate and devout petition
> the holy circles showed new joy
> in their turning and their wondrous song.
> (*Par.* 14:19–24)

This is the court of Amour and so the erotic underlies the religious. The voice likened to that of the angel's before the mother of a Messiah, "una voca modesta," "a modest voice" (*Par.* 14:35) is a gentle voice, but the voice that is also announcing to the lady her ravishment to come by the Holy Spirit. This is Dante, being playful, linking this *modesta* by simile with the voice that speaks now of the earthly body to Dante and Beatrice. They hear not the voice of the angel Gabriel, but that of the earthly king of pleasure, Solomon. It is his voice that psalmed the body, calling out of a circle of dancers, *"pinti e tratti,"* "thrust and drawn." Solomon of "The Song of Songs" is given the song of praise in the *Commedia* to the restored body at the long *"festa di paradiso"* (*Par.* 14:37), "the festival of paradise," which is and has and will be going on. Solomon's Song.

> "Quanto fia lunga la festa
> di paradiso, tanto il nostro amore
> si raggerà dintorno cotal vesta.
> La sua chiarezza séguita l'ardore;
> l'ardor la visïone, e quella è tanta,
> quant' ha di grazia sovra suo valore.

Come la carne glorïosa e santa
fia rivestita, la nostra persona
più grata fia per esser tutta quanta
per che s'accrescerà ciò che ne dona
di gratüito lume il sommo bene,
lume ch'a lui veder ne condiziona;
onde la visïon crescer convene,
crescer l'ardor che di quella s'accende,
crescer lo raggio che da esso vene.
Ma sì come carbon che fiamma rende,
e per vivo candor quella soverchia,
sì che la sua parvenza si difende;
così questo folgór che già ne cerchia
fia vinto in apparenza de la carne
che tutto di la terra ricoperchia;
né potrà tanta luce affaticarne;
ché li organi del corpo saran forti
a tutto ciò che potrà dilettarne."
Tanto mi parver sùbiti e accorti
e l'uno e l'altro coro a dicer, 'Amme!'
che ben mostrar disio d'i corpi morti;
forse non pur per lor, ma per le mamme,
per li padri e per li altri che fuor cari
anzi che fosser sempiterne fiamme.

"As long as shall last the feast
of Paradise, so long our love
shall beam about this vestment.
Its brilliance accompanies our ardor
the ardor, the vision, and each has just so much
as he has grace beyond his worth.
When the flesh, glorious and holy
will be again invested, our person
will be more gracious, for being more complete;
wherefore that which the Highest Good
gives of gratuitous light will increase,
light which is the means of our seeing Him;
so that vision must increase,—
the ardor—increase that it kindles—
the radiance—increase which comes from this.
But just as the coal which gives flame

> yet with its white glow outshines it[1]
> so that its appearance is maintained
> so this glow which already circles us
> will be overcome in appearance by the flesh
> which is still covered by the earth
> nor will so great a light be able to tire us
> since the organs of the body will be strong
> for everything able to delight us."
> So sudden and eager they appeared to me
> one choir and the other, to say, 'Amen!'
> to show indeed desire for their dead bodies;
> perhaps not for themselves alone but for mommas
> and for their fathers and for others that were dear
> before they became everlasting flames.
> (*Par.* 14:37–66)

The fourteenth canto, the canto of craving for flesh, that jest of Solomon's, Jewish wisdom, "Don't worry, 'our organs will be strong' enough for anything that's coming to delight us," is also the canto of the mysterious flash, double and triple exposure in the sky. "Sì che la vista pare e non par vera," "so that the sight seems and seems not real" (*Par.* 14:72), where Dante is moved to exclaim, "Oh vero sfavillar del Santo Spiro!" "Ah very spark of the Holy Breath!" (*Par.* 14:76). Sound and sight are confounded here, spark and breath in the white living glow. And at this moment, Beatrice smiles so brightly his memory is wiped out.

> Ma Bëatrice sì bella e ridente
> mi si mostrò, che tra quelle vedute
> si vuol lasciar che non seguir la mente.
>
> But Beatrice so beautiful and smiling
> showed herself to me, that among those sights
> it must be left that did not accompany my mind.
> (*Par.* 14:79–81)

The word *seguir* is the key. A moment ago, ardor was seen to "accompany," "*seguir*," vision. Here, however, ardor has outstripped vision.[2] Breath or spirit,

---

1. "*Vivo candor*" is translated "white glow" but carries the connotation of "living" and perhaps even "passionate" white.

2. Note the doubling of the word "ardor" in lines 40 and 41, its repetition in 50, and the image of the spirits' ardor for their bodies and their parents' bodies at the end of the passage.

spiro, has gone beyond sight. Dante has been ravished. And the mark of his rape is blindness. He has flamed, rises, *crescare,* been augmented in grace far beyond the dancing circle of Solomon. But the means of telling us that his sight went is curious.

His memory is wiped out—this is the mark of angelic intensity, as Dante teaches, to burn in an everlasting present.

The blackout, blindness is succeeded by an invocation to fire and lust, a mingling of Hebrew and pagan names for the Holy One, as if the God who calls for human sacrifice and the sun god were the same. Again "ardor," "l'ardor del sacrificio" becomes as real a stuff as flesh.

> Con tutto il core, e con quella favella
> ch'è una in tutti, a Dio feci olocausto,
> qual conveniesi al a grazia novella.
> E non er' anco del mio petto essausto
> l'ardor del sacrificio, ch'io conobbi
> esso litare stato accetto e fausto;
> ché con tanto lucore e tanto robbi
> m'apparvero splendor dentro a due raggi,
> ch'io dissi: "O Eliòs che sì li addobbi!"
>
> With all my heart and with that tongue
> which is one in all, to God I made a holocaust,
> such as was fitting to the new grace.
> And not yet in my breast was consumed
> the ardor of the sacrifice, but I knew
> that the offering had been accepted and fortunate;
> with such great brightness and so ruddy
> splendors appeared to me within two rays
> that I said, "O Elios who so adorns them!"
> (*Par.* 14:88–97)

Sacrifice at the moment of lust and ardor, *olocausto* (that word so frightening in its modern context), a burnt offering, a holocaust, I made of my breast and tongue to God. The desire to burn to charcoal? Recall the memory at the entrance into Eden, charred bodies, how strongly the recall of them disturbed Dante? Now he is eager to be charred. He sees the rays of the sun make a cross in the sky. But he calls out to the sight, ending his invocation with a coinage of Hebrew and Greek. "*Elios!*" The translator John D. Sinclair in his notes remarks, "Elios is his own coinage and is apparently meant to combine the Hebrew *El,* God—expressly referred to in the twenty-sixth canto—or *Eli,* my God—familiar from the cry of

Jesus in the story of the crucifixion—and the Greek *Helios,* the Sun. The verb *ad-dobare* has meanings varying from *adorn* to *furnish* and *equip,* and is cognate with the English 'dub' for the act of a sovereign in granting a knighthood."[3] C. H. Grandgent sheds additional light on this matter of Hebrew and Greek. "*Elios,* 'Sun'; God, the source of light. According to the *Magnae Derivationes* of Ugoccione da Pisa . . . the Greek word for 'sun,' comes from the Hebrew *Eli,* 'God.' " (Grandgent 754, note 96). The sacrifice transfixed at the intersection of the two rays adorns them. The Hebrew God in the persona of a scorching sun dubs the knight of love red and rosy with lust. Crucified, dubbed in the smile of Beatrice, Dante is willing to go up in flame.

The cross? It would seem that Dante is making excuses to his beloved for dreaming of following (the familiar *"segue,"* "accompanying," *Par.* 14:106) the sacrificial Messiah and his cross of pure spirit rather than looking into her eyes. But has he followed? Follow the final verses of the canto through their tortured convolution. What in fact is he doing but justifying his leaving the very sparkle of the Holy Breath and the flash in the dawn for his resting place in Beatrice's eyes? It is the body, not the spirit, that Dante is singing. And for this he has theological, not simply erotic justification. "The blessed will be more perfect after the resurrection than before and therefore more like to God, who is absolute perfection." The proof is brought from Saint Thomas Aquinas: "The soul rejoined to a glorified body is more akin to God than when separated therefrom, insofar as when rejoined it has more perfect being. For the more perfect a thing is the more it is like to God." The Grandgent edition notes this (*Commedia,* 748). "The bodiless soul in Heaven has full spiritual happiness; but when clad again in the flesh, it will possess bodily happiness as well: its joy will be increased 'extensively.'" The body will increase spiritual joy, for as Saint Thomas concludes. "Every imperfect thing, desires its perfection. Hence the separated soul naturally desires to be rejoined with the body."[4]

In Dante's *Paradiso,* not Thomas of Aquinas but a Hebrew king embodying wisdom of pleasure, plenitude of wives, Solomon—magnet of Sheba, is called on

---

3. *Par.* 1972b, 211. Sinclair does not note that the cry would be familiar to Jesus as the shout of King David, the prototype of the Messiah, from Ps. 22:1. Is Dante assuming the crown? My next chapter will speak to this. Perhaps the Tuscan hellenized the Hebrew to palliate the despair of its echo, "My God, My God, why have you forsaken me?"

4. *Summa Theologicae,* Tertia, Suppl. Qu. xciii, Art. I: "Anima conjuncta corpori glorioso est magis Deo similis quam ab eo separata, inquantum conjuncta habet esse perfectius: quanto enim est aliquid perfectius, tanto est Deo similius." The Grandgent edition quoting this, also gives the Latin of the second citation. "Omne autem imperfectum appetit suam perfectionem. Et ideo anima separata naturaliter appetit corporis conjunctionem."

to give the lecture on corporal joy. In this canto of mysterious vision, and theological joy, it is still in Beatrice's eyes that Dante finds rest. Her eyes become organs of sex. They burn. How suggestive his phrase, *"vivi suggelli,"* "living seals." How tight that resting place:

> Perhaps my words appear too bold
> "putting down" the pleasure of those beautiful eyes
> in which, staring, my desire has rest
> but he who perceives that these living seals
> of every beauty, do more as they go higher
> and that I had not turned there to them,
> can excuse me of that which I accuse myself
> to excuse myself, and may see that I speak truth
> since the holy pleasure is not shut out here
> but becomes, thus, mounting, purer.
> (*Par.* 14:130–39)[5]

This *"più sincero,"* "purer," is suspect. The loops and handsprings of his excuses, signal it. Dante has been blinded a moment before, and the blindness of Dante is never pure joy. Later on he will be truly frightened when he loses sight, is confounded by sound. Under the dancing circles of the fourteenth canto I hear a deep sadness. Dante makes the saints cry out for their bodies, cry out for pleasure, not for their own sakes, but for the sake of embracing parents. They desire to return to the happiness of infants. It is the cry of the Dante who lost his mother as a child hardly past infancy. In this paradise there is pathos. It is still a realm of death. Not until the body returns will its white winding bands of light be annulled into a wedding of absolute joy. Here he sees the sparkling of the Holy Breath, something unthinkable. Beatrice's smile flashes so that, as the reader learns in the next canto, within the burning of those "living seals" he thinks, "toccar lo fondo / de la mia gloria e del mio paradiso" "to touch the very depth of my glory and of my paradise" (*Par.* 15:35–36). Then why the cry, "Mammy!" a cry for the breast, for the flesh?

Though the holy pleasure grows more intense as they mount, only the holy body will crown the real Paradise, not the one that Dante is let into, *"mio par-*

---

5. "Forse la mia parola par troppo osa / posponendo il piacer de li occhi belli / ne' quai mirando, mio disio ha posa / ma chi s'avvede che i vivi suggelli/ d'ogni bellezza più fanno più suso / e ch'io non m'era lì rivolto a quelli / escusar puommi di quel ch'io m'accuso / per escusarmi, e vedermi dir vero; / ché 'l piacer santo non è qui dischiuso, / perché si fa, montando, più sincero" (*Par.* 14:130–39).

adiso," as he puns. And the promise of the body for which he, like Gilgamesh, has come wandering up these gyres, that promise eludes him.[6]

Why? Like an antique Wizard of Oz, Beatrice gives him an answer of sorts. In the twenty-first canto of *Paradiso*,[7] a theatrical hoax is practiced on Dante. The scantest sound of holy zeal fills him with terror of its thunder. "How could you endure my smile and song at its full power since a mere cry sends you rushing for my skirts," mocks Beatrice. How can you ask for your body, my body, when you cannot take the full measure of light and sound that awaits you in Heaven?

In the next canto, as if to compensate Dante for her trick, she seems to become palpable for a second. She actually thrusts him up the stairway from behind. Even Sinclair, a conservative commentator, notices this sexual push from behind.[8]

> La dolce donna dietro a lor mi pinse
> con un sol cenno su per quella scala,
> sì sua virtù la mia natura vinse.

> The sweet lady behind them thrust me
> with only a sign above, on that stairway
> so her power overwhelmed my nature.
> (*Par.* 22:100–102)

Thrust on by Beatrice, I am pushed past cantos to which I will return later.[9] For there is trouble in Paradise. Deeper pathos.

---

6. Not only the flesh of Beatrice is denied Dante. He encounters from his own family, among the spirits of Heaven and Purgatory, only Cacciaguida. That encounter is strategically placed after the fourteenth canto of *Paradiso*. It would seem as if his mother would be the one of the objects of his search. Is she omitted because admission of that need would detract from Beatrice? Dante's fleeing into Beatrice's skirts at the beginning of the twenty-second like a frightened child to a mother argues strongly that the poet deliberately chose not to encounter his own mother.

7. Note that this is three times seven.

8. Sinclair remarks that Beatrice "literally" thrusts Dante up the staircase to the higher heavens. (*Par.* 1972b, 328).

9. This push has the text whirling too fast now to stop at the sixteenth canto, where I would have liked to note the importance to the discussion of the courtly dance between Dante Alighieri and Beatrice Portinari. Dante's self-criticism, which sounds in the cough of Beatrice there, marks a constant of the *Commedia*. Dante regards himself as a character in his poem—one its author is willing to mock. Through Beatrice's as through Virgil's eyes, he sees himself. Her cough, her rebuke of his pride in birth, her smile, her mind reading—all distinguish between the poet as author and as character. The *Commedia* is a drama in which we can ask why a character says something and probe particulars of speech. The cough of Beatrice alerts us to Dante's sin of pride. The use of the honorific *voi*, signals his desire to alter the familiar *tu*, to give his ancestor and himself more honor. Dante's foible may not be

Ahi quanto ne la mente mi commossi,
quando mi volsi per veder Beatrice,
per non poter veder, benché io fossi
presso di lei, e nel mondo felice!

Ah, how agitated I was in my mind,
when I turned to see Beatrice,
and was unable to see her, though I was indeed
beside her and in the happy world!
(*Par.* 25:136–39)

How "happy" is Dante in this "happy world"? His cry comes in the twenty-fifth canto, where the souls talk not of faith but of hope, hope of restitution of the body, hope of consummation with the nuptial Beatrice who stands here, silent and motionless, tense as a figurehead. She is a bride staring into the fire of the dancing wedding guests, Saint Peter, Saint James, Saint John, prancing "sol per fare onore / a la novizia," "only to show honor to the new bride" (*Par.* 25:104–5). "E la mia donna in lor tenea l'aspetto, / pur come sposa tacita e immota," "And my lady fixed her glance on them, / as a bride silent and still" (*Par.* 25:110–11), and Dante is miserable.

The canto of hope begins with a description of his meager condition on earth, the disappointment of his hopes, and ends with the poet troubled and blind in Paradise, the "happy world."

Why?

Dante is finally told that Beatrice's body is not in Paradise. He is told it indirectly, by Saint John.[10] Dante has believed the folktale that Saint John was "bodily" transported to heaven. If John could do it, why not the "amanza del primo amante," "the beloved of the First Lover," Beatrice! Now staring passionately into the fire of Saint John for evidence of the body he had brought from earth, Dante is rebuked, goes blind.

Why do you dazzle yourself
to see a thing which has no place here?

---

as deadly as Lancelot's, but the parallel to Guinevere suggests that Beatrice may share the same adulterous tale. It is the warning of virtue but coupled with the smile of indulgence. It recalls Paolo and Francesca. This is the second time the tale of Lancelot is alluded to and so echoes Francesca's remark that the knight's story is a harbinger of adultery. Dante's lapse is not merely adultery but adultery and pride, *"la superba strupa,"* "the elevated adultery." Only in his confidence of an elevated courtship in the stars does he make light of nobility of blood on earth.

10. Beatrice, it would seem, cannot bring herself to tell him this painful fact.

> In earth, earth is my body and will be
> until with the others, our number
> equals the eternal proposal.
> (*Par.* 25:122–26)[11]

Can Dante be happy in heaven? He dazzles, blinds himself, looking for the impossible. Not only in Heaven. He is still hoping for the laurel crown on earth. It is a cruel canto of impossible hope. He recalls his miserable state among the living, lean for many years, barred from the fair sheepfold of Florence by the wolves. Now he learns that the body of Beatrice cannot be encountered on this trip. The earth is weighing him down. The downward look he took a few cantos before is dragging him with it, the glance to the threshing floor of our planet.

> As one who ogles and strains
> to see the sun a bit in its eclipse
> who, by seeing becomes without sight,
> so became I in that last fire.
> (*Par.* 25:118–21)[12]

Consider the image of Beatrice as bride, bride through sight, the emphasis on the nonpresence of the body. Why are you straining your sight after my body? And in the orgiastic fire of John, Dante loses sight—his sightless state becomes truly melancholy when he hears for certain that the body of Beatrice is not in the Catholic heaven. Bodies will not be given out until it tallies with heavenly purpose. And his blindness sets him in contradiction to the happy world.

Dante is miserable in Paradise. He has seen something, but it has the texture of a dream. Is it Beatrice? The corporal nature of souls after death—this was somewhat disputed in Purgatory. He had some hope of a more bodily reunion. Now it must be postponed. Too much light puts out his eyes.[13]

      •   •   •

IN A COMEDY, pathos cannot be the touchstone. Enter Adam, the original rude joker, rustling in his pants. "O ripe apple . . . speak to me!" cries Dante (*Par.*

---

11. "'Perché t'abbagli / per veder cosa che qui no ha loco? / In terra è terra il mio corpo, e saragli / tanto con li altri, che 'l numero nostro / con l'etterno proposito s'agguagli.' "

12. "Qual è colui ch'adocchia e s'argomenta / di vedere eclissar lo sole un poco, / che, per veder, non vedente diventa; / tal mi fec' ïo a quell' ultimo foco."

13. "And," an auditor notes, "his capacity for a physical approach."

26:91). And like a burlesque comedian the *"padre antico"* (*Par.* 26:92) mimes the essential message with a bump and grind before he "breathes forth."

> Talvolta un animal coverto broglia
> sì che l'affetto convien che si paia
> per lo seguir che face a lui la 'nvoglia;
> e similmente l'anima primaia
> mi facea trasparer per la coverta
> quant'ella a compiacermi venìa gaia.

> Sometimes an animal stirs under its covering
> so that its feeling must be apparent
> since its covering follows it
> and similarly the first soul
> made transparent to me through its cover
> how gaily it came to give me pleasure.
> (*Par.* 26:97–102)

The "stir in the pants" is significant.[14] As Sinclair notes "Dante deliberately breaks through the limits of classical poetic propriety in order to preserve the vigor of reality in the ethereal heights." What is this vigor and how vulgar is the imagery? Adam's covering is light but it is also skin, nudity. "O apple that ripe / alone was produced" (*Par.* 26:91–92) cannot but recall the fatal apple of Eden and Adam's nakedness before the Fall. The falcon which one edition suggests as the stirring animal (see my previous note) does not move "gaily" within or under a covering. *"Gaia"* recalls another animal, from the first canto of the *Inferno,* "quella fiera alla gaetta pelle," "that beast with the gay pelt" (*Inf.* 1:42), the leopard of lust and its spotted hide.

Shame is what made our first ancestors "cover up," but there is no shame here. Is it the motion of sex that Dante sees in Adam's nudity before his "father" breathes speech? A playful animal, Adam appears to "give pleasure" to Dante. It is an erotic

---

14. "It is not evident to us just what kind of creature Dante had in mind, but it is quite possible that he may have been thinking of a falcon" (*Commedia,* 863). Sinclair hints at something but leaves it ambiguous. "The surprising comparison of Adam's movements through his enveloping light with those of an animal that stirs under a covering cloth is an instance of what has been noted as a marked feature of the *Paradiso,* the use of homely, sometimes even vulgar imagery, like some of the Gothic figures in the stone and wood of the cathedrals. Dante deliberately breaks through the limits of classical poetic propriety in order to preserve the vigor of reality in the ethereal heights" (*Par.* 1972b, 383–84).

image that Dante may have borrowed from Saint Augustine and Saint Thomas Aquinas. The former spoke of Adam's ability to make his male organ rise at will before the Fall whereas the latter expounded the notion of a more intense sexual pleasure in that untainted Garden.[15]

Everything in the twenty-sixth canto qualifies the despair of the preceding twenty-fifth. Love reads the Scriptures to Dante, sometimes with whispers, sometimes with strength, "mi legge Amore o lievemente o forte" (*Par.* 26:18) and love for Dante is more than a spiritual light and sound show. Saint John relents so much as to give a theological love bite to his pupil. "Ma dì ancor . . . con quanti denti questo amor ti morde," "but say on . . . with how many teeth does this love bite you?" (*Par.* 26:49–51).

Dante returns the bite, "Tutti quei morsi / che posson far lo cor volgere a Dio / a la mia caritate son concorsi," "All those bites / which can make the heart turn to God, / have come together in my charity" (*Par.* 26:55–57). In a moment he will mention the "eternal Gardener." With leaves and fronds, Adam will burst upon the scene. The bite of Saint John is a playful grazing of the sinful apple. Poetry is setting off and theology must follow her, across the "mar de l'amor torto," "sea of perverse love" (*Par.* 26:62).

No wonder the word with which Dante begins his voyage appears at the head of this canto, the twenty-sixth, "*smarrita*," "confused." Saint John, blinding, confusing Dante Alighieri, recalls him to his purpose in ironic words.

> Begin then: and speak whence aims
> your soul, and be assured
> sight in you is confused but not destroyed.
>   (*Par.* 26:7–9)[16]

---

15. See Haberman's comment on Aquinas, which may shed light on Dante's image. "Against the prevailing attitude of the Doctors of the Church and his own contemporaries, Aquinas maintained that the pleasurable sensation in the male-female sex act felt by unfallen men would have been more intense and greater, not less, than that felt by fallen men (S.T. la, Q. 98, a. 2, ad 3). According to Saint Augustine, before the Fall, Adam had his 'membrum virile' directly under the control of his will, as we even now have such volitional control over our arms and legs. As a result of sin, however, this 'member' defied the control of the will and begins to rise and fall of its own accord and not, like the other organs, at the dictates of the 'owner's' will. But in Eden the unfallen sexual activity of man was different: 'Even if there had been no sin in the Garden, there would still have been marriages worthy of that blessed place and . . . lovely babies would have flowered from a love uncankered by lust' (*De Civitate Dei*, bk. 14, chap. 15, 24, and 26)" (Haberman 1979, 193).

16. "Comincia dunque: e dì ove s'appunta / l'anima tua, e fa ragion che sia / la vista in te smarrita e non defunta."

The answer is obvious. Dante is shooting for Beatrice and whatever is beyond. But that one knows already. Either the question is redundancy or a "cover" for something else. From the previous canto there is good reason to suspect why Dante is again, *smarrita,* bewildered, confounded. Beatrice was becoming so palpable he thought for sure he would be able to touch, to bite her, as he ascended higher.

Had she not implied that sight, at least, is almost corporal here?

Listen to the exchange between Saint John and Dante in this twenty-sixth canto.

> "Comincia dunque, e dì ove s'appunta
> l'anima tua, e fa ragion che sia
> la vista in te smarrita e non defunta
> perché la donna che per questa dia
> regïon ti conduce, ha ne lo sguardo
> la virtù ch'ebbe la man d'Anania."
> Io dissi: "Al suo piacere e tosto e tardo
> vegna remedio a li occhi che fuor porte
> quand'ella entrò col foco ond' io
> sempr' ardo."

> "Begin then: and say where aims
> your soul, and be assured
> sight in you is confused but not destroyed
> since the lady who through this divine
> region conducts you, has within her look
> the virtue which the hand of Ananias had." [17]
> I said: "At her pleasure, early or late
> let remedy come to the eyes which were gates
> when she entered with the fire whence I always burn."
> (*Par.* 26:7–15)

John, after disappointing Dante on the one hand, gives him a sly "assurance" on the other. You haven't grasped the contradiction yet, the *bewilderment.* Your sight is *bewildered* but not destroyed and so with your hope. Beatrice's look is just

---

17. "Ananias went his way, and entered into the house, and putting his hands on him, said, 'Brother Saul, the Lord, even Jesus, that appeared unto thee in the way as thou camest, hath sent me, that thou might receive thy sight, and be filled with the Holy Ghost.' And immediately . . . he received sight" (*Acts* 9:17–18).

like the touch of a miraculous hand, Ananias's, that gave sight. Sight will heal you. And if sight is touch in *Paradiso,* the contradiction will be resolved. You will have theologically what you can have poetically, the touch of Beatrice.

Saint John's remarks "bite" Dante. They are love bites, and Dante realizes that though the sea of love is somewhat twisted, *perverse,* he is being drawn in a direction previously imagined as contradictory. What had been specifically denied is now being given. Everything is coming together, *concorsi,* yet in a manner miraculous and beyond anticipation. And so he cries, sooner, later, let her sight heal, come in through the portals where she entered with the fire with which I always burn. If sight is sex, let sight be healing for the "wound." And when Saint John says, "Enough—where do you hope to go? What makes you hope?"

Dante's answer is a dream of the Garden where every frond is blessed with a measure of love. Hope—through the *Inferno, Purgatorio,* a voyage over the sea, to the shore, up to the Garden—has:

> tratto m'hanno del mar de l'amor torto,
> e del diritto m'han posto a la riva.
> Le fronde onde s'infronda tutto l'orto
> de l'ortolano etterno, am' io cotanto
> quanto da lui a lor di bene è porto.

> drawn me from the sea of twisted love
> and placed me on the bank of the straight way.
> The leaves whence is leafed all the Garden
> of the Eternal Gardener I love as much
> as has been given to them from Him of good.
> (*Par.* 26:62–66)

Though the Garden of Eden lies far behind in the cantos of *Purgatorio,* it blooms again here on the twenty-sixth round of *Paradiso,* in the eighth heaven of the constellations. Remember its warm zephyrs, the air blazing under the green limbs? Here, too, its fronds are waving, waving in line after line. One of those green reeds Dante bound around his waist when he left the cord of false chastity behind. Here he is in the living garden of sex. "Holy, holy, holy," sings Beatrice and the saints in Hebrew psalmody when Dante gives the Garden reality in utterance. Forthwith Adam appears, gay as a light and skipping leopard to give pleasure. What happens to the bent over Alighieri?

> Come la fronda che flette la cima
> nel transito del vento, e poi si leva

per la propria virtù che la soblima,
fec' io in tanto in quant' ella diceva,
stupendo.

As the frond which bends its head
in the passing of the wind and then springs up
with its own power which uplifts it,
so did I—while she was speaking—
astounded.
>   (*Par.* 26:85–89)

Dante bounds back. The frond's head snapping back, the elaboration of leaves in Paradise, the repetition of *fronda* and *infronda* suggest the spring of the male organ. The chorus of Beatrice and the great lights burst forth—"Santo, Santo, Santo," "Holy, Holy, Holy" (*Par.* 26:69). Hebrew psalm is woven into the foliage of lovemaking, and in a literal flash, Adam appears, the original inhabitant of Paradise and carefree ancestor of human sex. "*Torto*" and "*diretto,*" "twisted" and "direct," the adjectives emphasize the snake's path. Dante's path is through the *fronda* toward Adam, addressed as an apple, a ripe one. The sin gleams on his lips.

If at first Dante was confused, *smarrito,*—now he is amazed, *stupefatto,* as the sweetness of nectar, seed, eros, *dolcissimo,* drips from the song of the sky. He is *stupendo* (*Par.* 26:80, 67, 89), astounded, before the stirring animal force of Adam. And yet Adam, too, is caught up in contemplation, as Beatrice describes him, "Within these rays / looks longingly on his Maker, the first soul / that the First Power, ever created" (*Par.* 26:82–84). That "*virtù,*" "power" has a special significance. "*La prima virtù,*" "the first power" that created the apple and Adam, is the same "*virtù*" that made Dante snap back. From the Eighth Heaven, with the assurance of Saint John that sight can touch, flying from the slingshot of snapping frond of Eden with "*virtù,*" Dante is off for the very place he started from—Eden.

Non è pareggio da picciola barca
quel che fendendo va l'ardita prora,
né da nocchier ch'a sé medesmo parca.

It is not a passage for a little bark
that which the burning prow goes cleaving,
nor for a pilot who will spare himself.
>   (*Par.* 23:67–69)

Dante is going round. That is the shape of the route, "*torto*" and "*diretto,*" the shape of Paradise, the *Commedia,* a spherical whirligig. Skipping, pulled by that power, *virtù,* thrust into the swiftest of the heavens by a look of Beatrice's.

> E la virtù che lo sguardo m'indulse,
> del bel nido di Leda mi divelse
> e nel ciel velocissimo m'impulse.
>
> And the power that her look allowed me,
> from the fair nest of Leda plucked me
> and into the swiftest of the heavens thrust me.
> (*Par.* 27:97–99)

There is barely time to notice that Beatrice is blushing in this canto, supposedly before the whoredom of the Church, "like an honest woman," "*come donna onesta.*" Like? Why use this ambiguous "like"? The rest of the image is hardly reassuring. "Che permane / di sé sicura, e per l'altrui fallanza, / pur ascoltando, timida si fane," "who remains / sure of herself, but through the folly of another, / only hearing of it, becomes abashed" (*Par.* 27:31–33). An embarrassed Beatrice? Dante will sing at the beginning of the twenty-eighth canto, "riguardando ne' belli occhi / onde a pigliarmi fece Amor la corda," "staring into the beautiful eyes, / whence love had made the noose to seize me" (*Par.* 28:11–12). This is the voice of flirtation, not adoration. The image of love as the hangman or trapper, killing or capturing the poor beast, points up a courtly humor, deprecation for the familiar masculine entrapment, a note of complaint in the manner of Provence, not of *Paradiso.* It stresses the ongoing courtship between Beatrice and Dante and it prepares . . . ?

For "*L'alto disio,*" "the high desire"! The angels are boiling like liquid iron with sparks in circles of love, "non altrimenti ferro disfavilla / che bolle, come i cerchi sfavillaro" (*Par.* 28:89–90). This is an image sounded also in the first canto of *Paradiso,* "sfavillar dintorno, / com ferro che bogliente esce del foco" (*Par.* 1:59–60), and here, as there, it signifies the metamorphosis into a kind of divine flesh like Glaucus. Here it is the flesh of angels, "che sole amore e luce ha per confine," "that has only love and light for limits" (*Par.* 28:54), like the temple of the Heavens they inhabit. And what do they do in that temple?

They are playing games, sporting.[18] Of the circles, "l'ultimo è tutto d'Angelici

18. This "sporting" recalls the "disporting" of the pious with the Holy One in the *Zohar,* 3:166b, a passage that precedes the description of sexual intercourse among the dead in the heavens. (See my first chapter.) The parallels between the *Commedia* and *Zohar* in detailing radical ideas of sex in the Hereafter are striking and have their root, perhaps, in Neoplatonic ideas of mystical union.

ludi," "the highest is all of Angels sporting" (*Par.* 28:126). And to point the sexual nature of this "sporting" Dante describes the second triad, "che così germoglia / in questa primavera sempiterna / che notturno Arïete non dispoglia,"[19] "which thus blossoms in that perpetual spring, that the nightly Ram does not ravish" (*Par.* 28:115–17). The reader understands that a flower is being formed out of the ranks of angels. A flower is budding which the world of change, the ram, cannot penetrate, despoil, ravish.

Remember Beatrice's face as her blush faded and she broke into a smile again in the twenty-seventh canto?

> Ma ella, che vëdea 'l mio disire,
> incominciò, ridendo tanto lieta
> che Dio parea nel suo volto gioire:
>
> But she, who saw my desire
> began, smiling with so much happiness
> that God appeared in her face to be having joy:
> (*Par.* 27:103–5)

How does God have joy in a lady—so that His pleasure beams from her countenance? In classical myth and theology the fair nest of Leda is where Zeus finds his pleasure. In Paradise, God takes his joy in the fair nest of Beatrice. In Dante's religion, God's joy blossomed in the womb of Mary.

Out of the fronds, foliage of these cantos, a bud will burst, its metaphors of garden and leaf. Angels are sporting in the shape of a blossom. An image looms in the Empyrean, prepared by the Eternal Gardener, who brings forth—"plucks," "*divelse,*" the lushest of blooms.

"If my face enamors thee," cried Beatrice several cantos back, "rivolgi al bel giardino," "turn to the fair garden": (*Par.* 23:70–71)

> "Quivi è la rosa in che 'l verbo divino
> carne si fece; quivi son li gigli
> al cui odor si prese il buon cammino."
>
> · · ·

---

19. The use of this word in the *Commedia*, "ravish," "*dispoglia,*" (see also *Inf.* 16:54 and *Purg.* 32:38) points to another one of Dante's fruitful "confusions," for the sinful heart, the sinful tree, lechery and fronds of the Garden are interwoven in its employment.

> "Here is the rose in which the divine word
> was made flesh. Here are the lilies
> at whose odor, the good road was taken."
> (*Par.* 23:73–75)

This was the canto that opened with the joying of a bird sitting "Intra l'amate fronde," "among the beloved fronds," "posato al nido de' suoi dolci nati," "perched on the nest of her sweet little ones" (*Par.* 23:1–2). The nest of Leda nestles in the garden of Dante's Paradise. Here where the classical father, Zeus, made his *logos*, spirit, word, into flesh, the reader sees the rose "in which the divine word was made flesh."

What or who is this rose? Why do the lilies add their odor?

The answer comes a few lines on.

> "Io sono amore angelico, che giro
> l'alta letizia, che spira del ventre
> che fu albergo del nostro desiro."

> "I am angelic love who goes round
> the high bliss, which breathes from the womb
> that was the inn of our desire."
> (*Par.* 23:103–5)

A womb breathing bliss—hostel—a place where you may eat and sleep your full.

Now all is clear. Only two, Mary and her son, have come up to Heaven with their bodies, so Saint John tells Dante. If the poet seeks the womb of Beatrice and ultimate consummation, it must be through the rosy white sheath of Mary. Hers alone is real flesh and it awaits us.

Impossible?

Not for the ardent prow. The angels are forming up in the circles of Heaven. At first in the twenty-ninth and thirtieth cantos of *Paradiso*, they seem mirrors,[20] but this is only to create the stagecraft for that great religious circus!

---

20. There is a similar image of mystical ascension in the first and second centuries, C.E., Merkabah mysticism. See Gershom G. Scholem's *Jewish Gnosticism, Merkabah Mysticism, and Talmudic Tradition,* 14–19. The adept in the talmudic tradition as he climbs the seven heavens is apt to lose his life or be driven from the ascent if he cannot distinguish between the glittering of mirrors or "pure marble plates" and the illusion of water. Sinclair, in his notes to the thirtieth canto of *Paradiso,* discusses Saint Paul's ascension and Dante's use of the word *"circunfulgere,"* taken from the Latin Vulgate's description of Saint Paul's mystical ascent. Scholem discusses the parallels between Saint

"We have issued forth
from the greatest body to the sky which is pure light
light intellectual, full of love
love of true good, full of bliss
bliss which transcends every sweetness."
(*Par.* 30:38–41)

Beatrice is barking, ringmaster, circle mistress, the beauties of this heaven. Dante goes blind again. But he hardly notices it for his transcendence is so rapid, painless, not falling between cantos, but instant—light rising in the form of a river, sweeping him along in the imagery of the psalm, the river of death become that of eternal life.

And I saw light in the form of a river
golden with brilliance, between two banks
painted with marvelous spring.
(*Par.* 30:61–63)[21]

It is spring, the Florentine spring, he sees, he smells.

From that stream issued living sparks
and on each side they dropped upon the flowers
as rubies circumscribed by gold.
Then, as if inebriated from the odors
plunged back into the wonderful torrent
and as one entered, another issued forth.
(*Par.* 30:64–69)[22]

Paul, the Book of Enoch, and the early Jewish mystics. Did Dante receive the rabbinic tradition or a Christian form of it?

21. "Vidi lume in forma di rivera / fulvido di fulgore, intra due rive / dipinte di mirabil primavera." According to Sinclair (*Par.* 1972, 442–43), "The passage is Dante's version of the language of the thirty-sixth Psalm: 'Thou shalt make them drink of the river of thy pleasures. For with thee is the fountain of life: in thy light shall we see light.'" Other probable sources are detailed in Grandgent and Singleton's notes (*Commedia*, 897), "See Daniel 7:10, 'A fiery stream issued and came forth before him.' Also Rev. 22:1, 'And he shewed me a pure river of water of life, clear as crystal proceeding out of the throne of God and of the Lamb,' cf. Isaiah 66:12."

22. "Di tal fiumana uscian faville vive, / e d'ogne parte si mettien ne' fiori / quasi rubin che oro circunscrive/ poi, come inebrïate dal li odori / riprofondavan sé nel miro gurge:/ e s'una intrava, un'altra n'uscia fori." This repetition within seven lines of the word *uscire*, "to issue, come out," emphasizes the perpetual pollenlike eruption of joy and Dante's own coruscating emergence into the

Drunken, he plunges into the flood of light, sight, smell, in bliss, confounded, about to plunge into the divine *"albergo."*

> "The high desire which now inflames and urges
> you to have knowledge of that which you see,
> the more it swells the more it pleases me
> but of this water it is necessary that you drink
> first, before such great thirst in you be satisfied."
> (*Par.* 30:70–74)[23]

Why such a material requirement? What is the taste of this stream of living sparks, this torrent of glory? Milk! Beyond the material universe, light may turn into waters, into milk. Isaiah, 66:12: "Behold I will extend to her like a river, peace, and like a flowing river, the glory of the Gentiles: and you shall suck, ye shall be carried upon her side, and be dandled upon her knees." And how does Dante bend to taste the stream?

> Non è fantin che sì sùbito rua
> col volto verso il latte, se si svegli
> molto tardato dall' usanza sua
> com fec' io.
>
> No infant falls on the instant
> with its face toward the milk, if it wake
> long after its usage
> as I did.
> (*Par.* 30:82–85)

Isaiah 66:11, "[Y]ou may suck and be satisfied with the breasts of her consolation, that you may milk her out and be delighted with the abundance of her glory." Dante, Isaiah in mind, has a flood of glory and revelation stream from Beatrice's

---

stream of light. Now, he boasts, he is strong enough for any light. He seems himself to have become in part, a particle of light.

23. "Alto disio che mo t'infiamma e urge, / d' aver notizia di ciò che tu vei / tanto mi piace più quanto piu turge; / ma di quest' acqua convien che tu bei / prima che tanta sete in te si sazi."

breasts as milk.[24] "Suck me," she cries. "Suck me if you wish to go up!" The milk will bring him to a further revelation, the highest reach of his adulterous vision, "*superbe*," "exalted." For this is the canto where his sight will no longer be "*smarrita*," "confused," but rather that confusion will be exalted. His sight looking into his own fantasies, "non si smarriva ma tutta predeva," "was not confused but took all in" (*Par.* 30:119).

The river of bliss is watering the rose that is about to bud. The laughter of flowers, "'l rider de l'erbe" (*Par.* 30:77) on every side they bend and toss their blossoms, "shadowy forecasts of their truth." Tickling Peter, Paul, and James is the odor of the field, a Florentine spring, Messiah, perfume of a woman. No wonder Beatrice blushes. Dante uncovers her breasts.

Does he embarrass her?

Has he revealed her smile?

"O isplendor di Dio," "O Splendor of God" (*Par.* 30:97).

She uncovers her nakedness and between those flowered banks, she draws him into her petals, into the gold bole of Divine love and sun.

> Into the yellow of the eternal rose
> which expands and rises and is redolent of
> odors of praise to the sun which is always spring
> as one who is quiet and wishes to speak,
> Beatrice drew me.
> (*Par.* 30:124–28)[25]

If in courtship Dante and Beatrice are inflaming each other through their eyes (they are reflecting the primal love, but that is a synonym for its most powerful human manifestation, Eros), the whole of Paradise is one glorious mounting. If Dante is getting hotter and hotter, like "iron boiling," as he says, the temperature rising from Heaven to Heaven, relief must come. And it does—in the rose that flowers in the thirtieth and thirty-first cantos of *Paradiso* with the odor of perpetual spring. The problems of bodily love in Paradise are resolved through blinding sight in the fourteenth canto, when Dante is translated into the burnt flesh of angels, flesh with no memory, flesh of light. The other constituent of spiritual flesh is

24. Coleridge in "Kubla Khan" (See previous chapter, "The Milk of Paradise" note 4) seems to draw on the same intuition. It is "the milk of Paradise" that brings the speaker of the poem to his ecstatic height.

25. "Nel giallo de la rosa sempiterna, / che si digrada e dilata e redole / odor di lode al sol che sempre verna, / qual è colui che tace e dicer vole, / mi trasse Bëatrice."

smell, and now smell, the Messianic sine qua non, blossoms in the shape of what is described as an enormous sheath, vagina. Joy is cupped in the great white rose into which, inebriated by *"odor di lode,"* "odor of praises," the saints go buzzing.[26]

Sì come schiera d'ape, che s' infiora
una fïata e una si ritorna
là dove suo laboro s'insapora,
nel gran fior discendeva che s'addorna
di tante foglie, e quindi risaliva
là dove 'l süo amor sempre soggiorna.
Le face tutte avean di fiamma viva
e l'ali d'oro, e l'altro tanto bianco,
che nulla neve a quel termine arriva.
Quando scendean nel fior, di banco in banco
porgevan de la pace e de l'ardore
ch'elli acquistivan ventilando il fianco.

So like a swarm of bees which enflower [27] themselves
at one moment and the next return
there where their labor turns to sweetness [they],
descended into the great flower which adorns itself
with so many petals and thence remounted
there where their love always sojourns.
Faces they have all of living flame
and wings of gold, and the rest so white,
that no snow comes to that extreme.
When they descended into the flower, from rank to rank
they proffered peace and passion
acquired as they fanned their sides.
                    (*Par.* 31:7–18)

26. I find myself puzzling over the talmudic and rabbinic traditions that link the authentic Messianic experience and expectation to smell. In brief, the Messiah, according to the rabbis, will be distinguished by his capacity to judge by smell. The proof text is found in Isaiah 11:1–4. The ingenious interpretation of this can be located in the *Babylonian Talmud, Sanhedrin,* 93b.

27. Sinclair translates *"s'infiora,"* as "dip in the flowers," which gives the sense (perhaps following the suggestion of the Carlyle-Wicksteed, "plunge into the flowers,") but not the resonance of this moment for Dante. The poet uses the word specifically in the *Paradiso* when he wants to stress the metamorphosis of light into flowers. "Tell him if the light with which your substance flowers, bedecked," "Diteli se la luce onde s'infiora / vostra sustanza," Beatrice calls to Saint Thomas and the saints in the fourteenth canto. Also see *Paradiso* 10:91, 23:72, 25:46.

It is a womb into which all the saints go buzzing, "sporting," fanning their wings, pollinating a vagina flowering in the universe of the same flower-bedecked flesh that Dante has been promised.

It is the supreme symbol of courtly love, recalling to Dante's audience the *Roman de la Rose,* which Grandgent cites as "the greatest literary success of the 13th Century." The flower is the womb of Beatrice and of Mary, whom Dante regarded as the mother of Messiah. This link is made specific in the final, thirty-third canto, where Dante speaking through Saint Bernard, admits:

> "Nel ventre tuo si raccese l'amore,
> per lo cui caldo ne l'etterna pace
> così è germinato questo fiore."

> "In your womb was love lit again
> by whose heat in the eternal peace
> thus was this flower germinated."
> (*Par.* 33:7–9)

So behind the stagecraft, the courtly masque, is the light and odor of Beatrice's breasts; and the ecstatic mingling of the whole Empyrean of saints in the divine womb. Dante hints at this.

> Then as people who are under masks
> seem at first different—if they take off
> the semblance not their own, in which they were concealed–
> so changed for me into a greater festival
> the flowers and the sparks—so that I saw
> both courts of the sky plainly.
> (*Par.* 30:91–96)[28]

What is the plain reality behind the courtly masque? In the song of Provence, where lyric and romance originate for Dante, is it not the *"leis de con,"* "laws of cunt"?[29] This is the lesson of Guillaume, troubadour, count of Poitiers and duke of

---

28. "Poi come gente stata sotto larve, / che pare altro che prima, se si sveste / la sembianza non süa in che disparve, / così me si cambiaro in maggior feste / li fiori e le faville, sì ch'io vidi / ambo le corti del ciel manifeste."

29. See Frederick Goldin's, *Lyrics of the Troubadours and Trouveres* (Goldin 1973b, 22–23). "Pero dirai vos de con cals es sa leis," "But I shall tell you about that cunt, what its law is."

Aquitaine. But the light in Dante's heavens is so blinding that it is hard to see the reality.

Do not be "confused," or "confounded." Remember the cry of Dante as he is drawn into the petals of the rose.

> La vista mia ne l'ampio e ne l'altezza
> non si smarriva, ma tutto prendeva
> il quanto e 'l quale de quella allegrezza.
>
> My sight in the breadth and in the height
> did not confound itself, but took all in
> the quantity and quality of that joyousness.
> (*Par.* 30:118–20)

He has had Beatrice. The *"via smarrita"* is behind him. Now he desires more.

CHAPTER TEN

Messiah on Earth

WITH THE CONSUMMATION of Dante and Beatrice in the divine womb, the *Paradiso,* the comedy, and my book might end. Three cantos still remain. The gallant footing with his mistress that has whirled Dante Alighieri up to the heights of Paradise fades in these last circlings. His music is muted as the highest question, union with the Unknown, swims into ken. The Florentine wedded to pagan mythology brings Leda, the victim of rape, hand in hand with Beatrice, his mistress, as the two tutelary deities in the rarefied stratosphere of these high Heavens. Virgil may have been halted by the church at the gate of Eden, but the Greek gods enter the Catholic heavens through Dante's imagery.

Other critics imagine the humor of the *Commedia* is its slapstick, moments of buffoonery in Malebolge, the push of the poet into the burning fire of the Garden's gate. Dante has his moments of coarse laughter, particularly at himself, but it is his leap in a defeated middle age that draws my smile. In a dream autobiography he somersaults through classical myth and church martyrology from Hell into Heaven.

His final posture in the heavens is, "Look, I have squared the circle."

◆   ◆   ◆

WHERE OTHER POETS were content in the bosom of their beloved, Dante takes that final step into the *Ayn Sof,* the Without End. Why is it not enough to be one with Beatrice?

It is only the One Without End making stateless, homeless wanderers of all seekers after the Mystery, *"Evraim,* Crossers, Hebrews," who can finally redeem Dante. The poet desired to be with the One. Yet Dante's is not entirely the complaint of the Neoplatonic lover.[1] Suspicions of himself as prophet, Messiah, res-

---

1. See note 9, in chapter 4, "Dante Bewildered" and Guttmann's remark about Greek philosophy in its Neoplatonic guise as the source of "a kind of popular theology." This is what would have given

onate through his work. From the first he regards the Holy One as a rival for Beatrice. As the poet makes himself a sacrifice, he cries out in the language of Isaiah, of Jesus, *"Elios."*

Note Dante's jealousy of "l'etterno sire," in *La Vita Nuova*. The step that Dante takes in the thirty-third canto of *Paradiso* is prepared in the first canto of *Inferno*. Here presenting himself as a piteous figure, fleeing before a skeletal she-wolf, ravenous and wicked, he has Virgil reassure him with the prophecy of an obscure Deliverer:

> Molti son li animali a cui s'ammoglia,
> a più saranno ancora, infin che 'l veltro
> verrà, che la farà morir con doglia.
> Questi non ciberà terra né peltro,
> ma sapïenza, amore e virtute,
> e sua nazion sarà tra feltro e feltro.
>
> Many are the animals with whom she pairs
> and yet more will be, until the hound
> comes, that will bring her death with pain.
> He will not feed on earth or pewter [money]
> but wisdom, love and virtue
> and his home [birth] will be between felt and felt.
> (*Inf.* 1:100–105)

Who can this Deliverer be? Jesus, Can Grande, his patron in Verona? Scholars have tortured the problem for hundreds of years. Early commentators were aware of the terms of the riddle. Dante's ego, however, dazzled beholders. It could not be that. . . ? No, outrageous, thought Boccaccio, though he came closest to guessing. "Were it lawful to say so, I would declare that he had surely become a God upon the earth" (Boccaccio 1904, 31). It is not "lawful"; therefore, Boccaccio has to put his tongue in his cheek when referring to Dante's obvious Messianic aspirations. He cannot resist a little humor on the subject, reporting the dream of Dante's mother. In the obligatory prophetic prologue to a divine birth, (quoted previously) Boccaccio reports how the "gentle lady" first dreams of giving birth to a human son, but as this "shepherd" grows apace, he "feeding only on the berries

---

Dante and Moses De Leon a common language. For an amplification of the radical innovations of the new kabbalah of Moses De Leon and his circle, see the essay by Moses Idel, "No Kabbalistic Tradition" (1983, 51–73). Bernard Septimus makes reference to the Neoplatonic influences in the great predecessor of this circle, Nahmanides, "Nahmanides and the Andalusian Tradition" (1983, 28).

which fell from the laurel tree and the waters of the clear spring" (by the side of which he was born), finally, "he strove with all his power to have of the leaves of that tree whose fruit had nourished him." He "struggles" and his mother sees him "fall," but when "he rose again, he was no longer a man, but had become. . ."

What? What becomes of the shepherd who isn't content with the fruit of the tree of fame but wants to eat the very leaves thereof, the crown of his laureate? ". . . but had become a peacock."

Divine, yes, a metamorphosis, certainly, and yet is there a faint irony in the apotheosis of Alighieri according to Boccaccio, into the peacock? According to the bestiaries, the flesh of the peacock was impervious to death, "sweet smelling and incorruptible." The voice of Boccaccio in telling this legend of Dante's childhood has certain drollness in it. I am not convinced that this was "the god on earth" that Dante had in mind.[2]

Dante at the beginning of the *Commedia* sets his own pretensions in the context of his flight and cowardice. Licking the wounds of his exile, he dreams of a better day. He is only in the middle of his life. A Deliverer is coming, announces Virgil, between "felt and felt." But where is that?

The riddle of felt is solved in the short handbook of Leonard Olschki, *The Myth of Felt*. After exhausting a dozen alternatives and taking the reader through the whole of Tartary, Olschki assembles the evidence of Dante's messianic forecast from the sign of the poet's own birth date in the heavens.

> Dante made no allusion to an *election* of his *Veltro*. He speaks only of his *birth*, "tra feltro e feltro," and thereby excludes the geographical or ethnical definition of *nazione*. . . . The expression seems rather to contain a veiled allusion to a horoscope as it was usually cast in Dante's day at the birth of a child, and especially of a prince. Consequently, Virgil's prophecy of the *Veltro* must have some astrological implications and may refer to a celestial influence that will shape the character, deeds and personality of the coming Deliverer. . . . [3]

---

2. William Anderson, in *Dante the Maker*, remarks, "The peacock's flesh according to the bestiaries was sweet-smelling and incorruptible, meaning the immortal matter of the poem; its feathers were beautifully various, indicating how the expression of each part of the poem fitted exactly its subject-matter; its feet were ugly, meaning that it was written in the vernacular; and its voice was harsh, befitting the violent condemnation of crime and malpractice the poem contains" (Anderson 1980, 68).

3. Olschki, to confirm his astrological reading, cites the other allusion to a Deliverer in the *Commedia*, in *Purgatorio* 33:37–45 and its warning that "stars are already near," in announcing the prodigy's advent. Olschki quotes a host of early commentators, among them Dante's sons Pietro and Jacobo, who held that *"tra feltro e feltro"* meant *"tra cielo e cielo,"* "between heaven and heaven"; Boc-

The only constellations with which the idea of felt was associated in antiquity and in the Middle Ages . . . is the constellation of the Twins, the *pilleati
fratres* or felt capped brothers, Castor and Pollux, traditionally depicted with
their felt caps in the miniatures of medieval astrological treatises. . . . Dante . . .
must have contemplated with a particular intentness the features of those felt
capped brothers because the Twins were his own constellation. He was born in
1265, between May and June, *tra feltro e feltro,* that is, between the rising of the
one star and the setting of the other. (1949, 37–40)

Nor does Olschki miss Dante's other references to the Dioscuri or Gemini, the
invocation to *"Il geminato cielo,"* "the twin-bearing sky," in the canzone, "Io son
venuto al punto della rota"; the naming of Castor and Pollux in *Purgatorio,* 4:61
(when Dante is conspicuously dragging his steps); and of course, his passionate
apostrophe to them in the twenty-second canto of *Paradiso.*

> O glorïose stelle, o lume pregno
> di gran virtù, dal quale io riconosco
> tutto, qual che si sia, il mio ingegno,
> con voi nasceva e s'ascondeva vosco
> quelli ch'è padre d'ogni mortal vita,
> quand' io senti' di prima l'aere tosco;
> e poi, quando mi fu grazia largita
> d'entrar ne l'alta rota che vi gira
> la vostra regïon mi fu sortita.
> A voi divotamente ora sospira
> l'anima mia, per acquistar virtute
> al passo forte che a sé la tira.
>
> O glorious stars, o light pregnant
> with great power, from which I acknowledge
> all, whatever it may be, my genius!

---

caccio, who believed it, referred to "a celestial constellation"; Francesco da Buti ("between heaven and
earth"); and finally the most prominent Dante critic of the Renaissance, Cristoforo Landino, who
stated unequivocally, "I believe that the poet, as an excellent mathematician, has understood by
means of astrology how in the future there will be some revolutions in the Heavens, through the
clemency of which greed might end forever. Therefore the '*Veltro*' will be either that very influence,
which will originate between Heaven and Heaven [i.e., *tra feltro e feltro*], or else a sovereign who will
be produced by that influence" (1949, 39). Olschki feels that the origin of this exegesis is from the lips
of Dante himself.

with you was born and masked with you
he who is father of every mortal life
when I first felt the Tuscan air:
and then, when grace was allotted me
to enter into the high wheel that rolls you round
your region was drawn for me.
To you devoutly now sighs
my soul, to acquire power
for the strong step that pulls it to itself.
(*Par.* 22:112–24)[4]

His shout, a child's in a carnival swing, spins in the mocking joy of the canto's final lines.

Li aiuola che ci fa tanto feroci,
volgendom' io con li etterni Gemelli,
tutta m'apparve da' colli a le foci;
poscia rivolsi li occhi a li occhi belli.

The little threshing floor which makes us so fierce,
while I was turning with the eternal Gemini,
was all revealed to me from hills to river mouth:
then I turned back my eyes to the beautiful eyes.
(*Par.* 22:151–54)[5]

4. These lines contain several riddles. Among them is the identification of the "he" (line 116) that commentators have supposed to be the sun, or Helios. Apart from Dante's attraction to the pagan deities, note the implicit image of the wheel of fortune that has cast his lot, his birth, in the sign of Gemini, the sphere of the Dioscuri. Dante, however, pauses in his proper sphere, only to acquire the power to be spun to an even higher one. Is this ironic? For while willing to exploit his luck in being born under the Dioscuri, he is not content with the cast of the wheel of fortune but is using it to stake him to an ever higher throw. Recall the image of dice in *Purgatorio* 6:1, "Quando si parte il gioco de la zara." His career on earth destroyed, his hopes in ruin on the "little threshing floor," there is a melancholy cheer in this apostrophe, a taunting of his dreams for advancement above.

5. Jean Seznec discusses this dilemma which concerned Aquinas too. "While the fear of demons continues to haunt the popular (medieval) imagination, the astrological theory of causation remains in force as an intellectual concept: even the greatest minds do not repudiate it entirely. They do of course see that omnipotence of the stars could constitute a threat to human liberty, but like the apologists and the Fathers, they are satisfied with defining the limits of this power; they do not deny its existence. [Note 45—Pierre Abelard and Hugues de Saint Victor repudiate astrological predictions as suggestions of the devil; they do however recognize a "natural" astrology—that is to say, the influence

What do these references to Castor and Pollux imply? What does Dante's sign mean to him? What does it forecast? Olschki is aware of Castor and Pollux as the signifiers of liberty.

> In the first canto of the *Inferno* the allusion to felt as a celestial mark of the Twins is put into the mouth of Virgil, who knew the significance of the Roman *pilleum* not only as an attribute of Castor and Pollux, but also as a popular symbol of liberty. The world's new redeemer, whoever he might be, would be impressed so strongly by the constellation that he would secure to mankind the triumph of wisdom, love, and virtue embodied in the two felt-capped mythological brothers. (1949, 42)

He elaborates on this.

> Castor and Pollux were in Rome the tutelary divinities of the middle class, the *equites,* that is, of all men entitled to wear the undyed felt cap as a mark of their rank and privileges, and as a symbol of their civil liberties. . . . When a slave obtained his freedom, he put on that cap as a symbol of the newly acquired liberty. A coin celebrating Caesar's assassination shows that same cap flanked by two daggers. (1949, 45–46)

Olschki asks the question, "Can Dante himself be the Veltro announced in the prologue of the poem?" He dismisses the possibility. "The prophecy is intended for too undetermined a future to include the very protagonist of the epic vision displayed in the poem." Olschki rests his case with the assurance that the Gemini stand for a Deliverer in an undetermined future and the "reign of liberty" (1949 42–46).

---

of the planets on the temperature and on the human body. . . .] St. Thomas Aquinas admits that the stars determine individual character, at least in a physical sense, and since most men follow their passions—that is to say, their physical appetites—it is really by the stars that they are led into sin: '*Plures hominum sequuntur passiones, quae sunt motus sensitivi appetitus, ad quos cooperari possunt corpora coelestia. . . .* '[Note 46—*Summa*, 1:115, 4. ("The majority of men follow their passions which are movements of the sensitive appetite, in which movements heavenly bodies can co-operate. . .")] And Dante, on this point, faithfully follows in his master's footsteps: while affirming freedom of the will [Note 47—"*Lume v'è dato a bene e a malizia E libero voler.*" "Light is given unto you, for good and for evil, and for freedom of will" (*Purg.* 16:75–76)], he at the same time recognizes the influence of cosmic forces on the human soul: *Lo cielo i vostri movimenti inizia.* [Note 48—*Purg.* 16:73. "The stars initiate your movements." "*Astra inclinant: non necessitant.*"] With this reservation, astrology continues as the foundation of profane culture and the underlying principle of all science, '*la fin de toute clergie*'" (Seznec 1972, 48–49).

With the key of the Gemini, however, doors locked with this *trobar clus,* "hidden image," secret singing of the *Commedia,* spring open. The caps of Castor and Pollux may signify liberty, fraternal love, "the wisdom acquired through poetry and science," or as "represented in medieval miniatures with a weapon in one hand, a lyre in the other" (1949, 42–43). But Castor and Pollux themselves, their lives not just their caps, were the objects of Dante's brooding. Had his sign betrayed him? Was his destiny really reflected in theirs? He was conspicuously long on the lyre and short on the weapon.

In the preceding cantos, 20 and 21, Dante harps on the theme of predestination. He, who argued so strongly for the freedom of the will, cries out to his sign, the Gemini, "O light from which I acknowledge all my genius." But he goes on, calling to "he who is father of all mortal life . . . born and masked with you." Is he apostrophizing the sun god, Apollo, fate? Had Dante's astrological sign determined his destiny, not his acts? The doctrine of free will is struggling against an old Roman stoicism and superstition. At the beginning of the *Paradiso* Dante mocks Plato's belief that man's destiny is tied to his star by material connection and asserts free will. Now he bows before his tutelary deities. Dante wavers throughout the *Commedia* between the two halves of a conundrum that the Talmud states as, "All is foreseen but choice is given." What I would assert is not obvious to Olschki, or commentators who feel with a shiver the challenge to Orthodox Christianity—is Dante's psychology. This Florentine exiled from the Arno must have recalled the vaunt of his early lines, *"tra feltro e feltro,"* the hope that the weapon in his hand would be the equal of the lyre of his song—a song that had begun to hold Italy, the Italy he cared about, in sway. He had to have reflected on the myth of Castor and Pollux. Who were they—these sons of Leda? What did they signify to him? What did they predict of his life?

Their caps represent the two halves of the egg,[6] not just felt liberty caps, the egg out of which the children of a divine rape, Leda by Zeus, sprang—Helen of Troy, Pollux. The eggshells were symbols of the messianic dream as well, which mesmerized Christianity—to be half-human, half-divine. Olschki follows the references to the Gemini in the *Commedia* but disregards manifold allusions to their mother, Leda.

What were the Gemini or Dioscuri most famous for? I quote Bullfinch's dry collection, "Castor was slain, and Pollux, inconsolable for the loss of his brother, besought Jupiter to be permitted to give his own life as a ransom for him. Jupiter

---

6. Olschki mentions this in a single line: "Since late antiquity . . . the two conjoined felt caps of the Dioscuri were deemed to represent the egg from which they were born, or else singly the two hemispheres of the world," but he hints at its connection to Leda in footnote 131 (1949, 44–45).

so far consented as to allow the two brothers to enjoy the boon of life alternately, passing one day under the earth and the next in the heavenly abodes. According to another form of the story, Jupiter awarded the attachment of the brothers by placing them among the stars as Gemini, the Twins.

"They received divine honors under the name of Dioscuri (sons of Jove)" (Bulfinch 1894, 193).

The most common version of the story of Leda is that one of the two brothers, Castor, is wholly human and the other, Pollux, with his sister Helen, the offspring of a Divine rape (Graves 1978, 206–7).[7] The elevation into the stars of Castor through the fraternal love of his divine brother, who refuses to live without his companionship, must ring familiar. The plot of Dante's *Commedia* is that an erring, confused, only too human Dante passes through the love of his angelic partner, Beatrice, into the other world. The *Commedia* fulfills both versions of the myth of Castor and Pollux. The human Dante passes from the world of the earth into the other world, from Hell to Heaven. Here, like Castor, Dante is elevated by his Beloved into the stars.

Is Beatrice a proper stand-in for Pollux? Is it really Jesus who ought to be Dante's twin? Or has Alighieri flipped male into female, bringing the ardor of Catholic worship to the still life of her dead body?

Dante's attraction to astrology has to do with his dream world. His sign, the Gemini, directs him to " 'l poema sacro / al quale ha posto mano e cielo e terra," "the sacred poem, to which heaven and earth have put hand" (*Par.* 25:1–2). The poem, like the tale of the Dioscuri, of Messiah, is compounded of Heaven and earth. Olschki notes the line when for a moment he entertains the notion of Dante regarding himself as the *veltro* (1949, 42).

That Dante is flirting with his own Messiahship as a child born under the sign of the Dioscuri, the sons of Jupiter, high-judging Jove, becomes clearer when I look back over the whole of the *Commedia*. In this long, autobiographical romance, commentators have struggled with the absence of parents. Dante, bereft of his mother at a tender age, ought to be eager for a sight of her. Only the generalized cry of the blessed souls for their "mommas" touches this. It is not a Florentine mother who is mentioned with filial piety, but Leda, the mother of the Dioscuri.

> E la virtù che lo sguardo m'indulse
> del bel nido di Leda mi divelse
> e nel ciel velocissimo m'impulse.

---

7. For Graves's version of Castor and Pollux see his *The Greek Myths* (Graves 1978, 246–48).

. . .

> And the power which her look allowed me
> from the lovely nest of Leda plucked me
> and into the swiftest heaven thrust me.
> (*Par.* 27:97–99)

From "the lovely nest," the womb of Leda, Dante is upthrust and impelled into his final round of discovery. Leda and Beatrice compete to be his mother. That is not to slight the breasts of Beatrice, for it seems important even to the latter that Dante should be hatched out of the nest of the Gemini. Beatrice thrusts him out just as she thrust him in—the language of the passage quoted above foreshadowed in the twenty-second canto as the poet is "pushed" or "thrust" into the heaven of his birth sign, nativity, his astrological sign. La dolce donna dietro a lor mi *pinse* . . ."

> The sweet lady behind them thrust me
> with only a sign, above on that stairway
> so her power overwhelmed my nature.
> (*Par.* 22:100–102)

The twenty-third canto of *Paradiso,* when Dante is firmly secured in the brooding place of the Gemini, begins with the twitter of the mother bird and an apostrophe to nesting. Beatrice seems to be standing in for Leda.

> As the bird among the beloved fronds,
> has perched on the nest of her sweet little ones
> during the night that hides things from us,
> who to see their longed for looks
> and to find the food with which to feed them,
> in which hard labors are a relish to her,
> anticipates the time upon the open branch,
> and with burning affection awaits the sun,
> fixed, staring through the hatching dawn;
> thus my lady stood erect and eager.
> (*Par.* 23:1–11)[8]

8. "Come l'augello, intra l'amate fronde, / posato al nido de' suoi dolci nati / la notte che le cose ci nasconde, / che, per veder li aspetti disïati, / e per trovar lo cibo onde li pasca / in che gravi labor li sono aggrati, / previene il tempo in su aperta frasca, / e con ardente affetto il sole aspetta, / fiso guardando pur che l'alba nasca; cosi la donna mïa stava eretta / e attenta." I have translated *fronde* as

The twenty-second and twenty-seventh cantos, in which the Gemini and then their mother, Leda, are mentioned, show another curious parallel. The little "threshing floor," "*aiuola,*" is alluded to in both. As if claiming a patrimony with Jupiter and Leda, Dante cannot resist a contemptuous gaze downward to the earth. The sense of sexual push, "*mi pinse,*" noted in the twenty-second as Dante came into this heaven, puts Beatrice in the role of Jupiter. And it is echoed in his exit when she "upthrusts" and "pushes" him even higher. But at that moment, he casts a quick glance to the "little threshing floor" below, its hills and river mouths. Whirling, he speaks sardonically—something about earth makes us, Man, "so fierce," ferocious. Now, in the twenty-seventh, Dante's description is far more detailed. He gives us the origin of that ferocity.

> Da l' ora ch'ïo avea guardato prima
> i' vidi mosso me per tutto l'arco
> che fa dal mezzo al fine il primo clima;
> sì ch'io vedea di là da Gade il varco
> folle d'Ulisse, e di qua presso il lito
> nel qual si fece Europea dolce carco.
> E più mi fora discoverto il sito
> di questa aiuola: ma 'l sol procedea
> sotto i mie' piedi un segno e più partito.

> From the hour when I first stared
> I saw I had moved through all the arc
> which the first climate makes from the middle to the end;
> so that I saw from there beyond Cadiz the mad track
> of Ulysses and on the other side nearly to the shore
> on which Europa made herself a sweet burden.
> And more would have been discovered to me of the site
> of that little threshing floor: but the sun was proceeding
> under my feet a sign and more away.
>   (*Par.* 27:79–87)

He sees now not merely topography, but the fierceness of the European character, begun in the rape of Europa by Jupiter, "*dolce carco,*" "a sweet burden." Does the "bel nido di Leda," "lovely nest of Leda," a few lines on not echo this?

Two rapes are described in the space of a few lines, the same divine perpetra-

---

"fronds" rather than "branches," for I believe the belt of Dante is being alluded to in the interweaving of the nest, the *fronda* alluded to again some cantos on in the persona of Adam.

tor, Jupiter. Dante, dreaming on the Gemini, is dreaming of himself as the child of one of these rapes. But he is also being ravished, overcome, as well. He is the child of love.

> I am one whom, when
> Love breathes in me, note,—and in the way
> it speaks within—go set it down.
> (*Purg.* 24:52–54)

And whence does that Love breathe most intensely, angelically? I hear a common music. "*Spira,*" "breathes," strings both these passages together.

> "Io sono amore angelico, che giro
> l'alto letizia che spira del ventre
> che fu albergo del nostro disiro."

> "I am angelic love, who goes round
> the high bliss, which breathes from the womb
> that was the inn of our desire."
> (*Par.* 23:103–5)

In the heat of Beatrice's smile, he fuses the womb of Mary and Leda and his own inspiration.

> "Open your eyes and regard what I am:
> you have seen things, which have made you
> able to sustain my smile."
> (*Par.* 23:46–48)[9]

The Messianic laughter.

"One day under the earth, the other in the heavenly abodes," this characterization of the Gemini is a description of Dante's passage from the *Inferno* to the *Paradiso*. Is it not also the dream of humankind, to pass freely from earth to paradise, the dream of Messiah? His stars spur Dante to the voyage. The constant reiteration of this charge, the courage to go after Ulysses, to attempt the "*folle volo,*"

---

9. "Apri li occhi e riguarda qual son io: / tu hai vedute cose, che possente / se' fatto a sostener lo riso mio."

"mad flight," over the perverse sea, is done under the tutelary sign of the protectors of voyages.[10] Did not Saint Paul sail in a ship under the sign of "Castor and Pollux?"[11]

No wonder Dante leaves the footpath once he has departed Hell and embarks on a ship. The ship is the skiff of his dreams guided by desire for Beatrice under the benignity of his pagan emblem in the heavens, the messianic stars, Gemini. But I would fall short of Dante ringing only his metaphors of voyage. As a brother of Castor and Pollux, he is a child of Leda. In Dante's mythos, the Father of the Universe has conceived him. Dante is less a son of the Hebrew unknown, the mysterious Jesus of the Gospels, more like a child of Jove, of the thirteenth century's fascination with Greek mythology. Did Dante dream of that rape of illumination painted by Yeats, "the great wings beating still / Above the staggering girl, her thighs caressed / By the dark webs, her nape caught in his bill. . . / her helpless breast upon his breast"? Did Dante ask Yeats's conundrum? "So mastered by the brute blood of the air / Did she put on his knowledge with his power?" (Yeats 1958, 211–12).

Yeats's riddle is answered by Leda's children, among whom Dante counts himself. All through *Paradiso,* Dante speaks of being vanquished by light, overcome, overthrown. He is pushed from the "lovely nest of Leda." It is meant in a figurative and literal sense. He is pushed from the Heaven of Leda, but he is also a child, a fledgling, of Leda's. He looks down from the heavens and sees another divine rape taking place, Europa's.

This bestiality is the accompaniment of messianic dreams. Howard Nemerov notes it.

> Ulysses and the fall of man both relate to knowledge and lust. Whenever Ulysses turns up, three times in all, it is in the company of some sort of sexual enchantment. When he tells his story, he begins with leaving Circe, who had kept him for over a year, and his exhortation to his crew includes a denunciation of bestiality. In Purgatory, Dante dreams of a siren who mentions having enchanted Ulysses just before she is revealed by Virgil as a creature of falsehood and filth. The last memory of Ulysses and his *varco folle,* high in heaven is companioned in the next line by a reminiscence of Europa's rape. So sexuality, bestiality and the voyage are

---

10. "Castor and Pollux came . . . to be considered the patron deities of seamen and voyagers" (Bulfinch 1894, 193).

11. "We departed in a ship of Alexandria . . . whose sign was Castor and Pollux" (Acts 28:ll).

brought together in these fleeting and riddling allusions, which echo over great spaces of the poem. (Nemerov 1974, 131–32)

The riddle of lust, knowledge, and deliverance is to be read in the sign of the Gemini. The rape on the threshing floor is twinned by the rape that results in the elevation of man into the heavens. "The uncontrollable mystery on the bestial floor," says Yeats as the Magi exit from the stable where Jesus of Nazareth is born.

Dante's is the personal story of the hero raised to divinity. He has harrowed Hell just by visiting it. He has outboasted Theseus and deserved the fate of Castor, "disposto a salire alle stelle," "disposed to go up to the stars!" What irony that last line of *Purgatorio* has, in the light of the Dioscuri.

So Dante born anew in his sign refers to the Gemini; he goes whirling in the heavens with them.[12] They are his birth sign. The inference, however veiled, is asking the question—am I intended as a redeemer? All those curious references to bird and nest—his very bestiality, lechery, is tied to the rape, the "sweet rape" that gives birth to one of the twins of his sign, the messianic sigh.

Had the *Paradiso,* the *Commedia,* been solely about the search for Beatrice, it would have ended with her enthronement high above him after his passage through the divine vagina of the rose. But Dante has come after more than a woman. A woman for Dante, for the Kabbalist, Moses de Leon, as "beauty" is for Plotinus, is a means to the Almighty.

In the fourteenth canto of the *Paradiso,* Dante accused himself to excuse himself (*Par.* 14:136). Why? Because he temporarily left his winding embrace of Beatrice to fly after the sparkling of the Holy Breath, Spirit, the messianic promise. This canto, as Sinclair notes, is filled with the echoes of the preacher Joachim, who readied the twelfth century for the coming of Messiah. At the lower levels of Paradise, still hoping he may embrace his mistress in the body, Dante is torn between flight toward the Apocalypse and flight toward her. That is why he makes her the stern handmaiden of Joachim, announcing the coming Armageddon high in the

---

12. There is a tradition that there were three Dioscuri. "In Samothrace . . . there stood on both sides of the entrance to the All-Holiest two brazen phallic statues like our statues of Hermes. They were said to be twin brothers, sons of Zeus, the Dioskouroi. In the All-Holiest itself stood—so much even an uninitiate may guess—the third brother, who was worshipped both as a small and as a great Kabeiros, as a small Kadmilos and as the great and mysterious Korybas. His relationship with the great Mother was kept secret" (Kerenyi 1950, 87).

Empyrean. Beatrice's hint that the seats are almost full in the choir: "Vedi li nostri scanni sì ripieni, / che poca gente più ci si desira" (*Par.* 30:131–32), that high Henry's (the Emperor of Dante's dreams) seat awaits him, is a prophecy of impending Judgment. (Again the hope for Henry as political redeemer speaks to the ambivalence of Dante's questions about his own role.) Beatrice's breasts are taut, anticipating Armageddon, strapped with the reins of war. Embracing her, Dante is free at the end of lust and revenge, or cheated of both. For one cannot hear his final fig to Fiorenza from the highest heavens without wondering:

> I, that to the divine from the human
> to the eternal from time had come
> and from Florence into a people just and sane
> with what a stupor must I be filled!
> (*Par.* 31:37–40)[13]

The echo of "*sano*," "sane," taints his cry a few moments later that Beatrice has made his spirit "sane" or whole, for the "*anima sane*," "healthy (or sane) spirit," like the "*popol sano*," "sane people," must be separated, untied, the former from the body, as the latter from the earth. "'Sì che l'anima mia, che fatt' hai sana, / piacente a te dal corpo si disnodi," "So that my spirit, which you have made healthy, / may be untied from the body so pleasing to you'" (*Par.* 31:89–90).

He is flying up at the end of Paradise, beyond body, out of the rosy womb of Mary and Beatrice, the flaming rose of consummate female love. He has moved beyond the womb through the walls of a joy that can hardly be conceived, beyond the speed of light, appearance, the measurements of physics, ancient and modern. He is going up. Beatrice has been beyond Dante, "nel terzo giro / dal sommo grado," "in the third gyre / of the highest rank," but now Dante is beyond Beatrice (*Par.* 31:67–68).

Since they are at a safe distance, Dante may utter an outrageous admission. "Piacente a te dal corpo," "My body so pleasing to you" (*Par.* 31:90). It would be too baldly erotic if she were not far up in the sky. And it recalls Beatrice's boast in Purgatory, "*piacer*," like Dante's "*piacente*."

---

13. *Par.* 31:37–40. "ïo, che al divino da l'umano / a l'etterno dal tempo era venuto / e di Fiorenza in popol giusto e sano / di che stupor dovea esser compiuto!"

"Mai non t'appresentò natura o arte
piacer, quanto le belle membra in ch'io
rinchiusa fui."

"Never did art or nature present you
a pleasure equal to the beautiful limbs in which
I was enclosed."
(*Purg.* 31:49–51)[14]

Does Dante answer that boast here in a breath of thanksgiving or complaint? The well-pleasing bodies are now well separated as the poet mounts to a holiness and intensity beyond human limbs. Saint Bernard flies to his side. They swirl through a cone of biblical ladies and matriarchs, Beatrice in their midst: Eve who opened the wound, "'La piaga che Maria richiuse e unse,'" "'the wound[15] which Mary closed and anointed'"; Rachel, Sarah, Rebecca, Judith, Ruth (described as the mother of David, which recalls Dante's link to the "supreme singer"); saints like John, Francis, Benedict, Augustine. Moses comes into sight for a moment, his epithet echoing the Florentine fig, for he is the leader of "a thankless, shifty, retrograde people," "la gente ingrata, mobile e retrosa" (*Par.* 32:132). Bernard (notorious for his anti-Semitic remarks)[16] utters a reminder about the inadequacy of

14. Notice that the admission falls in the thirty-first canto of both books.

15. The *"piaga"* was the object of discussion in my chapter "Ocean" on the pages of *Purgatorio* (*Purg.* 25:136–39). The wound here stands for sin, but the stress on its opening through Eve and its healing through Mary, whose womb is the inn of love, give emphasis to its sexual meaning as well.

16. See Joachim Prinz, *Popes from the Ghetto,* quoting Saint Bernard's attack upon Anaclet II, a descendant of the Jewish Pierleoni family of Rome: first in the *Vita Prima:* "Charity compels us to speak because *that robe of the Lord which at his passing neither the Gentile nor Jew could tear, Peter Leonis with the approval of the Jew, his master, tears and divides. . . .* " And again in *Epist.,* 139, "It is undeniable that it is an injury to Christ for the spawn of a Jew to have usurped the throne of Peter" (Prinz 1966, 233–34). Bernard in some ways is the most complex and ironic figure of the *Commedia.* Gilson cautions us to regard Saint Bernard carefully since with Virgil and Beatrice he completes the triumvirate of guiding spirits. "The length of the parts entrusted to the actors in the *Divine Comedy* is not everything. . . . Most certainly Saint Bernard's part is short, but it is decisive, since without it the poem would remain incomplete. Is it an exaggeration to count among the protagonists of the sacred poem this Saint Bernard whom we cannot omit without truncating the poem? I do not think so" (Gilson 1949, 238). Gilson warns us that Dante often plays tricks on the historical reality of the characters he portrays, *"A character in the* Divine Comedy *conserves only as much of its historical reality as the representative function that Dante assigns to it requires."* The poet enjoys twisting that reality to his purpose, as Gilson points out in his remarks about the praise of Joachim of Fiori Dante puts in the mouth of

circumcision for grace, followed by lines which condemn the unbaptized to limbo [17]—and then, as in agony of faith, the saint cries:

> "Look now in the face which to Christ
> is most like, since its brilliance
> alone is able to dispose thee to see Christ."
> (*Par.* 32:85–87)

What does Dante see in the final canto of the *Commedia?* Does he see what Bernard expects him to—the face of Jesus?

Or does he see something else? Bernard was the conservative enemy of Abelard: a racist in denunciation of a Jewish pope, Anaclet II, a reactionary against the bent toward free inquiries in philosophy at the liberal monastery of Cluny. At the end of the thirty-second canto, Dante has Bernard refer to the coming vision, after the cry, look on the Christ family face, as a direction of the eyes *"al primo amore,"* "to the primal love." This is language closer to Aristotle (i.e., the Prime Mover) and to the poet's.

Twinned with Saint Bernard, Dante rises for the climax of the poem "to the primal love." The scholar Thomas Bergin notes that Dante has a companion

---

Joachim's adversary, Saint Bonaventure. "He desired to amuse himself at the expense of the earthly Bonaventure. . . . Dante was not sorry to teach him a mild lesson" (Gilson 1949, 267, 268–69).

17. These lines, "sanza battesmo perfetto di Cristo / tale innocenza là giù si ritenne," "without the perfect baptism of Christ, / such innocence was held back there below," are puzzling to the commentators as they imperfectly represent Saint Bernard's sentiments. See the Carlyle-Wicksteed edition of *The Divine Comedy;* footnote 9, of Dr. H. Oelsner and Philip H. Wicksteed (Dante 1932, 600). "It is noteworthy that Bernard, himself, in a treatise addressed to Hugo of St. Victor, shrinks from this appalling conclusion. 'We must suppose that the ancient sacraments were efficacious as long as it can be shown that they were not notoriously prohibited. And after that? It is in God's hands. Not mine be it to set the limit!' " Why should Dante desire to cast Saint Bernard in a more conservative theological position? I don't believe Dante does.

In fact the *"'l forte legame,"* "the hard knot" (*Par.* 32:50) that Bernard promises to untie is not the knot of infant baptism but free will, to which he seems to oppose himself, asserting that the King, "a suo piacer di grazia dota / diversamente; a qui basti l'effetto," "at His pleasure endows diversely with grace: and here—enough—the effect!" (*Par.* 32:65–66). That final tag—*"basti,"* "enough," so typical of Saint Bernard's breathless style, qualifies everything. "Bastavasi ne' secoli recenti," "it was enough in recent centuries" (*Par.* 32:76). We hear the *"basti,"* again in a few lines. It is an expression of frustration, impatience, not of a man skilled in untying knots. The cry, "Look in the face of Christ," in the face of a problem to which the historical Bernard cried, "Not mine be it to set the limit. It is in God's hands," is equally ironic. *"Basta!"* "Enough! Stop reasoning!" This is hardly a victory against the argument for Free Will. I cannot escape the conclusion that in these lines as well as in others, as Gilson suggests, Dante is amusing himself at Saint Bernard's expense while at the same time paying the saint homage.

throughout the *Commedia*[18] but does not draw the conclusion that in view of Castor and Pollux it may have symbolic weight. Dante has a habit of twinning opposites, Siger and Saint Thomas Aquinas, Dominican and Franciscan, apocalyptic heretic and church conservative. Has a sly reference to his own bent for the unorthodox tied him to Saint Bernard, the persecutor of the philosophical tendency in the church?[19] For the final canto of *Paradiso* is a vision of philosophy, not of Jesus. In that vision, after the saint's prayer, he leaves Bernard behind.

18. "Masterly too is the device of a companion and a guide. Dante always is *with* someone, Virgil or Beatrice or Saint Bernard, who can instruct him, reason with him, discuss with him, and, on occasions, participate with him" (Bergin 1969, 11).

19. Gardner in *Dante and the Mystics* notes with surprise that the poet represents Saint Bernard in the guise of a contemplative and a mystic rather than a statesman of the church and makes no mention of his great opponent Abelard. "The saint's own contemporaries and successors . . . were more impressed by his career as an ecclesiastical statesman and preacher of righteousness" (1968, 111). Is it Abelard for whom Dante is stealthily standing in? "Dante is completely silent on the subject of Saint Bernard's most famous opponent. Peter Abelard, indeed, is the figure that, even more than Plotinus, one most misses in the *Divina Commedia*." Gardner seems to be hinting at some form of twinning a few sentences on. "It is obvious that his relation to Saint Bernard is somewhat analogous with that of Siger of Brabant and Joachim of Flora to St. Thomas Aquinas and St. Bonaventura, beside whom respectively these two supposed heretics appear in the fourth heaven." And again, "Abelard profoundly influenced the method of the later schoolmen, and, through them, Dante" (1968, 112–13).

It is not Bernard, the church statesman and fanatic, but rather the mystic Dante twins himself to. It is the Saint Bernard who speaks in the morning hours at the Abbey of Clairvaux of the kiss, the divine kiss of the *Song of Songs,* explicating its first sentence. "'Let him kiss me with the kiss of his mouth,'" thus "that prerogative of Christ, on whom uniquely and in one sole instance the mouth of the Word was pressed, that moment when the fullness of the divinity yielded itself to him, as the life of his body. A fertile kiss therefore, a marvel of stupendous self-abasement that is not a mere pressing of mouth upon mouth; it is the uniting of God with man" (Bernard of Clairvaux 1971, 10).

In Bernard's desire to share that "stupendous kiss" we have the old dream of uniting with God. In Bernard's case, there is constant talk about the "breasts of the bridegroom." Man is cast into the female position. "Prostrate yourself on the ground, take hold of his feet, soothe them with kisses, sprinkle them with your tears and so wash not them but yourself." He is "lying prone at God's feet of flesh, kissing these same feet with her [the penitent's] lips of flesh" (1971, 17, 35). It almost seems that in the ecstasy of the kiss by the Bridegroom, Bernard experiences a metamorphosis into a woman with breasts. "For so great is the potency of that holy kiss, that no sooner has the bride received it than she conceives and her breasts grow rounded with the fruitfulness of conception, bearing witness, as it were, with this milky abundance. Men with an urge to frequent prayer will have experience of what I say. . . . Our breast expands as it were, and our interior is filled with an overflowing love; and if somebody should press upon it then, this milk of sweet fecundity would gush forth in streaming richness" (1977, 58).

The *Commedia* in its image of Divine sex chose a way to union through a female rather than a male spirit. Worshiping the young Beatrice, a lady learned in Philosophy, Dante freshens the aged dame of Boethius, Lady Philosophy. Though rejecting the specifics of Saint Bernard's approaches to

"A woman is the means to the Almighty." The Florentine seizes the mistress of Saint Bernard, Mary. For that moment, "Nel caldo suo calor," "in the heat of his hotness" (*Par.* 31:140), he is a Christian after the French saint's fashion. Yet in the rush of wings he hears other voices, the Sibyl's.[20]

> And yet there drips within
> my heart the sweetness which was born of it.
> Thus the snow to the sun unseals
> thus to the wind in the light leaves
> was lost the saying of the Sibyl.
>   (*Par.*33:62–66)[21]

A drop of sweetness—he is twinned again with the pagan world of Virgil. But it is light he is pursuing, light beyond the appearance of light.

"Non si smarriva," "I was not confounded," he cried in canto 30, "My sight in the breadth and in the height did not confound itself but took all in, the quantity

---

Divinity, foot kissing, metamorphosis into female, still Dante honored the intuition of the Catholic saint about Divinity's sexual nature. (Bernard, who confesses that he has "many times received the visits of the Word," reports its departure as a form of postcoital depression. "Once he leaves, everything falls back into slumber, all grows cold, like a boiling pot of oil withdrawn from the fire" (Halflants 1971, xxi, quoted from Sermon 74).

Think of the composer of the *Commedia* reading these lines of Bernard and imagining the scope of the epic. "Only the touch of the Spirit can inspire a song like this, and only personal experience can unfold its meaning. Let those who are versed in the mystery revel in it; let all others burn with desire rather to attain to this experience than merely to learn about it. For it is not a melody that resounds abroad but the very music of the heart, not a trilling on the lips but an inward pulsing of delight, a harmony not of voices but of wills. . . . It is preeminently a marriage song. . . . Disciplined by persevering study, only the man whose efforts have borne fruit under God's inspirations, the man whose years, as it were, make him ripe for marriage—years measured out not in time but in merits—only he is truly prepared for nuptial union with the divine partner" (Bernard of Clairvaux 1971, 6–7).

20. "This tendency of the Middle Ages to establish parallels between pagan wisdom and the wisdom of the Bible has long been recognized. It came clearly to light when study was first undertaken of the representations on cathedral portals associating Sibyls and Prophets, and of the legend of Virgil, whom the medieval imagination had transformed into a kind of sorcerer or mage. The Sibyls and the author of the Fourth Eclogue, it is true, had intuitive foreknowledge of Christian verity, and had foretold its coming. Applied to the divinities of paganism, this tendency has, as will be seen, surprising results. Not only does it 'justify' the false gods by recognizing in them certain real virtues, but it even goes so far as to re-endow them with at least part of their supernatural character" (Seznec 1972, 16–17).

21. "E ancor mi distilla / nel core il dolce che nacque da essa. / Così la neve al sol si disigilla; / così al vento ne le foglie levi / si perdea la sentenza di Sibilla."

and quality of that joyousness." Now the light is so great that with ironic inspiration he declares, "ch' i sarei smarrito," "I would have been confused," if I had looked away from it.

> Io credo, per l'acume ch'io soffersi
> del vivo raggio, ch'i' sarei smarrito,
> se li occhi miei da lui fossero aversi.

> I believe, by the sharpness I endured
> of the living ray, that I would have been bewildered,
> if my eyes had been averted from it.
>   (*Par.* 33:76–78)

The dazzling of the light is clarity. The optical contradiction[22] of this image serves to show his present divine confusion, bewilderment, confounding—for what he sees is the great simplicity, the lamp, light, that ends all confusion—a pantheistic whole. The edges of the apparent world lose their clarity, just as once before, dazzled by philosophy, straining his eyes, "the stars appeared to him to be shadowed by some white mist." Now that blur becomes reality, clarity—in his final paean, Apollo is not apostrophized, yet neither is Jesus perceived as other than a shadow. Neither name is mentioned. Instead, with a final wave at the world of books, at the Argo, which symbolizes the whole of classical spiritual history, he enters the realm of pure light, fearing to look away.

> E' mi ricorda ch'io fui più ardito
> per questo a sostener, tanto ch'i' giunsi
> l'aspetto mio col valore infinito.
> Oh abbondante grazia ond'io presunsi
> ficcar lo viso per la luce etterna . . .

> And I recollect that I was more ardent
> because of that to sustain it, so that I joined
> my gaze with the Infinite Worth.
> Oh abundant grace whence I presumed
> to fix my look on the Eternal light.
>   (*Par.* 33:79–83)

22. "When we turn from gazing on a very bright light, our eyes are blurred for everything else" (*Commedia*, 926).

In these final dazzling circles of the *Paradiso,* when Dante stares and stares deeply into the "vero sfavillar del Santo Spiro," "very sparkling of the Holy Breath" (*Par.* 14:76) and *"giunsi,"* breathing rib of light, brushes by so many familiar figures: the Argonauts, his twins, Castor and Pollux, Neptune lost in the sea, the birth of history, the milk of Beatrice, circling higher in the Heavens—Bernard signals him to look up but he needs no guide here, "Ma io era, / già per me stesso tal qual ei volea," "but I was / already by myself doing what he wished" (*Par.* 33:50–51). Seeking to fix his ruthless scientific gaze on the Holy of Holies, Dante is a Florentine mapmaker in Paradise, drawing the circle of Divinity out of the skies—a Galileo—unable to recall much more than the passion (he claims) of what he remembers and of that:

> More short by speech
> still of what I recollect, than a baby's
> who moistens yet the tongue by the tit.
> (*Par.* 33:106–8)[23]

But not merely the speech of an infant at his mother's tit, but like the tongue lolling on the nipple, speech of the womb, of birth, falling short of what it recollects—but now reaching back, into his birth, oblivion, he sees three rings. This, and a shadowy image, *"parve,"* "appearing," only appearing! "Pinta de la nostra effige," "painted in our effigy" (*Par.* 33:131), this abstraction is as far as he will go in imaging the Light Eternal.

For he wants to experience identity not with man, but Light, and—he understands light as motion. The circling he has done is the very motion of the Godhead, and to be caught up in that motion is his aspiration, to take the line, the logic of human reason and send it whirling in the circles of Love, light, planets.

To gather all, mother's milk, confusion, courtship, holiness, substance, accidents, in the *"profundo,"* "depth," of that light, in the depth of "un volume," "one volume," "legato con amore," "bound with love" (*Par.* 33:86), all the laws and knowledge scattered through the Universe and then to leave even the image of the book, *his* book, behind, too literal for

> Lor costume
> quasi conflati insieme, per tal modo
> che ciò ch'i dico è un semplice lume.

23. "Più corta mia favella, / pur a quel ch'io ricordo, che d'un fante / che bagni ancor la lingua a la mammella."

Their relations
fused together in such a way
that what I speak of is one simple lamp.
(*Par.* 33:88–90)

In this pantheism, he must give deference to the mysteries of his patrimony, the church of Rome, and so he strains his sight into the great light and sees in threes, circles that seem to be and not to be, distinct yet one, colored yet rainbow-like, a single spectrum of diversity. This is the Florentine religion—an abstract of the myth that Paul and Mary have bequeathed into circles, squares. It is a preoccupation with purity of line as divinity, line sensuous and circling in the domes, ovals, columns of her chapels, Duomo, libraries, hospitals, as close as Dante, the first conductor of his city's hymn to the Tuscan heavens, this abstract, can come. A high, awestruck music filled with the *e*, *"come iri da iri,"* "as rainbow by rainbow," color echoes like sound.

Ne la profonda e chiara sussistenza
de l'alto lume parvermi tre giri
di tre colori e d'una contenenza;
e l'un da l'altro come iri da iri
parea reflesso, e 'l terzo parea foco
che quinci e quindi igualmente si spiri.

In the profound and clear being
of the high light appeared to me three circles
of three colors and of one dimension;
and the one by the other as rainbow by rainbow
appeared reflected and the third appeared fire
that from here and there equally breathed forth.
(*Par.* 33:115–20)[24]

How far are we from a point at which the Universe begins in the world of the *Zohar?*

When the King conceived ordaining
He engraved engravings in the luster on high.
A blinding spark flashed

24. Note as in the line just quoted from canto 14, the confounding of breath or spirit and light.

> within the Concealed of the Concealed
> from the mystery of the Infinite
> a cluster of vapor in formlessness,
> set in a ring,
> not white, nor black, nor red, not green,
> no color at all.
>
> (*Zohar* 1983, 49)[25]

The mysterious power strikes the void, and there is a brightness from which the world issues forth. We are beyond the world of quantum mechanics, Bell's theorem; the visible universe issues from the world that is beyond the speed of light knocking in the void, and becoming light. These thirteenth-century philosophers, poets, are the physicists of the imagination, their science rude but already implacable—Arabs, Christians, Jews. Dante's study of Averroes shines forth—in the triumph of geometry, geometry Dante's poetry, his toy, his dream. His descendants, Brunelleschi, Donatello, in their severe and playful lines will create the Protestant, the Arabic chapels as the canopies of Florence.

So, as Dante stares at the "image fitted to the circle," seeking to break the Universe's metaphysical code, the image that comes to his mind is not of an inspired saint but of a geometrician. He is light years from Saint Bernard.

> Qual è 'l geomètra che tutto s'affige
> per misurar lo cerchio, e non ritrova
> pensando, quel principio ond' elli indige,
> tal era io a quella vista nova:
> veder voleva come si convenne
> l'imago al cerchio e come vi s'indova;

25. I have chosen Daniel Matt's translation here. The passage goes on: "When a band spanned, it yielded radiant colors / Deep within the spark gushed a flow / imbuing colors below, / concealed within the concealed of the mystery of the Infinite . . . / It was not known at all / until, under the impact of breaking through / one high and hidden point shone. / Beyond that point, nothing is known. / So it called Beginning, / the first command of all." (Here the Soncino's translation is interesting. "Beyond that point there is no knowable, and therefore it is called *Reshith* [beginning], the creative utterance which is the starting-point of all.")

"'The enlightened will shine like the *zohar* of the sky, and those who make the masses righteous / will shine like the stars forever and ever' (Daniel:12:3).

"*Zohar*. Concealed of the Concealed, struck its aura. / The aura touched and did not touch this point. / Then this Beginning emanated" (*Zohar* 1983, 49).

ma non eran da ciò le proprie penne:
se non che la mia mente fu percossa
da un fulgore in che sua voglia venne.

Such is the Geometer who sets his all
on squaring the circle, and can not discover
thinking, the principle he needs for it,
so was I at that new sight:
wishing to see how it fit
the image to the circle and how it was set there;
but without the proper wings for that
had not my mind been struck
by a flash in which its wish came!
(*Par.* 33:133–41)

The reduction of all to a single principle of light; the reference to the obliteration of time in which Neptune stares at the track of the Argonauts—an image recalling the mad track of Ulysses, Castor, and Pollux among the shipmates of the Argo searching for the golden fleece; the "*percossa,*" "blow," familiar to us from the sexual flush of Beatrice, the percussion of the look that ravishes—this is the sight that stuns, stupefies, leaves one first "bewildered," "*smarrito,*" and then "clear," "*chiara*" (*Par.* 33:77, 115). Only Beatrice's smile has no power to stun him now. Who is staring at Dante?

Il Primo Amore, the Primal Light! He has sexual congress, knowledge of the unknown, squares the circle. O mad geometer.

At the very last moment of *Paradiso,* he is granted what he has asked, like Moses, a look at the face, backside, of the Holy One, the smile of God.

Now he has leapt beyond heresy into a madness that sends him whirling through the stars.

The madness of going round and round like a geometric principle or circle— beyond Spinoza, the reach of Florentine science, squaring the circle—what marvelous laughter, the last push and he is spinning with the stars:

A l'alta fantasia qui mancò possa;
ma già volgeva il mio disio e 'l velle,
sì come rota ch'igualmente è mossa,
l'amor che move il sole e l'altre stelle.

· · ·

Power here failed the high fantasy;
but already my desire and will were turned,
like a wheel which is evenly spun,
by the Love which spins the sun and the other stars.
                    (*Par.* 33: 142–45)

Is he between the Twins, "*tra feltro e feltro,*" an angel, a star, a deity translated to the sky?

"*Qual Marvaviglia!*" comes the shout from Hell.

CHAPTER ELEVEN

Dante in Exile

THE ARGUMENT OF MY BOOK is at an end. I
cannot glide away however, from the shadow of
Dante. Clinging, it recalls his exile in this world,
and then from the "other." The shade whispers of
other ghosts, speaks of a kingdom of shadow that extends from antiquity to the
century now fading behind us.

◆   ◆   ◆

DANTE THE EXILE—the deep chord of the Hebrew sounds in his poetry. A person, a nation, in exile, remembers every building, sets each stone in place in memory. Helpless, wandering, one embraces the Presence or *Shechinah* that goes with
us when we leave our partner, our city and travel from place to place. A man must
remain ever male and female, that mingling of identities that brings the Divine
Presence so close he can feel it hovering over him. It is through his beloved, his
partner, that the Holy One draws in honeyed proximity. If he ventures from home,
while still bound up in that union: he must pray to God, to draw to himself the
Presence.[1]

To Florence Dante Alighieri was never to return. In his imagination, the Holy
One came with the face and body of Beatrice, to ease the poet's tears and take him

---

1. "Before starting [on a journey, a man] must pray to God, to draw unto himself the Presence of
his Master. After he has prayed and offered thanksgiving, and when the Presence is resting on him,
then he may go, for by virtue of his union with the Presence he is now male and female in the country,
just as he was male and female in the town, for it is written, 'Righteousness [*zedek,* feminine of *zaddik,*] shall go before him and shall make his footsteps a way' " (Ps. 85:14).

"Remark this. The whole time of his traveling a man should heed well his actions, lest the holy
union break off, and he be left imperfect, deprived of the union with the female. If it was needful
when he and his wife were together, how much greater the need when the heavenly mate is with him?
And the more so, indeed, since this heavenly union acts as his constant guard on his journey, until his
return home" (*Zohar* 1970, 34–35).

on high. In the judgment of his contemporaries, it was to Hell he went. Dante's dear friends, Bosone da Gubbio, with whom he lodged according to legend, and Cina da Pistoia, whom Alighieri addressed as "fair master," in an exchange of sonnets between them on love and lechery, admitted that the Florentine's blatant sin, common gossip of Ravenna's gutter, could consign him to a pouch deep in his own elaborate *Inferno.*

What was Dante's offense? His biographer, Boccaccio, speaks of it with pain, but makes it plain.

> And assuredly I blush to be forced to taint the fame of such a man with any defect, but the order of things which I have begun in some sort demands it; because that if I hold my peace concerning those things in him which are less worthy of praise, I shall withdraw much faith from the praiseworthy things already recounted. So do I plead excuse to him himself, who perchance, even as I write looketh down with scornful eye . . . [It is not Boccaccio who will send Dante to Hell for such a peccadillo.] from some lofty region of heaven. Amid all the virtue, amid all the knowledge, that hath been shewn above to have belonged to this wondrous poet, lechery found most ample place not only in the years of his youth but also of his maturity; the which vice though it be natural and common, and scarce to be avoided, yet in truth is so far from being commendable that it cannot be suitably excused. But who among mortals shall be a righteous judge to condemn it? Not I. Oh the infirmity, oh the brutish appetite of men! What power cannot women exercise over us when they choose, seeing what great things they can do even when they choose not. Attractiveness and beauty and natural appetite and many other things are working for them without pause in the hearts of men. (Boccaccio 1904, 55)

"Who among mortals shall be a righteous judge to condemn it?" Obviously Cina da Pistoia felt he had that right. Was he still rankling at Dante's condescension many years before, first to his rhymes?

> Io mi credea del tutto esser partito
> da queste nostre rime, messer Cino
> ché si conviene omai altro cammino
> a la mia nave più lungi dal lito:
>
> I thought I had quite departed from
> these, our rhymes, Master Cino

since now another way is suitable
for my boat, further from the shore:

And then to his personal life:

Ma perch'i' ho di voi più volte udito
che pigliar vi lasciate a ogni uncino,

But since I have heard several times of you
that you allow yourself to be caught on every hook.
                    (*Rime* 163)[2]

He, Cino, thought now to set the record straight. In his youth he had borne
lightly Dante's accusation:

Chi s'innamora sì come voi fate,
or qua or là, e sé lega e dissolve,
mostra ch'Amore leggermente il saetti.
Però se leggier cor così vi volve,
priego che con vertù il correggiate,
sì che s'accordi i fatti a' dolce detti.

Whoever falls in love, as you do,
now here, now there, binds and looses himself,
shows that Love but lightly shoots him.
So if a light heart thus revolves you
I pray you that with virtue you correct it,
That among themselves they may agree,
the deeds and sweet words.   (*Rime*, 163)

To which Cino had courteously replied:

Since I was, Dante, from my native place
made by a harsh exile, a wanderer
and put at a distance from the purest beauty

2. The Italian text may be found in the edition of *Vita Nuova/Rime*, of Fredi Chiappelli (*Rime*,
163). The scholar and translator Professor Frederick Goldin, of CUNY, pointed out to the author in
conversation that "nostre rime" refers to the "dolce stile" and that "uncino" puns on Cino's name.

that ever the Infinite Beauty formed
I have gone grieving through the world
disdained by death like a beggar
and if when I have found near me one like her
I have said that this one has wounded my heart—.
Never from those first pitiless arms
from which firmly rooted despair releases me
have I moved, even though I expect no help;
but one beauty always binds and winds me round
which beauty in whatever is like it
in many different women must delight me.
                    (*Rime* 163–64)[3]

Cino has taken up Dante's phrase, "e sé lega e dissolve," "binds and looses himself," echoed it, "ch'un piacer sempre me lega ed involve," "but one pleasure [or beauty], always binds and winds me round." In fact, far from loosing me, says Cino, it winds me tighter, the same Beauty, though I find it in different women.

But now, in old age, the lines of mockery, "Let them agree, the deeds and sweet words," must irritate Cino. Who put him up to straying from one woman after others? Was it not Dante Alighieri whom he had asked about pursuing the One through the many?

Dante, when the longing of love
comes to abandon hope—
hope that the eyes bring forth from the sweet seed
of that beauty which opens in the mind—
then I say: if death spares her,
and Love rules her more than the two extremes
the soul, alone now and afraid no more
can indeed turn to another person.
And she who is mistress in all things
makes me say this, because of One I feel again

3. "Poi ch' i fu', Dante dal mio natal sito / fatto per greve essilio pellegrino / e lontanato dal piacer più fino / che mai formasse il Piacer infinito / io son piangendo per lo mondo gito / sdegnato del morir come meschino / e s'ho trovato a lui simil vicino / dett'ho che questi m'ha lo cor ferito. / Né da le prime braccia dispietate, / onde 'l fermato disperar m'assolve, / son mosso perch'aiuto non aspetti; / ch'un piacer sempre me lega ed involve, / il qual' conven che a simil di beltate / in molte donne sparte mi diletti."

entered, alas, at my window.
But before the black and white slay me,
from thee, who have been within and without
I would know—if my creed is wrong.
(*Rime* 161)[4]

To which Dante replied, "Your creed is right—Love is in the saddle and to him we surrender even free will."

Thus within the circle of his arena
free will was never free
so that reason bends its bow in vain there.
Indeed he can with new spurs prick the flank
and whatever the pleasure may be which now leads us
follow we must, if the other is played out.
(Goldin 1973a, 404)[5]

"'L piacer ch'ora n'addestra, / sequitar si convien," "the pleasure [beauty] which now leads us, / follow we must," what right then did Dante have to excoriate him, one of the singers of the "sweet new style" with the remark that his acts did not accord with his "sweet" words? Did Dante reform?

"Lechery found most ample place not only in the years of his youth but also of his maturity." Was Dante any different from Cino da Pistoia? Not according to Boccaccio's testimony some sixty years later. He couples Cino and Dante in the *Decameron*.

Some of my critics say, young ladies, that I am wrong to dedicate myself to such an extent in seeking pleasure, and claim that I go out of my way in trying to win your favor. . . . As for those others who inveigh against my age—they simply show their ignorance of the truism that though the leek has a white head, it has a green tail. To these worthies I say, laying jesting aside, that as long as I love, I shall never think it shameful to ingratiate those beings whom Guido Cavalcanti and Dante Alighieri honored, and whose approval they prized in their old age, yes, and Cino da Pistoia, too, when he was a very reverend old man. . . . I could quote

4. See also Goldin 1973a, 432–33. Goldin in his footnotes points out the ambiguity of "her" in the fifth line, which may refer either to "hope," or to the "soul."
5. For the Italian and Goldin's fluent translation refer to his edition (1973a, 404–5).

plenty of instances of noble oldsters who did their utmost, in their hoariest years to win the favor of the ladies. (Boccaccio 1955, 224)

This is what explains Cino's fury in his poem, *Messer Boson, lo vostro Manoello.* Under it seethes his dialogue with the dead Florentine. Dante! You hypocrite. Heaven? What good did your passage through Hell, bath in Eden, vows in Paradise, do? Right up to the end on earth, "eyes purging thick amber and plum tree gum" you were flattering and seducing, just like me, showing a "green tail."

Going to Heaven? Cino did not think it likely. Men were still naming Dante Alighieri's peccadillo in the streets of Italy, and those who knew the *Commedia* would understand when Cino sang, dunking the Florentine in the same bolgia of the *Inferno* as the notorious Immanuel, the Jew, a common friend of Bosone da Gubbio and himself:

> Con Dante si sta sotto al cappello
> del qual come nel libro suo si legge
> Vide coperto Alessi Interminello.

> With Dante he is under that cap
> of which as we read in his book
> he saw Alessi Interminello covered.

Cecil Roth, who was the first to draw conclusions from the evidence of Immanuel and Dante's common bonnet in the line of Cino's, refers us to *"il libro."* It is in the *Commedia,* canto 18 of the *Inferno,* that we find Alessio Interminei, as Dante saw him, "un col cap sì di merda lordo, / che non parëa s'era laico o cherco," "one with a head so thick with shit, / one could not tell whether he was lay or cleric." Cino's *cappello* echoes Dante's "cap." Not laurels but excrement would adorn Dante's brow in the world to come. Cino is too discreet to heap the ordure on directly—the passage, the reference to Alessio will do. Let Dante's own description fix him in his place.

> Già erevam là 've lo stretto calle
> con l'argine secondo s'incrocicchia,
> e fa di quello ad un altr' arco spalle.
> Quindi sentimmo gente che si nicchia
> ne l'altra bolgia e che col muso scuffa,
> e sè medesma con le palme picchia.
> Le ripe eran grommate d'una muffa,

per l'alito di giù che vi s'appasta
che con li occhi e col naso facea zuffa. . . .
Quivi venimmo: e quindi giù nel fosso
vidi gente attuffata in uno sterco
che da li uman privada parëa mosso.
E mentre ch'io là, giù con l'occhio cerco,
vidi un col capo sì di merda lordo,
che non parâa s'era laico o cherco.
Quei mi sgridò: "Perché se' tu sì gordo
di riguardar più me che li altri brutti?"
E io a lui: "Perché, se ben ricordo,
già t'ho veduto coi capelli asciutti,
a se' Alessio Interminei da Lucca:
però t'adocchio più che li altri tutti."
Ed elli allor, battendosi la zucca:
"Qua giù m'hanno sommerso le lusinghe
ond' io non ebbi mai la lingua stucca."
Appresso ciò lo duca, "Fa che pinghe,"
mi disse, "il viso un poco più avante,
sì che la faccia ben con l'occhio attinghe
di quella sozza e scapigliata fante
che là si graffia con l'unghie merdose,
e or s'accoscia e ora è in piedi stante.
Taïde è, la puttana che ripuose
al drudo suo quando disse, 'Ho io grazie
grandi apo te?': 'Anzi maravigliose!'
E quinci sian le nostre viste sazie."

Now we were there where the narrow road
with the second dike is crossed
and makes of this to the other arch, a span.
Here we heard a people whimpering
in the other ditch and with snouts puffing
and thumping themselves with their palms.
The banks were encrusted by a mold
by the breath below which sticks
yet fights with the nose and eyes. . . .
Here we came, where in the trench below
I saw a people dipped in turd
that seemed from human privies stirred.
And while my eyes below there searched

I saw one with a head so thick with shit,
one could not tell whether he was lay or cleric.
He shouted at me, "Why art thou so greedy
to regard me, more than the other brutes?"
And I to him, "Because if I remember right
I have seen you before with dry hair.
You are Alessio Interminei of Lucca.
Therefore I fix my eyes on you more than all the others."
And he then, beating his dome,
"Thus below have my enticements submerged me
with which my tongue was never cloyed."
After that the leader, "Thrust forth,"
he told me, "your face a bit further
so that your eyes may indeed reach
to that foul and rumpled wench
that there scratches herself with shitty fingernails,
now she squats and now stands on her feet.
Thais it is, the whore who replied
to her lover when he said, 'Do I have a big
thank you from you?' 'Please, too marvelous!' [6]
And with that let our sight be sated."
                                        (*Inf.* 18:100–136)

Who is in this pit and what for? What links Thais's big thank-you for her romp in the hay with Alessio's smelly pate? Cecil Roth explains,

It is important to realize, however, that he [Alessio/ Alesso] is not a mere flatterer, but (as the context suggests on the one hand and the ancient commentaries emphasize on the other) one who seduced women by his flattery. (C. F. Bambl., *"Ex multis banditiis coloratis et verbis ipsius multas mulieres decepit"*; A. Asel. *"Tenne bordello di puttane,"* and other glosses cited by the authorities.) This accords to some extent with what we know about Immanuel (or rather, what he informs us about himself). His Hebrew poetry is perhaps the most lascivious written in that language in the Middle Ages: he boasts his amatory conquests, though indeed not very realistically, at every opportunity: and the Rabbis of a later age forbade his book even to be read. ("He dressed up the sober Hebrew muse in the skirts of

---

6. *"Maravigliose!"* here recalls Brunetto Latini's greeting of Dante in a previous canto—its import I will discuss in a moment. It seems, however, to be a word with levels of irony that we might in a modern context call "camp."

a ballet dancer," as it has been expressed.) . . . It may have been boasting only: but it was the sort of boasting that he obviously indulged in when he was in the company of his Italian acquaintances. This apparently made a lasting impression on the minds of the author of the sonnet ascribed to Cino da Pistoia, who considered that he would be eternally punished for it, together with Alesso Interminelli [sic] of Lucca and Dante Alighieri. The language of the sonnet, as of Bosone's reply, is as I have indicated so obscure as almost to defy interpretation. But it seems obvious that in the eyes of the writer, Dante was no ascetic. (Roth 1953, 31)[7]

Dante—forever in Hell, yoked to his fellow, the Jew, Immanuel? Bosone da Gubbio, in his reply to Cino, held out a better hope. To save his friends, Dante and Manoello, Bosone denied the very premise of the *Commedia*, that Hell, the Catholic Hell, was exclusive and eternal. It is true that Alighieri and Ha-Romi, must—I blush. It is too crude,—sit in sh. . . . But hope, the Hebrew hope that the "happy laughing soul," Immanuel had preached in his own version of the *Commedia, Ha Tophet Veha-Eden*—all souls, Jew, Christian and Moslem would have their thrones in the hereafter. It is that idealism which animates Bosone. He proves himself a disciple of the broad-minded Immanuel, and paying tribute to "la mente tua, che già ridea," "that mind of yours which already smiles,"[8] Bosone predicts, "Dante e Manoello compiono lor corso. Ov'è lor cotto lo midollo e il buccio, Tanto che giunga lor lo gran soccorso," "Dante and Manuel run their race together. There where the marrow and the rind of theirs are baked so much, they gain by it, the great Deliverance" (Roth 1953, 29).

"Lo gran soccorso," "the great Succor," is Bosone punning on the "*corso*," "race," the race of the sinners and the "*soccorso*," great Succor racing toward them.

7. In view of Cino's gloss, I re-read with a raised eyebrow Rossi's remark, which Sinclair approvingly quotes in the notes of his edition, "The misbegotten breed of these paltry offenders guilty of private crimes awakes no storm in the lofty moral consciousness of the Poet. He feels toward them an olympic, one might almost say a serene, contempt" (*Inf.* 1972, 235). On the contrary, Virgil urges Dante to practically put his nose into the mess. The Poet's stare, which Alesso feels, hardly seems "olympic." Honesty, perhaps, forbids Dante making any superior moral reflections at this moment. Reflect on the act of sexual flattery in the book that Paolo and Francesca read—their accusation that its author as panderer, was responsible for their sin. The writing of the *Commedia* itself may be Dante's greatest crime, for it facilitates a tryst in the "other world," the seduction of Beatrice. The seduction of the reader, in any case, is a crime that many writers are at risk for.

8. See Israel Zinburg's sketch of Immanuel where he quotes with approval Bosone's characterization "la mente tua, che già ridea" (1972, 203).

Yes—they may expect it. And the *corso* recalls the race to victory by Brunetto Latini. Dante has been rewarded by his own moment of hope in Hell.

Reading Dante through Cino and Bosone, the melancholy of the comedy rings through. In Thais's "Too marvelous!" I hear the cry of Brunetto, *"maravigliose,"* "marvelous!" It is the degradation of sex in excrement. "Fair needs foul," the commentary of Yeats—without Dante's own experience, terror of incarceration in the *Inferno,* he could never have risen to the dream of salvation in *Paradiso.* The smile of Beatrice has come to a man crowned in ordure and restored him, girt with a frond of Eden, to his laurels. Adorned in the feathers of the peacock, he has a place beyond the stars. That smile, its grace, inspiration, can only be refraction, a wind of the nameless Spirit, not alone of mercy but of laughter.

Rimbomba

"RIMBOMBA," RESOUNDS, RE-ECHOES from the judgment before eternity one final note which Dante heard. It dogs my ear, booming along the shore.

Walking the stony beach, the Atlantic headland of my summer cottage in that "sublimely dreary" coast, as Thoreau concisely named it,[1] the South Shore stretching away from Boston to Cape Cod, I think of the sage in his last year. Dante was already prematurely, as his Ulysses had been, "old and slow," subject to the fevers of the marshes across which the Florentine exile had to ride and walk. His footsteps, ague ridden, took their way over pebbles and sands along the strand at Ravenna. The questions of the poem speak in the ocean's seething as I stop to wonder at his final refuge at this eastern Italian harbor, across the sea from the shore that descended to Greece. A boat carrying the poet slides in with the tide.

Dante and Homer—what did the former know, how much had he read of the latter? As I read the *Odyssey* again after a lapse of years, the Greek epic seemed to me more than an echo heard by Dante from far away. The *Odyssey's* story was not just an influence received from Latin shades, fragments, but a counterweight to the Florentine's poem. Had Dante discovered Homer, or had Homer's hero, Odysseus, escaped from confinement in the condescending lines of Virgil and, a shadow soul, accompanied Dante in his dream?

I recalled from the very first chapters of *La Vita Nuova* the quotation of Homer's lines, "She did not appear as the daughter of a mortal man but of a god." The quote puts the words of Odysseus into the mouth of Dante, as the latter looks on Beatrice. It is a prophetic quote, the aged mariner looking at the princess, Nausicaa, a nubile teenager. Dante must have felt his kinship—a man standing naked, having stepped out of the woods, holding a bush to mask his private parts.

---

1. See Henry David Thoreau's *Cape Cod,* where he characterizes the wintry shore south of Boston (Thoreau 1961, 31). Walking the beach at Ravenna in 1977, I felt the same cold breeze.

Where had Dante come across these lines? Fredi Chiappelli in his notes to *Vita Nuova Rime* theorizes that he had found the description of the dialogue with Nausicaa in the *Odyssey* of Homer, 6.149.[2] They recall also, Chiappelli adds, the description of Hector in the *Iliad*.[3] Why had Dante Alighieri remembered them, identified with them, so early in his career? When Dante came to write the *Divine Comedy* he would see himself again as Odysseus, in spite of his master, Virgil, and the latter's hostility toward Greek heroes. Virgil, as a scion of an imperial Rome that traced descent from Trojans, had a natural antipathy to Odysseus, who symbolized the glory of Greece, a man who brought destruction to the purported mother of the Romans, Troy. Dante so far deserts not only Virgil, but his own sympathies with Roman dreams of legitimacy, to tremble before the Greek captain, not once but many times. The lines of Howard Nemerov *rimbomba,* resound, and speak of that timbre in Dante's music when it sings of Ulysses. I quoted them in a previous chapter and now read them over. "Ulysses and the fall of man both relate to knowledge and lust. Whenever Ulysses turns up, three times in all [the critic, David Thompson, points out a fourth possible allusion],[4] it is in the company of some sort of sexual enchantment" (Nemerov 1974, 131–32).

Sexuality, bestiality, the voyage, these are three deep concerns in Dante's writing about the world beyond, its reference to a world around us. The very setting

2. For a discussion of this see J. A. Scott on the twenty-sixth canto of the *Inferno* and Dante's Ulysses. "The quotation from Homer in *Vita Nuova,* 2 ("che certo di lei si potea dire quella parola del poeta Omero: 'Ella non parea figliuola d'uomo mortale, ma di deo'") was derived from the Seventh Book of Aristotle's *Ethics* which was well known to Dante (cf., *Conv.* III, vii, 7, IV, xx, 4: *Mon.,* II, iii, 9). The description of Homer in *Inf.* IV, –88, and his appellation *'poeta sovrano'* merely echo the praises found in Latin writers" (1971, 146, fn. 4). Scott's conclusion about Dante's praise of Homer as a "mere echo," has, however, been challenged. I will quote in the following pages, from David Thompson's *Dante's Epic Journey.* Thompson enumerates a number of medieval sources where Dante can be expected to have encountered Homer.

3. "Si allude forse al discorso tenuto da Ulisse a Nausicaa nell'*Odissea*, VI, 149, segg.; o alla descrizione di Ettore che 'non pareva figlio di un uomo mortale, ma di un dio' cfr. Iliade, XXIV, 258, che Dante poteva aver trovato nell'Etica di Aristotele" (*Rime,* 20, n. 12).

4. Thompson points out that in that in the first canto of *Purgatorio,* after Virgil washes Dante's face, they walk along the shore, which calls up in the poet's mind the ill-fated journey of Ulysses toward Purgatory: "Vennimo poi in sul lito diserto, / che mai non vide navicar sue acque / omo, che di tornar sia poscia esperto. / Quivi mi cinse sì com' altrui piacque."

"We came then to the desert shore, / which never saw any one sail its waters / who was afterwards able to return. / There he girded me as it pleased another" (*Purg.* 1:130–33). The line in which Ulysses accepts his fate, to be drowned in sight of the "promised land," *"com'altrui piacque"* (*Inf.* 26:141) is repeated here in Purgatory. Thompson remarks on a number of other echoes of that moment of despair in the *Inferno* that tie the two passages together (1974, 46–47).

out is fraught with misgiving. The medievalist Fredrick Goldin pointed out to me in conversation that the writing itself of the *Commedia,* a description of the world beyond, is an act of heresy, "the ultimate transgression which must make the poet tremble. . . . What Ulysses did on the sea, he [Dante] is doing with the poem. The book is Odysseus's voyage. Writing about the supreme truth, and he [Dante] is writing a lie, a fiction, and he knows it." In that sense, Goldin comments, "Ulysses is really a representative of the poet," and that is why he is "such a powerful and unforgettable figure in the *Inferno.*"

Writing of a visit to Hell, Purgatory, Heaven, presuming to describe those worlds with authority, Dante Alighieri has gone on a journey toward an end that his own conscience questions.[5] Behind the mask of sarcasm (echoing Ulysses' own sardonic reference to a "little speech" by which the Homeric hero taunts his men into the unknown), Dante calls the Greek captain's dash across the waves, *"folle*

---

5. Scott identifies several sources for Dante's knowledge of the controversy over Odysseus's ultimate destination. "Homer himself had left the question open in the *Odyssey* by mentioning that his hero's death would 'come off the sea ' and this cryptic reference had given rise to all manner of conjecture. Dante was probably aware of this through two authorities, Servius and Seneca. In the eighty-eighth epistle to Lucilius, Seneca argues against the useless pedantry of grammarians and literary critics. Rather than ask such otiose questions as 'where did Ulysses' wanderings take him?' we ought instead to open our eyes to the moral implications behind the word *errare* and do our best to avoid the storms of the spirit that buffet us every day, surrounded as we are by false allurements, shipwreck and evil of every kind" (Scott 1971, 146–47). Scott is arguing that Ulysses represents for Dante a type of absolute folly, but the critic ignores the obvious. Dante does exactly what Seneca proscribed. Dante speculates on where Ulysses' wanderings took him. Scott's article, while balanced in arguing its position, the condemnation of Ulysses and the opposition of Cato, the pious pagan, to Ulysses, the impious one, takes no notice of the laughter of Dante, which teases the question. While quoting T. S. Eliot on sympathy, Scott misses Dante's sympathies as a poet. Cato remains a dead figure in the *Commedia* no matter how correct his point of view. Ulysses' lines echo over and over, disturbing the reader. The poet Blake's observation that Milton wrote "at liberty when of Devils & Hell because he was a true Poet and of the Devil's party without knowing it" has a curious echo here. Dante, however, in never allowing Satan as the ruler of Hell a real dramatic existence, and taking himself, Dante, through the circles of Hell, creates a more complex, ambiguous situation. Dante, I believe, understood, only too well, his slippery footing in the Inferno. See note 6 of this chapter.

Dante's attitude toward Ulysses is, I admit, ambivalent. Reading Statius's *Achilleid,* one of Dante's sources for his portrait of the "Ithacan," I wondered what Dante's personal response to the treachery of Ulysses/Odysseus would have been. Is there some residue of anger in Dante's condemning of Odysseus together with Diomedes in the same flame—an echo of the Greek captains' common journey in Statius to trick Achilles into joining them for the Trojan War? Achilles will leave his new bride and peaceful life behind. Though Dante may identify with Odysseus, Dante also has been talked into leaving Florence to join a political cause—and this has cost Dante his home. Ulysses' being punished together with Diomedes, is after all, the focus of the Greek captains' torment, and Diomedes is innocent of a trip to the borders of the unknown.

volo," "mad flight" or "flight of folly"—but it is precisely the flight of the poem. The word, *folle,* in the context of a questionable journey should be familiar to our ears. In the second canto of the *Inferno* Dante exclaims in terror of starting out to Virgil, "Per che, se del venire io m'abbandono, / temo che la venuta no sia folle," "so that if I give myself over to going, / I fear that my going may be folly," remarking piteously, "I am not Aeneas, I am not Paul" (*Inf.* 2:34–35). And Dante wants to know, "Who allows it?"

John Scott, in his essay, "Dante's Ulysses," observing this repetition of *folle,* folly, wishing to see Ulysses not as the poet's shadow but as his antithesis, writes, "Dante's reluctance to fall into the trap set by *follia* of which he had been guilty in the past, adds further weight to the parallel between the pilgrim's successful journey, assisted by divine grace, and its antithesis, the *folle volo* of Ulysses" (Scott 1971, 168). Such a reading ignores what follows Dante's admission of self-doubt at the beginning of the *Inferno,* his so-called, prudent speech. Virgil accuses Dante of being a coward for talking thus. The response is so strong as to suggest that Ulysses' voice is echoing through the Mantuan's. For indeed pious, prudent Aeneas is scolded for not going on his journey with more dispatch in Virgil's epic.[6]

Both the adventure and the folly of Dante lie on the road to the world beyond. As Dante and Virgil approach the gates of Dis, one of the devils speaks to the poet's anxiety, that he will be "abandoned" or "given over" in Hell to the punishment of the "road of folly." Mocking fiends invite Virgil to come in and leave his friend outside: "'Quei sen vada, / che sì ardito intrò per questo regno. / Sol si ritorni per la folle strada," "Let him go off / who was eager to enter this kingdom / Let him return by his mad road" (*Inf.* 8:89–91). To underscore this terror, Dante follows with the comment, "Imagine, reader, how discomforted I was / at the sound of the cursed words, / that I thought never to return here."

The poem is the road over land and sea, the *"folle volo"* and its words are steps, then oars, which become "wings for the mad flight." In detailing the heretical act of Ulysses, however, the imagery speaks of angels, mocking the evil, the anxiety, "De' remi facemmo ali al folle volo," "of the oars we made wings for the mad flight" (*Inf.* 16:125). Just how subversive this is, may be appreciated by noting what

---

6. In opposing Cato's refusal to go beyond the limits of the habitable, known world, to Ulysses' voyage, Scott does not acknowledge that Dante's voyage takes him to exactly the place, Purgatory, to which Ulysses, piously or impiously, has been heading—which suggests some fellow feeling at the least. Cato's trip, for all its piety, is a dead end. As to the assertion that Dante is condemned for going beyond the boundary of human knowledge, again, as Frederick Goldin notes, the very writing of the *Commedia* is an act of impiety, of going beyond the bounds of what can be described or imagined truthfully by man.

"wings" stand for in the *Commedia*. David Thompson in *Dante's Epic Journeys* cites the following, seeing the flight on wings as the image that reveals the concept of Dante's poem.

> "Non v'accorgete voi che noi siam vermi
> nati a formar l'angelica farfalla.
> che vola a la giustizia sanza schermi?"

> "Do you not realize that we are worms
> born to form the angelic butterfly
> which flies to judgment without defense?"
> (*Purg.* 10:124–26)

Thompson points out that "Dante advances gradually to flying on the wings afforded him by Beatrice" (1974, 10).

And scanning the Italian, the *"vola"* in this key passage, clearly echoes the *"volo"* of Ulysses. The lines above read as a cry of anxiety, recalling Kafka pleading for a metamorphosis from a cursed human existence, man as insect.

Not only the composition of the poem, but the language in which it is written is part of the poet's "mad" venture. Dante, writing a poetic epic in Italian not Latin, adopting the language of the street, of the merchant and tradesman, rather than the cleric, has Virgil, greatest of the Latin poets, serve as his guide. This is part of the book's "comedy." An imitator of Virgil, Dante uses the Latin poet as a guide in the writing, but Dante has broken with Rome by deserting Virgil's language. Virgil, over a thousand years before, had taken Homer as a guide, in an affectionate embrace despite Roman imperialism. (Dante, however, inherits bad habits from Virgil, the baroque trumpet blasts of Roman patriotism, prophecies of future greatness. The *Aeneid* is propaganda for the state. Homer, although partial, is free of this.)[7]

What is common to Homer, Virgil, and Dante is their fascination with the underworld. Hades will be one-third of Dante's *Commedia* but only one-twelfth of Virgil's *Aeneid*. In Homer, the kingdom of the dead occupies even a smaller fraction of Odysseus's epic. (Though the conversation of the dead in the last book of

---

7. The rage and pathos of exile temper Dante's reflections on Florence and qualify his patriotism. Memories like the statue of Mars by the Arno are embedded as folklore in the *Commedia*. Even Dante's shout for the imperial banner of Henry is forlorn. (Virgil, at least for this reader, spoils the genius of the Aeneid's sixth canto, its portrait of the underworld and meeting with Dido, with the theatrical Hollywood ending, a pan across future Roman greatness. This flash forward diminishes the tension.)

the *Odyssey* is a partial return to the shadow realm.) Odysseus goes to the underworld to find directions to go home. This is exactly what Dante denies the Greek
hero wishes to do! In the course of the journey in Homer to the other world
Odysseus meets his mother. It will be a moment of overwhelming pathos for
Odysseus in his journey to his home, a reminder that he is subject to time.

Virgil, rewriting Homer, reversed the order. Aeneas goes to the underworld to
see his father, Anchises, and receives, not directions, but a reassuring vision of the
rightness of his course.

Dante, the chief persona of his own drama, is closer to Homer. Dante is *smarrito*, bewildered, in his course, not in a literal voyage but in life itself. His journey
to the underworld is a correction of the bewilderment. He finds not so much directions, but guides. (It can be argued, however, that Athena is Odysseus's guide.
Venus fulfills this role for Aeneas.) In both the *Odyssey* and the *Commedia* however, the experience of the realm of shadows, its hopelessness, changes the hero.
Odysseus is not reassured but receives a tragic vision of life. Dante is warned of
what awaits the impenitent. Therefore Dante's journey takes new directions. This
modern notion, implicit in the *Odyssey* is explicit in the *Commedia*. Not what
Dante is told in the *Inferno*, but the experience of passing through it, changes him.
I doubt whether the trip through the *Aeneid*'s underworld in any way transforms
its pious captain, even though Virgil writing of Aeneas's encounter with the dead,
in imitation of Homer, stresses the tragic distance between the dead and the living.

In both Homer and Virgil, however, the unburied dead make claims upon the
living. The myth of the funeral pyre and proper funeral rites would too obviously
contradict the beliefs of Christianity based on the Jewish customs of interment, and
so this cannot figure in Dante directly. Nevertheless, in the promise of the Sibyl to
the drowned pilot, Palinurus,[8] that he will receive fame from the surrounding cities
charged to rebury his bones, Dante receives from Virgil a strong hint about the
emotional life of Hell. What can the dead ask from the living? Virgil in this incident
from the *Aeneid* would have indicated to Dante that the dead interrogated would
wish for fame after interment. In the *Inferno* many of the dead beg to be remembered, and Virgil promises them that Dante will do it in the bright world above. The
vision of the forgotten, at the very portals of Hell as the worst of punishments, the
cieca vita resounds through the poem. The *Commedia* is a paean to memory, that
mysterious trait of life that "arises out of aeons of rotting matter" but has made bio-
logical life possible. Memory rises in man to self-awareness, perhaps *the* human
achievement. The fact that Dante made himself, the memory of himself, his autobiography, the *Commedia*'s principal drama, speaks to a new funeral rite.

8. See Virgil's *Aeneid*, book 6 (1986, 375–83).

Dante, in the tradition of Augustine, elevates confession to the status of a religious art form. Dante has the wit to see that Homer and Virgil's imaginative descents to the underworld are the mysterious centers of their poems and to make himself, Dante Alighieri, the hero of the epic he writes. At issue in the *Commedia* is not bravery, but honesty. It is through the honesty of his confession that Dante can make sure he is remembered.

It is therefore not just Odysseus who fascinates Dante, but Homer, the writer, and the *Odyssey* as a confession of Homer's. Homer becomes the mysterious, missing author, like the missing father of the *Commedia*. For Homer had gone before Dante, before Virgil, as a writer, to the other world. One of Dante's sources for Homer was Statius. Thompson remarks that together with Virgil's *Aeneid*, "Statius's *Achilleid*, afforded Dante an account of the sins for which Ulysses (with Diomedes) will be punished among the false counselors" (Thompson 1974, 14). Statius, like Virgil, will play a pivotal role in the *Commedia*.

What was Dante's knowledge of Homer? Grandgent thinks that Dante knew about Homer through Horace.[9] Dante, as one critic points out, "conceals his sources as he does his education, and the story of his youthful years." [10] Homer and the story of Ulysses, however, as Thompson points, out were well known to Dante and his contemporaries.

Dante has invented the entire account of Ulysses, not only the final voyage but also the quoted version of his encounter with the siren. And he has invented these episodes not to fill gaps in the story as known to himself and his Greekless contemporaries, but in direct opposition to a perfectly clear tradition.

From Dares and Dictys, or from the extensive literary texts dependent upon them, Dante could easily have learned about Ulysses' return to Ithaca and how he died there. And these were not the only obvious sources of information. Classical texts cast considerable light upon Ulysses' fate, but if we consider these sources

9. The notes of the Grandgent and Singleton edition of *La Divina Commedia* state flatly, "Dante did not know Homer directly." They trace Dante's knowledge of Homer to the former's reading of Horace, quoting *Ars Poetica*, 73–74: "Res gestae regumque ducumque et tristia bella / quo scribi possent numero, monstravit Homerus," "The deeds of kings and captains and sorrows of war / The measure of what may be written, Homer has shown."

Citing a reference to Homer by Dante in *La Vita Nuova*, chapter 25, that appears in Horace *De Arte Poetica*, 141, "In Horace a man speaks to his own learning, as though to a person: and not only are they the words of Horace, but he gives them as a quotation from the good Homer, in his Poetics: *Dic mihi Musa, virum*" (Reynolds 1969, 74), the Grandgent and Singleton edition remarks that the same constellation of ancient poets appear "grouped" in the Inferno as in chapter 25 of *La Vita Nuova* (40, n. 88).

10. Curtius, *European Literature*, 360, as quoted by Thompson (Thompson 1974, 28).

too vague, we need only turn to the various mythographers. Hyginus, for example, gives us the several stages of Ulysses' homeward voyage, step by step. After
lying with Circe and siring Telegonus, Ulysses proceeds to Avernus for his *descensus ad infernos*. Then, warned by Circe, he passes successfully by the sirens,
reaches home, destroys the suitors, and eventually dies at the hands of Telegonus.

Thompson remarks that "if Dante was the least bit curious about Ulysses, he
may be expected to have found his way to one or another of these sources" and he
quotes Benvenuto da Imola, "I cannot be persuaded to believe that Dante was ignorant of what even schoolboys know; so I say that rather the author devised this
on purpose" (Thompson 1974, 49–50).

> Dante and his contemporaries could not read Homer in the original. The tale of
> Troy had come down to Dante only through various Latin filters. . . . There was
> available to him, however, a compendium that remains handy even today—Mac-
> robius's *Saturnalia*, the fifth book of which quotes numerous passages that Virgil
> allegedly borrowed from Homer. (Thompson 1974, 57–58)

Dante's use of Homer can hardly be described as Vossler did as "decorative." [11]
The *Commedia*'s regard to Homer goes to the poem's deepest stratum, a search for
the body of Dante's mistress. Despite the lack of a Greek original, Homer was not
an obscure figure to the medieval writers who preceded Dante, but in the center of
their debate about literature and life. "Just as Homer's work lies behind Virgil's, so
behind allegorizations of Virgil's there lies a long history of Homeric interpretation, which ultimately also provides part of the context in which we should view
Dante's enigmatic depiction of Ulysses" (Thompson 1974, 3). Dante had access to

---

11. See Karl Vossler, *Mediaeval Culture:* "Already in the *Vita Nuova,* the canon of Dante's taste is
anticipated. Virgil, Horace, Ovid, and Lucan are cited as models. Homer, the Greek whom Dante
never knew, stands beside them merely as a decorative greatness." On the other hand, Vossler is ful-
some in his appreciation of the importance of Ulysses for Dante. "Dante, the Christian poet who was
the first to recognize in him [Ulysses] the evil-doer, described the triumphant hero on his way to destruction. He set the tragedy over against the epic. . . . So the Dantesque Ulysses stands, a many-sided
figure, at a point where the remotest perspectives in the history of the human spirit meet: Homer, the
Fall, Christopher Columbus; Hellenism, mediaevalism, and the Renaissance; unbroken natural force,
terrible guilt, and the bold spirit of discovery. Meantime strength and courage are infused into the
will, abysmal evil into the intellect, of this hero. Flickering lights of divine truth play over his utterance, and the epic tale is illuminated, not merely from without, in tragic firelight. In short, deceit is, in
Ulysses, so consistent and intellectually so clear, that he is at the point of discovering the truth.

"Among all the frauds of Hell, Ulysses is the greatest, most brilliant, most beautiful, the most like
Lucifer" (1958, 2:182, 281–82).

texts like that of John of Salisbury, the great twelfth-century Humanist, and of Bernard Silvestris, which implied not only that Virgil was an allegorist, but an allegorist in imitation of Homer, and specifically, of Homer in the *Odyssey*. Odysseus was the pattern, as Aeneas was in the *Aeneid*, of man on a spiritual voyage of ascent located in a physical kingdom. It is part of Dante's subtle and secret art that not Virgil, the imitator, but Homer, the originator, and Homer's hero, Odysseus, should therefore represent Dante Alighieri's shadow self. Again what is apparent when looking back from the careful balancing act of the *Paradiso*, where saints with conflicting claims are twinned, is that in the *Inferno* Homer and Virgil are brought into harmony—Virgil in his own persona, as guide, Homer in the guise of his hero, Odysseus.

If Dante has identified with Homer's hero, not Virgil's, and regretfully left Virgil behind but taken the hand of Statius to go into Paradise (though part of Statius's fitness to accompany Dante seems to be the former's reverence for Virgil), revision of conventional notions of the *Commedia* are in order.

Who was Statius? How did he represent Ulysses in the *Achilleid?* What would have attracted Dante to him and to what purposes did Dante put the Latin poet in the *Commedia?*

Statius is not among the current pantheon of great authors, but he was far better known in Dante's world. "The fame that Statius so anxiously yearned for was his throughout the Middle Ages" (Mozley 1961, xxvi). It is not clear why Dante attributed a Christian conversion to him. In Dante's world many writers had seen Virgil as an inspired prophet of Jesus. Virgil's birth and death made it almost impossible to think of him as a secret Christian. Statius, however, in a number of places talks about his debt to Virgil and names himself as a faithful follower of the Latin poet. Mozley, in his introduction to the "silver" poet's work, repeats the assertion of D. A. Slater in the latter's introduction to the Oxford Press 1908 translation of the *Silvae*.

Statius as we know from *Silvae*, iv, 4. 53, was in the habit of frequenting the tomb of Virgil outside Naples; he suggests that this fact, together with the well-known tradition of St. Paul's visit to that spot, may have given rise to a story of the meeting of the two, and of Statius's conversion to Christianity as the result.

It is quite possible, however, that Dante originated the idea for his own purposes; this was the opinion of Benvenuto, the commentator on Dante . . . and there seems to be no earlier tradition. When Dante and Virgil meet Statius, he is in the Circle of Avarice, where he has been 500 years, having previously spent 300 in the Ante-Purgatory, and 400 in the Circle of Sloth. . . . Statius enlightens Dante on two matters, first, the natural causes of winds and earthquakes . . . and

second, the nature of the soul when separated from the body. This latter knowledge depended to some extent on revealed truth, for which Statius needs to be a
Christian. If it be asked why Statius was chosen, the answer may be (i.) that he
was highly esteemed in the Middle Ages, (ii.) that his Epic [the *Thebaid*] contains
similar discussions. . . . (Mozley 1961, xxvii-xxviii)

Ulysses appears in Statius's *Achilleid* as one of its major actors. This compels
attention.

Statius's attitude in the *Achilleid* toward Ulysses is quite different from
Virgil's, despite their common language, Latin. Statius is obviously writing a poem
about a Greek hero, Achilles, rather than a Roman one. (Statius's father, a poet and
teacher of literature, "had won prizes in the Grecian contests at Delphi, Nemea
and the Isthmus" [Mozley 1961, 7]). Taking up the *Achilleid,* I tried to read it
through Dante's eyes and found many curious moments.

Statius's first mention of Ulysses is in sharp contrast to Virgil's. The *Aeneid*
seems to disparage Ulysses. Aeneas asks Dido, about to introduce his tale, "What
soldiers even of the hard Ulysses [of harsh Ulysses], could keep from tears in
telling such a story?" (Virgil 1986, 2.7)[12] (Virgil follows this with disparaging allusions by Laocoön and the Greek agent, Sinon.)[13] Statius's speaker is a god, Neptune, and in a god's mouth, the poet's epithet is a backhanded compliment. "I will
allow you to raise the streaming waves, when the Danaans return and Caphereus
stretches out his nightly signals, and we search together for fearsome Ulysses"
(*Achilleid* 1:92–94).

Thetis and Neptune search the sea off the promontory where Greek ships returning from Troy are lured in the night toward the rocks by false signals. Neptune
talks of the "fearsome" or "terrible Ulysses"[14] (an adjective borrowed from Virgil),
but in fact it is he and Thetis, two gods, who represent the dark powers of destruc-

12. The Loeb translates *duri,* the adjective that modifies Ulysses as "stern." This shades Virgil toward a more neutral attitude. Allen Mandelbaum (Virgil 1981, 2.10) translates it as "harsh," but I was
intrigued by "hard" since it seems to put iron in the Greek hero's face. "Quis talia fando / Myrmi-
donum Dolopumve aut duri miles Ulixi / temperet a lacrimis?" "What Myrmidon or Dolopian, or
soldier of stern Ulysses, could in telling such a tale refrain from tears?" (Virgil 1986, 2.7).

13. *Aeneid* 2.7; Laocoön, cautioning the Trojans to beware of free gifts from the Greeks, warns of
Ulysses' craftiness (*Aeneid* 2.44): "Is it thus you know Ulysses?" Sinon, in order to gain credence with
the Trojans, claims to be a victim of Ulysses, through his friendship with Palamedes, who fell to "the
malice of subtle Ulysses" (*Aeneid* 2.90). The insults are then heaped on Ulysses but there is some irony
since Ulysses is being insulted by his own agent.

14. Virgil uses this adjective as well. See *Aeneid* 2.762, where the shade of Creusa, Aeneas's wife,
refers to *"dirus Ulixes,"* "dread Ulysses."

tion lurking for the Greek captain. The fact that he is "fearsome," "*dirum*," even to Neptune, bent on tossing him about, has a dire nobility about it rather than harshness or craftiness.

Ulysses when he next appears in the *Achilleid* (excepting a reference to him as "sleepless in counsel, and deeds of arms" joining in the clamor for Achilles to be brought to the Greek camp [*Achilleid*, 1:472]), is not presented as a forward schemer. Ulysses has to be cajoled by Diomedes, the "Calydonian hero," before he sets out to find Achilles, who is hiding in a woman's dress.

> Then the Calydonian hero falls upon the hesitating Ithacan; "This labor calls us; for indeed I could not refuse to go as companion, should your care so draw you. Though he be sunk in the echoing caves of far off Tethys and in the bosom of watery Nereus, you will find him. As a man of foresight, in your cunning just extend your sleepless mind and rouse your fertile breast; no prophet, as far as I am concerned, would dare in a doubtful case, to see fate before you."

Ulysses flattered by the speech, after weighing the disgrace of failure, assents.

> "Let omnipotent God prove it so, and the virgin guardian of your father agree with you! But slippery hope gives me pause; for sure it is a great enterprise to lead armed Achilles to our camp, but should the fates say no, how disgraceful and sad to return! Yet I will not leave untried the fulfillment of the Danaan's vows. And now either the Pelean hero shall accompany me so, or the truth is hidden deep and Calchas is without Apollo."

The departure of the Ithacan, however, does not sound either of the "harsh Ulysses" or even "fearsome Ulysses" but rings with merriment, or good cheer, "*hilaris*," as the Latin states. "Without delay the Ithacan sail is already calling for a favorable breeze, and the cheerful young men are seated at the oars" (*Achilleid* 1:539–59).

Statius slowly develops the drama of Ulysses evading Thetis, Achilles' frightened mother, approaching the kingdom in which her son has been concealed, "Quod non erueret pontum ventisque fretisque / omnibus invisium iam tunc sequeretur Ulixem," "She [Thetis] with all the winds and waves could not tear up the sea and immediately pursue the hated Ulysses" (*Achilleid* 1:686–87) referring to him as "the Laertian chieftain" (*Achilleid* 1:693). The poet takes pains to describe Ulysses, his caution, his poise, preparing himself for the task of enlisting Achilles. "Then the hero with foresight, lest they alarm the hospitable walls with a sudden mob, orders his crew to remain on the poop. . . . So the heroes, slow, move on the open plain that lies between the port and the high walled town, talking back and forth." Statius has deserted the point of view of Thetis. Achilles' natural curiosity as a young man becomes the foil for Ulysses and the sympathies of the reader are clearly meant to be with the manly "hero," the "Laertian chieftain." Indeed it is Thetis, in choosing to disguise her son as a girl, who has become the crafty one, and Statius has not been shy to point this out.

"What god endowed the terrified mother with deceit and *cunning?*"[15] It is the same word, cunning, *astum, astu,* that Statius later uses as one of Diomedes' epithets for Ulysses, as the former urges the latter to his task, "in your cunning, extend your sleepless mind" (*Achilleid,* 1:542–43).

Divinities of the sea in the mythology of antiquity have a changeable, "cunning," nature.[16] Thetis, as a sea goddess, is a perfect counterpart to Ulysses. She masks her son's masculinity with fraud. Ulysses uncovers the disguise and will later practice a masquerade upon the city of Troy.

Through the whole of the uncovering of Achilles' disguise, the humor that accompanies the guile of Ulysses' strategy can only enlist the audience to his cause. Diomedes inquires about the wands, cymbals, fawn skins decked with patterns of gold, that Ulysses has brought. The Ithacan responds, "smiling a little, his face relaxing" (*Achilleid,* 1:718), by explaining how these articles will draw Achilles, "self-confessed," out of his concealment. And it is so, of course, for Achilles alone of the band of maidens in which he is hiding, comes to grasp not the feminine wands, skins, bowls, but the great battle shield.

If Ulysses is seen in the imagery of Statius as a ravening wolf who conceals his hunger (*Achilleid,* 1:704–98), a man of many tricks (*Achilleid,* 1:846–47), he is also the hero who cannot sleep anticipating the day's trials: "but to the keen [shrewd] Ithacan the night is long; he desires the light and sleep only oppresses him" (*Achilleid,* 1:817–18). It is the voice of the heroic that speaks through the Laertian chieftain to Achilles, and the vaunt must have rung in Dante's ears. "Cities and

---

15. See *Achilleid,* 1:283–84, "Quis deus attonitae fraudes astumque parenti / contulit?" Scott, in his attempt to portray Ulysses as the representative type of "Greek guile" quotes Statius out of context. See his article on Ulysses (1971, 157), note 36, quoting, Statius: "Heu simplex, nimiumque rudis, qui callida dona, / Graiorumque dolos variumque ignorat [ignoret] Ulixem!" "Alas, how simple and untaught, who of the gifts' cunning / were ignorant, and the Greeks' and Ulysses' repertoire of tricks!" (*Achilleid,* 1:846–47). The passage in Statius, however, is touched with as much comedy as pathos and breathes no ill will toward Ulysses.

16. This was pointed out to me by Professor Jacob Stern of CUNY, who also remarked that the epithet for cunning in the Greek is *dolos,* from which Statius evidently derives the Latin *astus.*

fields are empty, we have spoiled the high mountains, the whole sea is hidden under the long shadow of our sails" (*Achilleid,* 1:789–90).[17]

This Ulysses, clever, but sagacious rather than just cunning—this boast of sails over the extent of the sea—must have aroused Dante's admiration and prompted the Florentine to push Ulysses forth on a new adventure.

Another passage in Statius would have touched Dante. It refers to the deep feelings between mother and son. The image of the breasts attacked by beasts Dante could not read indifferently. Thetis, mother of Achilles, cries out her terror.

> Isn't it right that the sleep of his mother is troubled by terrible and black signals from the gods—would that they are merely deceiving—my great fear? For just now I catch sight of hostile swords at my womb, I see my hands bruised with lamentation, now savage beasts rush upon my tits; now I see myself—a thing not to be spoken of—carrying off for a second time my son under the void of Tartarus to dip him in the springs of Styx. The Carpathian seer orders me to rid myself of these terrors by the ordinance of a magic rite, and purify the boy in secret waters beyond the bound of heaven's vault, where the furthest shore of Ocean lies and father Pontus is warmed by the inflowing stars. There, horrible rites of expiation and gifts to gods unknown—but to enumerate the whole is too long, and I am forbidden. (*Achilleid* 1:129–40)

This is a further reason for Dante's choice of Statius. "The relations of mother and son seem to have had a particular attraction for Statius," J. H. Mozley remarks, "e.g, Atalanta and Parthenopaeus, Ismenis and Crenaeus in the *Thebaid* (notice too, how many times he refers to Ino and Palaemon), Thetis and Achilles in the *Achilleid*" (Mozley 1961, 15). In fact the pathos or tragedy of the *Achilleid* is just that, the terrible grief of Thetis, anticipating her son's fate, trying to avoid it. And again this refers us to Homer. The insubstantial shade that Aeneas goes to find in the underworld is his father. Ulysses seeks his mother. It is to the mother, the mother he has never known, that Dante cries out first, in one of the *Commedia*'s great lines of pathos, "ma per le mamme!" "The dead showed their desire / not perhaps alone for themselves, but for their mammas, / their fathers, and for the others dear to them / before they became eternal flames" (*Par.* 14:64–66). The anxious care of the mother, so obvious in the images of Beatrice as milk giver, would echo in Dante as he read Statius.

---

17. "Rura urbesque vacant, montes spoliavimus altos, / omne fretum longa velorum obtexitur umbra."

Thetis's description of the underworld was of particular interest to Dante. The Florentine dreaming of making himself immortal, recovering the flesh of Beatrice, would listen carefully to the rites of the underground for immortality. The details of the kingdom of death, to which Achilles' mother brings him and pretends to Chiron she will bring him again, seem borrowed from Homer's account of Odysseus's sailing toward the shore of death, "The extreme shore of Ocean." Dante knew that Ulysses had sailed there once, and the question of what Ulysses found is echoed in Virgil.[18] For a religious man, woman, of the Middle Ages, Christian, Muslim, Jew, it was a scene of great pathos. Antiquity confessed its helplessness before death.

> But, deep in a green valley, Father Anchises was surveying with earnest thought the imprisoned souls that were to pass to the light above, and, as it chanced, was telling the full tale of his people and beloved children, their fates and fortunes, their works and ways. And he, as he saw Aeneas coming toward him over the field, held out both hands, eager, while tears streamed from his eyes, and a cry fell from his lips: "Finally you have come, and has the piety that your father expected of you overcome the difficulty of the journey? Is it given me to see your face, my son, and hear and utter familiar tones? Even so I thought and imagined the hour would come, counting the moments, nor has my yearning failed me. Over what lands, what wide seas have you journeyed to my welcome! What dangers have tossed you, O my son! How I feared the realm of Libya might harm you!"
>
> Then he: "Your . . . your sad shade, my father, meeting me so often, drove me to reach these portals. My ships ride the Tyrrhenian sea. Give me the grasp of your hand, give me, father, and do not withdraw from my embrace!"
>
> His face wet with flooding tears, thus he spoke. Three times there he tried to throw his arms about his neck. *Three time the Shade vainly clasped, fled from his hands, even as light winds, or most like a winged dream.* (Aeneid 6.679–702)

Aeneas's frustration, "ter frustra comprensa manus effugit imago," "three times the Shade vainly clasped, fled from his hands," is exactly Dante's throughout the whole of the *Commedia*. He cannot get his hands on Beatrice—a philosophical and theological problem is at the center of the erotic quest. The moment of grimmest pathos in Virgil, when the piety of Aeneas, the plea, *"Da,"* "give," repeated twice, "Give me," or "Let me! Let me clasp your hand," is met by the reality

---

18. Dante could have read this in *The Chronicles of Dictys of Crete*, "Then they [Ulysses and his shipmates] had gone to that place where, having performed the requisite rites, they learned of the future from the shades of the dead" (*Dictys and Dares* 1966, 123).

(or unreality) of death. The word carries the connotation of error, deception, and yet Aeneas hopes somehow to overcome the reality of death.

It is a familiar moment to antiquity. It echoes in its "frustration," the moment in Homer's *Odyssey*, book 11, when Odysseus attempts to grasp his mother. The moment is that much more affecting because the hero himself narrates it, becoming the bard, hearing his mother chide him for causing her death as his absence broke her heart.

> So she spoke, but I wished—my heart anxious—my mother's spirit, to seize, dead.
> Three times I sprang forward, wishing to seize her as my heart exhorted,
> three times out of my hands, like a shadow or dream
> she flits. The grief grew even sharper in my heart.
> And I spoke and addressed her with winged words.
> "My mother, *why* do you not stay still for me who to seize you is so excited.
> That even in Hades we may throw loving hands about each other
> Together, take pleasure in ice cold weeping?
> Or is this a phantom before me that awesome Persephone
> quickens; that I may mourn and groan yet more?"
> So I spoke, and immediately she answered, my revered mother,
> "O me! My child, ill fated beyond all men
> it is not Persephone, daughter of Zeus who cheats you,
> but this is the way of mortals, when one dies
> for the muscles no longer hold together the flesh and bone
> but the force of fierce fire blazing subdues these,
> when first it has dissipated from the shining bones, consciousness;
> the soul, like a dream, flies away and flits about."
>   (*Odyssey* 11.204–22)[19]

The three passes of the arms toward the shade, the wavering like a dream, all show the influence on Virgil of Homer. Virgil makes use of this in a passage almost as vivid and pathetic, earlier in the poem, in the second book, when Aeneas missing his wife, Creusa, in the disordered flight from Troy, "the unhappy likeness and

---

19. The sense of the insubstantial in Homer is underscored by the sound of the Greek *apoptameney* and *pepoteytay*, "flies away" and "flits about," or "hovers," emphasizes the frustration of Odysseus's attempt to seize or grasp his mother's image. This is reinforced by the contrast in apposition of the two nouns; the consciousness, spirit, life, *thumos* of man, which is tied to the bones, and the soul, *psyche*, which remains. There is a mocking humor in Homer (Odysseus's remark that he and his mother take pleasure in ice cold weeping), more akin to Dante than to Virgil's sobriety. For the Greek see the Loeb Classical Library text (Homer 1984, 11.204–22).

shade" of Creusa, larger than life, suddenly floats before him as if responding to his cries. Aeneas reaches out for her, and in language identical to that in the passage in which he attempts to grasp his father, is frustrated. Here, as in Homer, the hero speaks as bard in the first person.

> When she had spoken so, she left me, weeping, wanting
> to tell her so much, and drew back into thin air.
> Three times there I tried to throw my arms about her neck;
> three times Shade vainly clasped, fled from my hands,
> even as light winds, or most like a winged dream.
>   (*Aeneid* 2.790–94)

Dante had to be struck by this, for it was the stumbling block in his pursuit of Beatrice. How could he clasp her in the other world?

The Florentine poet had a partial answer in Neoplatonic philosophy. Virgil, whose characters could not progress past the relatively happy fields of limbo, would not have been aware of it. By converting Statius to Christianity, he could link the latter poet to himself.

Statius, as the fervent admirer of Virgil, his child, so to speak, was the perfect Christian link to Virgil. Dante's language is explicit on the subject of this paternity. Statius speaks of Virgil's *Aeneid* "la qual mamma / fummi, e fummi nutrice," "as his momma and his nurse." The second epithet, with its milky connotations, shows how important the corporal link was to Dante between Virgil and Statius. The author, to call attention to this connection, plays a practical joke on Statius by having the latter praise the poet Virgil without realizing that Virgil is standing before him.

The deeper reason for the choice of Statius, however, is Dante's need to link the question of corporal reality in his poem to the passages in Virgil and Homer. At the end of the practical joke, Statius so far forgets the nature of the world of the dead as to embrace Virgil. It is clear that in writing these lines, the passages in Virgil about the embrace of Aeneas and his father, based on that of Ulysses and his mother, were vividly before Dante's eyes.

Was it through Statius that Dante hoped to link himself with Homer—solve Homer's riddle? Substance and the journey through death—Dante sees himself as a cointerpreter of the ancient epic—an identification that is for him a passport to the realm beyond death.

The laughter of Dante is particularly acute at the moment of this embrace. Even Sinclair, a conservative commentator, notices and remarks on a "playfulness approaching as near as Dante ever does approach to humor" (*Purg.* 1972c, 281).

Remember that it has been preceded by the practical joke of Dante and Virgil's concealment of the latter's identity. And it is emphasized by Statius's reaction to Virgil's rebuke—which ought to have recalled to Statius the pathos of death. It is not with pathos, the touchstone of both Virgil and Homer's scenes of embrace in the underworld, but with a certain mocking passion that Statius responds.

> Ed ei surgendo; "Or puoi la quantitate
> comprender de l'amor ch'a te mi scalda,
> quand' io dismento nostra vanitate,
> trattando l'ombre come cosa salda."

> And he, rising, "Now you are able the measure
> to understand of the love which scalds me for you
> when I forget our vain emptiness
> treating the shade as a solid thing."
> (*Purg.* 21:133–36)

At the same moment that Statius reminds himself he is beyond the body, he speaks of how love "scalds," a strong image of the body and its capacity to feel. These lines "bite." They conceal a paradox that eludes Dante's translator, Sinclair. When Dante chose Statius, the Florentine's sense of humor mantled this lesser classical poet. The soul of Statius is released in a tremor like an earthquake, from the toils of Purgatory to go up to Paradise. Dante lets us know that he has read both the *Thebaid* and the *Achilleid* of Statius. In the former, Statius, as J. H. Mozley points out, speaks specifically to the nature of earthquakes (*Thebaid,* 7:809–17). Dante and Virgil feel a tremendous shock: "I felt like a thing that falls, / the mount shake; so that a chill seized me / like that which takes a man who goes to his death" (*Purg.* 20:127–29). And this shaking of the world beyond recalls the line of Statius, "in a gaping chasm the ground yawns, sheer and deep, and stars and shades feel mutual terror" (*Thebiad* 7:816–17). Statius himself mentions the "*tremoto*," "earthquake," which has released him. "*Sentisti il tremoto*" (*Purg.* 21:70), "you heard the earthquake," he tells Dante and Virgil. There are a number of other references to natural phenomena in Statius's work,[20] and he will be chosen to enlighten Dante on the nature of the spiritual world as opposed to the natural.

All this points to Dante's reason for Statius's mistake in embracing Virgil. Of all men or women, Statius ought to have known better. Sinclair notices the contradiction the scene offers but can give no explanation.

---

20. Mozley details them in his introduction to the volume *Statius* (Mozley 1961, 1:27–28).

Statius is Dante's fellow in spirit, flesh. Therefore, he commits the very mistake that Dante is committing in coming to the underworld. It is a mistake Dante will not give up until far into the *Paradiso,* and for the same reason as Statius here in *Purgatorio.* Scalded by love, Dante will forget the nature of spiritual reality. For love makes all things palpable, and especially those of the spirit. This is the reason for the laughter, the good humor, the delay of pathos, until much later.

Sinclair has pointed out that Virgil's rebuke of Statius for attempting to embrace him is a conscious contradiction on Dante's part of the scene between Sordello and Virgil, in canto 6, line 75 of *Purgatorio,* where the two embrace, and as we learn in canto 7, lines 1 and 2, not once, but four times. Why doesn't Virgil point out the futility of embracing "fictitious flesh" in these cantos? The answer can only be that Dante "deliberately" made the question of the shade's corporal reality ambiguous. Obviously the flesh of those condemned to the Inferno feels pain, cold, heat, pressure. In the spiritual realm of the *Purgatorio,* the very nature of punishment demands suffering, and suffering that is only spiritual is not vivid enough for the poet's purpose, too disembodied. Yet the theology that promised the actual flesh only at the last moment of Judgment was an absolute that Dante had announced at the very beginning of his poem, in the passage which *rimbomba* "echoes, sounds," throughout.

Dante means us to pay attention, however, to a strange transformation of the "fictitious flesh." Statius after all has now been released by the great sonic boom, the sound barrier, of salvation. He is somehow changed, just as Dante's flesh is changed and cleansed, and will be cleansed again, by passing through the fire. When he tries to embrace Virgil, the latter feels it as folly. This would be curious enough, but it is precisely Statius who will lecture Dante, given Virgil's unfitness, on the theology and metaphysics of the body after death.

Is the error of Statius the hope of Dante? Given the latter's wish to embrace Beatrice in the flesh, it is a hope that we see is not abandoned until, high in the circles of the *Paradiso* itself, Dante Alighieri receives the final "no." It is curious that quietly, unobtrusively, Dante goes blind in canto 24 of *Purgatorio,* just as he will go blind in Paradise, when the absolute "no" is announced to him, in regard to grasping Beatrice's real flesh to his own.

Statius's speech about the insemination of soul and body in canto 25 is dry, but such abstractness may be a cover for a deep erotic intention in Dante. The euphemisms about the sexual act blur the fact that it is semen that creates the spiritual body as well as the physical one—that "perfect blood."

·   ·   ·

THE CANDLEPOWER OF LIGHT is one of Dante's solutions. If he cannot grasp Beatrice in the body, he can feel the heat of her blessedness, even smell it. This is a considerable step beyond the vain or mistaken grasp of Ulysses and Aeneas. Still, it is a bitter disappointment to Dante not to have Beatrice in the body absolute. In the canto where it is unambiguously announced to him, Dante describes himself as blinded. He has been told what Bruno Schulz's character will be informed of in *Sanatorium under the Sign of the Hourglass,* a sanatorium at a Polish hospital where the dead may be encountered. "'Is my father alive?'" the narrator asks, "anxiously, staring into his [the doctor's] calm face.

"'Yes, of course,' he answered calmly, meeting my questioning eyes, 'That is, within the limits imposed by the situation,' he added. 'You know as I that from the point of view of your home, from the perspective of your own country, your father is dead. This cannot be entirely remedied. That death throws a certain shadow on his existence here'" (Schulz 1979, 116).

The pathos of this "certain shadow" is cast through the *Commedia* to its very last line. The shadow of a fictitious existence before the Judgment, announced in its very first cantos:

> "Più non si desta
> di qua dal suon de l'angelica tromba
> quando verrà la nimica podesta:
> ciascun rivederà la trista tomba,
> ripiglierà sua carne e sua figura,
> udirà quel ch'in etterno rimbomba."

> "He wakes no more
> until the sound of the angelic trumpet
> when comes the adverse judge
> each one will revisit the sad tomb
> put on his flesh and his figure
> hear that which in eternity resounds."
>   (*Inf.* 6:94–99)

REFERENCES

INDEX

References

Anderson, William. 1980. *Dante the Maker.* London: Routledge and Kegan Paul.

Barbi, Michael. 1966. *Life of Dante.* Translated and edited by Paul G. Ruggiers. 1954. Reprint, Berkeley and Los Angeles: Univ. of California Press.

Bergin, Thomas Goddard. 1965. *Dante.* New York: Orion Press.

———. 1969. *A Diversity of Dante.* New Brunswick, N.J.: Rutgers Univ. Press.

Bernard of Clairvaux. 1971. *On the Song of Songs I, Volume Two.* Translated by Kilian Walsh. Introduction by M. Corneille Halflants. Kalamazoo, Mich.: Cistercian Publications.

Bleibtreu, John. 1968. *The Parable of the Beast.* New York: Macmillan.

Bloom, Harold. 1987. *The Strong Light of the Canonical.* No. 20. New York: City College Papers.

Boccaccio, Giovanni. 1904. *Life of Dante.* Translated by Philip Henry Wicksteed. Boston: Houghton Mifflin.

———. 1955. *The Decameron.* Translated by Frances Winwar. New York: Modern Library.

Brown, Peter. 1999. *Augustine of Hippo.* Rev. ed. Berkeley and Los Angeles: Univ. of California Press.

Buber, Martin. 1965. *Tales of Rabbi Nachman.* Translated by Maurice Friedman. Bloomington: Indiana Univ. Press.

Bulfinch, Thomas. 1894. *The Age of Fable.* Boston: S. W. Tilton.

Cassuto, Umberto. 1974. *A Commentary on the Book of Exodus.* Jerusalem: Magnes Press.

Chaucer, Geoffrey. 1957a. "The House of Fame." In *The Works of Geoffrey Chaucer,* edited by F. N. Robinson. 1933. Reprint, Boston: Houghton Mifflin.

———. 1957b. *The Works of Geoffrey Chaucer.* Edited by F. N. Robinson. 1933. Reprint, Boston: Houghton Mifflin.

Chubb, Thomas Caldecot. 1966. *Dante and His World.* Boston: Little, Brown.

Cross, Frank Moore. 1976. *Canaanite Myth and Hebrew Epic.* Cambridge, Mass.: Harvard Univ. Press.

Dahlberg, Edward. 1967a. *Because I Was Flesh.* New York: New Directions.

———. 1967b. *Can These Bones Live?* Ann Arbor: Univ. of Michigan Press.

———. 1967c. *The Edward Dahlberg Reader.* Edited by Paul Carroll. New York: New Directions.

Dante Alighieri. 1932. *The Divine Comedy.* Translated by John Carlyle, Thomas Oakey, and Philip H. Wicksteed, New York: Modern Library.

———. 1965. *La Vita Nuova.* Translated by Mark Musa. 1957. Reprint, Bloomington: Indiana Univ. Press.

———. 1966. *Dantis Alagherii Epistolae (The Letters of Dante).* 2nd ed. Translated by Paget Toynbee. Oxford: Clarendon Press.

———. 1967. *Dante's Lyric Poetry.* 2 vols. Edited by K. Foster and P. Boyde. Oxford: Oxford Univ. Press.

———. 1969. *La Vita Nuova.* Translated by Barbara Reynolds. London: Penguin Books.

———. 1972a. *Dante's Inferno.* Translated by John D. Sinclair. 1939. Reprint, New York: Oxford Univ. Press.

———. 1972b. *Dante's Paradiso.* Translated by John D. Sinclair. 1939. Reprint, New York: Oxford Univ. Press.

———. 1972c. *Dante's Purgatorio.* Translated by John D. Sinclair. 1939. Reprint. New York: Oxford Univ. Press.

———. 1972d. *La Divina Commedia.* Edited and annotated by C. H. Grandgent, revised by Charles S. Singleton. Cambridge, Mass.: Harvard Univ. Press.

———. 1973. *Vita Nuova Rime.* Edited by Fredi Chiappelli. Milan: Mursia.

———. 1977. *La Vita Nuova.* Translated by D. G. Rossetti. In *The Portable Dante,* edited by Paolo Milano. New York: Viking Portable.

Dictys and Dares. 1966. *The Trojan War: The Chronicles of Dictys of Crete and Dares the Phrygian.* Translated by R. M. Frazer Jr. Bloomington: Indiana Univ. Press.

Dick, Steven J. 1982. *Plurality of Worlds.* Cambridge: Cambridge Univ. Press.

Feldman, Seymour. 1999. *Notes to* The Wars of the Lord *by Levi Ben Gershom (Gersonides).* Translated by Seymour Feldman. Philadelphia: Jewish Publication Society.

Freccero, John. 1986. "The River of Death." In *Dante: The Poetics of Conversion.* Cambridge, Mass.: Harvard Univ. Press.

Friedrich, Werner P. 1950. *Dante's Fame Abroad.* Rome: Edizioni Di Storia E Letteratura.

Gardner, Edmund G. 1968. *Dante and the Mystics.* 1913. Reprint, New York: Octagon.

Gilson, Etienne. 1949. *Dante the Philosopher.* Translated by David Moore. New York: Sheed and Ward.

Glatzer, Nahum N. 1946. *Time and Eternity.* New York: Schocken.

Goldin, Frederick. 1973a *German and Italian Lyrics of the Middle Ages: An Anthology and a History.* New York: Anchor Books.

———. 1973b *Lyrics of the Troubadours and Trouveres.* New York: Anchor Books.

Graves, Robert. 1978. *The Greek Myths.* Middlesex, Eng.: Penguin Books.

Greenberg, Moshe. 1969. *Understanding Exodus.* New York: Behrman House.

Guttmann, Julius. 1973. *Philosophies of Judaism.* New York: Schocken.

Haberman, Jacob. 1979. *Maimonides and Aquinas.* New York: Ktav.

Halflants, M. Corneille. 1971. Introduction to *On the Song of Songs I, Volume Two,* by Bernard of Clairvaux. Translated by Kilian Walsh. Kalamazoo, Mich.: Cistercian Publications.

Holy Bible, The. Containing the Old and New Testaments. Authorized King James version. Oxford: Oxford Univ. Press.

Holy Scriptures According to the Masoretic Text, The. 1916. Translated and revised by Alexander Harkavy. New York: Hebrew Publishing Company.

Homer. 1984. *The Odyssey, 1.* Translated by A. T. Murray, Loeb Classical Library. 1919. Reprint, Cambridge: Harvard Univ. Press,

Horace. 1927. *Horace Odes and Epodes.* Translated by C. E. Bennett. Loeb Classical Library. London: William Heinemann.

Idel, Moses. 1983. "No Kabbalistic Tradition." In *Rabbi Moses Nahmanides (Ramban): Explorations in His Religious and Literary Virtuosity,* edited by Isadore Twersky. Cambridge, Mass.: Harvard Univ. Press.

Immanuel of Rome. 1957. *The Cantos of Immanuel of Rome.* Vol 2. Edited by Dov Jarden. Jerusalem: Bialik Institute.

Ivry, Alfred L. 1986. "Islamic and Greek Influence on Maimonides' Philosophy." In *Maimonides and Philosophy,* edited by S. Pines and Y. Yovel, 139–56. Dordrecht/Boston/Lancaster: Martinus Nijhoff Publishers.

———. 1991. "Neoplatonic Currents in Maimonides' Thought." In *Perspectives on Maimonides: Philosophical and Historical Studies,* edited by Joel L. Kraemer, 115–40. Published for The Littman Library by Oxford Univ. Press.

———. 1995. "Ismai'li Theology and Maimonides' Philosophy." In *The Jews of Medieval Islam,* edited by D. Frank. Leiden: E. J. Brill.

Kay, Richard. 1978. *Dante's Swift and Strong.* Lawrence: The Regents Press of Kansas.

Kerenyi, C. 1950. *The Gods of the Greeks.* Myth and Man. London: Thames and Hudson. Reprint, New York: Book Collector's Society.

La Piana, Angelina. 1948. *Dante's American Pilgrimage, 1800–1944.* New Haven: Yale Univ. Press.

Maimonides, Moses. 1963. *The Guide of the Perplexed.* 2 vols. Translated by Shlomo Pines. Chicago: Univ. of Chicago Press.

Mandelstam, Osip. 1971. "Talking about Dante." Translated by Clarence Brown and Robert Hughes. *Delos* 6:65–106.

McCarthy, Mary. 1963. *The Stones of Venice.* New York: Harcourt Brace Jovanovich.

Midrash Rabbah. 1977. Vol. 1, *Genesis.* Translated by H. Freedman. New York: Soncino Press.

Milton, John. 1957. *The Student Milton.* Edited by Frank Allen Patterson. 1930. Reprint, New York: Appleton-Century-Crofts.

Mirsky, Mark Jay. 1984. "Dante, Kaballah, and the New World." *Denver Quarterly* 19, no. 1:33–70.

Mozley, J. H. 1961. Introduction and notes to *Statius,* Vol. 1. Loeb Classical Library. 1928. Reprint, Cambridge: Harvard Univ. Press.

Nemerov, Howard. 1974. "The Dream of Dante." *Prose,* no. 9. (fall):113–33.

Olschki, Leonard. 1949. *The Myth of Felt.* Berkeley and Los Angeles: Univ. of California Press.

Pines, Shlomo. 1963. Introduction to *The Guide of the Perplexed.* Vol. 1, by Moses Maimonides. Chicago: Univ. of Chicago Press.

Plato. 1921. *Theaetetus Sophist.* Translated by H. N. Fowler. Cambridge, Mass.: Harvard Univ. Press.

Poggioli, Renato. 1965. "Paolo and Francesca." In *Dante: A Collection of Critical Essays,* edited by John Freccero. *PMLA* 72, no. 3 (June 1957), 61–77. Reprint, Englewood Cliffs: Prentice Hall.

Pope, Maurice. 1999. *The Story of Decipherment.* Rev. ed. New York: Thames and Hudson.

Prinz Joachim, 1966. *Popes from the Ghetto.* New York: Horizon.

Reynolds, Barbara. 1969. Introduction and notes to *La Vita Nuova,* by Dante. London: Penguin Books.

Roth, Cecil. 1953. "New Light on Dante's Circle." *The Modern Language Review,* 48.

Sayers, Dorothy L. 1954. "The Comedy of the Comedy." In *Introductory Papers on Dante.* New York: Harper and Brothers.

Scholem, Gershom G. 1961. *Major Trends in Jewish Mysticism.* New York: Schocken Paperback.

———. 1965. *Jewish Gnosticism, Merkabah Mysticism, and Talmudic Tradition.* New York: The Jewish Theological Seminary of America.

Schulz, Bruno. 1979. *Sanatorium under the Sign of the Hourglass.* Translated by Celina Wieniewska. New York: Penguin Books.

Scott, J. A. 1971. "Inferno XXVI, Dante's Ulisses." *Lettere Italiane* 23, no. 2 (April-June).

Septimus, Bernard. 1983. "Nahmanides and the Andalusian Tradition." In *Rabbi Moses Nahmanides (Ramban): Explorations in His Religious and Literary Virtuosity,* edited by Isadore Twersky, 11–34. Cambridge, Mass.: Harvard Univ. Press.

Seznec, Jean. 1972. *The Survival of the Pagan Gods.* Bollingen 38. 1953. Reprint, Princeton: Princeton Univ. Press.

Shiur Koma. 1976. In *The Secret Garden: An Anthology in the Kabbalah.* Translated and edited by David Meltzer. New York: Seabury.

Southern, R. W. 1964. *The Making of the Middle Ages.* New Haven: Yale Univ. Press.

Statius. 1961. 2 vols. Translated by J. H. Mozley. 1928. Reprint, Loeb Classical Library. Cambridge: Harvard Univ. Press.

Stokes, Adrian. 1968. *The Quattro Cento, a Different Conception of the Italian Renaissance. Part 1: Florence and Verona, An Essay in Italian Fifteenth-Century Architecture and Sculpture.* New York: Schocken Books.

Strauss, Leo. 1973. *Persecution and the Art of Writing.* 1952. Reprint, Westport, Conn.: Greenwood Press.

Thompson, David. 1974. *Dante's Epic Journey.* Baltimore: John Hopkins Univ. Press.

Thoreau, Henry David. 1961. "Stage Coach Views." In *Cape Cod.* New York: Thomas Crowell.

Unamuno, Miguel de. 1976. *Our Lord, Don Quixote.* Rev. ed. Vol. 3, *The Selected Works of Unamuno.* Translated by Anthony Kerrigan. Bollingen Series 85. Princeton: Princeton Univ. Press.

Virgil. 1981. *The Aeneid of Virgil.* Translated by Allen Mandelbaum. 1961. Reprint, New York: Bantam Books.

———. 1986. "Aeneid." Book 6. In *Eclogues Georgics Aeneid, 1–6.* Translated by H. R. Fairclough. Loeb Classical Library. 1916, revised 1935. Reprint, Cambridge: Harvard Univ. Press.

Vossler, Karl. 1958. *Mediaeval Culture.* Vols. 1 and 2. Translated by William Cranston Lawton. 1929. Reprint, New York: Frederick Ungar.

Warburton, William. 1846. *The Divine Legation of Moses Demonstrated on the Principles of a Religious Deist, from the Omission of the Doctrine of a Future State of Rewards and Punishments in the Jewish Dispensation.* 10th ed. 3 Vols. Edited by James Nichols. London: Thomas Tegg.

Wolfson, Harry Austryn. 1961. "The Pelagian Controversy." In *Religious Philosophy.* Cambridge, Mass.: Harvard Univ. Press.

———. 1968. *Philo.* Rev. ed. Vol. 1. Cambridge, Mass.: Harvard Univ. Press.

———. 1977a. "Hallevi and Maimonides on Prophecy." In *Studies in the History of Philosophy and Religion,* edited by Isadore Twersky and George H. Williams, 2:60–119. Cambridge, Mass.: Harvard Univ. Press.

———. 1977b. "Maimonides and Hallevi: A Study in Typical Jewish Attitudes Toward Greek Philosophy in the Middle Ages." In *Studies in the History of Philosophy and Religion,* edited by Isadore Twersky and George H. Williams, 3: 120–60. Cambridge, Mass.: Harvard Univ. Press.

Womack, Jack. 11 April 2002. E-mail correspondence with Mark Jay Mirsky.

Yeats, William Butler. 1958. "Leda and the Swan." *Collected Poems.* New York: Macmillan.

Zinberg, Israel. 1972a. "Immanuel of Rome." In *A History of Jewish Literature.* Vol. 2, pt. 3, *The Jewish Community on Medieval Italy,* translated from the Yiddish by Bernard Martin, 201–17. Cleveland: The Press of Case Western Reserve Univ.

———. 1972b. *A History of Jewish Literature.* Vol. 2. Translated from the Yiddish by Bernard Martin. Cleveland: The Press of Case Western Reserve Univ.

Zohar, the Book of Splendor: Basic Readings from the Kabbalah. 1970. Edited by Gershom G. Scholem. 1949. Paperback reprint, New York: Schocken Books

Zohar. 1978. Vol. 1. Translated by Harry Sperling and Maurice Simon. 1934. Reprint, London: Soncino Press.

Zohar, the Book of Enlightenment. 1983. Translated by Daniel Chanan Matt. The Classics of Western Spirituality. New York: Paulist Press.

Zohar. 1985. "Love in the Afterlife." Translated by Yaakov Elman with assistance from Michal Govrin and Mark Jay Mirsky. *Fiction* 7, no.3–8, no. 1:322–30.

Index

Abelard, Peter, 169–70n. 5; Dante's identity with, 181–82n. 19

Abigail (wife of King David), 105

Achilleid, 205, 207–11, Diomedes in, 209–10; mother and sons in, 211; Ulysses in, 201n. 5, 205, 208–11, 208n. 14. *See also* Statius

Achilles, 36n. 6, 201n. 5, 209–11

Acts, 153n. 17, 176n. 11

Adam, 122, 126n. 5, 138, 140, 150–52, 154–55; movement under covering, 151n. 14

adultery, 30, 34, 38–39, 60–61, 63, 66–67, 99–108, 111–13; exalted, 123n. 3, 148–49n. 9; Chaucer and, 60n. 1; thirteenth-century attitudes toward, 66–67n. 11; translation of, 63n. 6, in works of Boccaccio, 60n. 3. *See also* Bathsheba; David (king of Israel); Francesca and Paolo

Aeneas, 6n. 3, 202, 204, 207–8, 211, 217; and meeting with Anchises 212–14. *See also* Virgil

Aeneid, 54, 202–4, 204n. 8, 208, 208n. 12–14, 212–14. *See also* Aeneas; Virgil

afterlife: light and smell in, 161, 161–62nn. 26–27; substance and dream, in, 22n. 16, 211–17. *See also* Beatrice; body in afterlife; Homer; Maimonides; Statius; Virgil

Alcibiades, 1

Anaclet II (Jewish pope), 180, 179–80n. 16. *See also* Bernard, Saint

Ananius, 153–54, 153n. 17

Anderson, William, 67n. 13, 167n. 2

Andreas, 116n. 4

Apollo, 183, 209

Aquinas, Thomas, 67, 74, 88, 95, 97, 110; and astrology, 169n. 5; and attitude toward Jews, 136–37n. 10; etymology of Jordan in, 6–7; and new worlds, 68–70n. 17; revision of Augustine in, 71–73n. 18, 152n. 15; sexual life in Eden, 146, 146n. 4, 152n. 15; state of souls after resurrection in, 141, 146, 146n. 4; as student of Maimonides, 18, 67, 67n. 15, 75n. 22; as twinned with opponent, 181–82n. 19

Argo, 183, 187

Argonauts, 184, 187

Aristotle, 68, 132, 180, 200nn. 2–3; fifth substance, 89, 89n. 8; influence on Maimonides of, 18–19n. 12, 65–66n. 10, 67n. 14, 75n. 22; and one world, 68–70n. 17; quote from, 36n. 6

Armageddon, 177–78

Arnaut, Daniel, 92, 94

Atalanta, 211

Atlantic Ocean, 3–7, 17, 32, 78

Augustine, Saint, 68, 70–74, 76, 95, 179; biography, 71–73n. 18; concept of confession, 205; and free will, 73n. 19; Eden's sexual power and, 71–73n. 18, 152, 152n. 15; as a young and old man, 71–73n. 18

Avernus, 206

Averroes (Ibn Rashid), 186

Barbi, 11

Bathsheba, 38, 102, 105, 107

Beatrice (Beatrice Portinari), 3, 23, 29–58, 60, 64–66, 81, 83–85, 87–88, 91, 95–96, 99, 108–11, 121–23, 165; age of, 33n. 4; attitude toward Jews of, 135–38; and the body, 17, 26–27, 27n. 3; 64, 117n. 6, 118n. 7, 141–50, 153–54, 161, 212, 216; blush of, 156–57, 161;